KT-381-572

Kevin Dundon

GREAT FAMILY FOOD

bor 10

20. NC

16.

28.

013492691 0

Kevin Dundon

GREAT FAMILY FOOD

More than 120 recipes for
delicious home-cooked food

Collins

Contents

introduction

With two young daughters and a toddler, food plays an integral part in our family life. My mother and grandmother were extremely good cooks and instilled in us a sense of passion for the food we ate – many of the recipes in this book are my childhood favourites. As children we always took an active role in the preparation of family meals and I've made sure this trend continues with my own children. After homework is done there is a mad dash to prepare the evening meal and everybody has their own special role. Sophie sets the table, Emily peels vegetables or stirs a pot while my wife, Catherine and I chop the meat and peel the vegetables!

The quality of ingredients is close to my heart and I always use the very best seasonal products I can find. *Great Family Food* features the recipes and the ingredients that Catherine and I use on a regular basis. You'll find a mixture of healthy and indulgent meals so all occasions are covered. In our house desserts are only served after the main course has been finished – that's our secret incentive for empty plates!

Being busy shouldn't mean missing out on good food. If you're leading a hectic life, juggling family, friends, work and play, it's important that the food you eat is as nourishing as possible. And even more importantly, food should be shared with the people you love. Happy reading and family cooking!!

Kevin

PS. The recipes in this book include both Metric and Imperial quantities. It is better to stick to one system, not a mix of two. I've also included cup measurements for American cooks. If any of the ingredients sound unfamiliar, you will find a short glossary of UK/US terms on page 218.

one-pot wonders

There's nothing more satisfying than easy-to-prepare casseroles and delicious one-pot dishes that can be made ahead of time and heated up just before serving.

Tucking into a warming bowl of soup or stew on a cold winter's day is my idea of heaven, and I guarantee that these recipes will be winners every time.

Tomato and Pesto Soup

This is a delicious way of making the most of tomatoes when they're at their juiciest and best at the end of the season. The pesto garnish turns this light and summery soup into something very special.

Serves 6–8

2 tbsp olive oil

1 small onion, peeled and finely chopped

2 garlic cloves, peeled and finely chopped

1kg/2lb 4oz ripe plum tomatoes, halved

700ml/1¼ pints/3 cups chicken stock or water

pinch of light brown sugar (optional)

200ml/7fl oz/generous ¾ cup double cream

salt and freshly ground black pepper

crème fraîche, to garnish

Basil Pesto:

50g/2oz/scant 1 cup fresh basil leaves

2 tsp toasted pine nuts

25g/1oz/¼ cup grated Parmesan cheese

2 garlic cloves, peeled

150ml/5fl oz/⅔ cup olive oil

1 For the pesto, place all the ingredients in a liquidizer and blend to a smooth paste. Transfer to a bowl, cover with clingfilm and store in the refrigerator until required.

2 Heat the olive oil in a large saucepan over a medium-high heat. Add the onion and garlic and sauté for a few minutes, or until golden. Tip in the tomatoes and continue to sauté for another 5 minutes, or until well heated through and just beginning to break down.

3 Stir in the chicken stock and allow the mixture to come to the boil and to reduce by half. Remove from the heat and blitz with a hand-held blender to a smooth purée. Alternatively, use a liquidizer. Season to taste and add the sugar, if using.

4 To serve, add the cream to the soup and warm through over a medium heat. Check the seasoning and ladle into warmed serving bowls. Garnish each bowl with some basil pesto and crème fraîche.

Potato and Thyme Soup with **Crispy Bacon**

This soup is a twist on the classic leek and potato; it's as delicious and warming as ever.

Serves 6–8

oil, for cooking

6 bacon rashers, cut into small pieces

50g/2oz/½ stick butter

5–6 large potatoes, peeled and chopped

3 celery sticks, chopped

1 leek, trimmed and sliced

½ medium onion, peeled and chopped

2 garlic cloves, peeled and finely chopped

3 large fresh thyme sprigs, leaves stripped from stems, plus smaller sprigs to garnish

1.2 litres/2 pints/5 cups chicken or vegetable stock, plus extra if needed

250ml/9 fl oz/generous 1 cup pouring cream

salt and freshly ground black pepper

1 Heat a little oil in a large frying pan and fry the bacon bits until well cooked and crispy. Drain them on kitchen paper and keep in a bowl until required.

2 Heat the butter in a large saucepan and toss in the chopped potato, celery, leek, onion and garlic together with the three thyme sprigs. Allow them to cook very gently (and without browning) for 8–10 minutes, or until the smaller of the vegetables are glazed. Add the chicken or vegetable stock to the pan and bring the mixture to a slow boil, then reduce the heat and simmer for 15–20 minutes, or until all of the vegetables, including the potatoes, have completely softened.

3 Remove the pan from the heat and use a hand-held blender to blitz the soup until it is nice and smooth. Stir in the cream, then return to the heat and bring back to a very gentle boil. If you prefer a thinner soup, now is the time to add some additional stock or cream to thin the consistency.

4 Season with salt and pepper to taste, then transfer the soup into bowls or cups and garnish with the crispy bacon pieces and the extra sprigs of thyme.

5 Alternatively, if you want to freeze the soup, allow to cool down completely, then transfer into containers and put in the freezer until required.

Roasted Butternut **Squash** and **Cinnamon** Soup

This lovely soup is really easy to prepare in advance, and it's ideal for freezing. The cinnamon gives it quite an unusual finish – it will definitely be the talk of any dinner party. If you don't like cinnamon, you can just leave it out.

Vegetarian
Serves 8

½ medium onion, peeled
3 garlic cloves, peeled
2 carrots, peeled
1 leek, trimmed
2 celery sticks
1 large potato or sweet potato, peeled
1 large butternut squash, peeled
50g/2oz/½ stick butter
1 cinnamon stick
½ tsp ground cinnamon, plus extra to sprinkle
100ml/3½fl oz/scant ½ cup pouring cream, plus 2 tbsp whipped cream, to garnish
1.2 litres/2 pints/5 cups vegetable or chicken stock
salt and freshly ground black pepper

1 Cut all of the vegetables into chunky pieces.

2 Set a large saucepan over a medium heat, add the butter and allow to slowly melt. Add the vegetables to the pan and mix thoroughly to coat. Add the cinnamon stick to the pan and sprinkle in the ground cinnamon to give the vegetables a nice, spiced flavour. Allow to cook for 6–8 minutes, stirring the vegetables continuously to prevent them from sticking to the bottom of the pan. Season lightly with salt and pepper.

3 When the vegetables are lightly browned and glistening, add the cream and two-thirds of the stock to the pan. Bring the mixture to the boil, then reduce the heat to a constant simmer. Simmer for 15–20 minutes, or until all of the vegetables have softened.

4 Remove the pan from the heat. With a slotted spoon, lift out the cinnamon stick and discard, then use a hand-held blender to blitz the soup until smooth, adjusting the consistency to your liking by adding more stock as required. Taste the soup and add more salt and pepper accordingly. You can also add a little additional cinnamon at this stage, if you wish.

5 Transfer the soup into small bowls or teacups to serve, and garnish the top with a swirl of whipped cream and a light sprinkling of cinnamon.

Roast Carrot and Garlic Soup

This is a highly flavoured soup, great for those cold winter days. You can vary the basic recipe depending on your preferences. Try substituting the carrot for pumpkin, butternut squash, sweet potato, parsnip or an extended mixture of vegetables (carrot, leek, celery, onion, etc). The soup freezes quite well so it's a great recipe to have on standby.

Vegetarian
Serves 6–8

50g/2oz/½ stick butter

½ medium onion, peeled and chopped

1 whole bulb of garlic, cloves peeled and chopped

1 leek, trimmed and sliced

2 celery sticks, chopped

5 carrots, peeled and cut into chunks

1 large potato, peeled and cut into chunks

75ml/2½fl oz/scant ⅓ cup pouring cream

1.2 litres/2 pints/5 cups vegetable or chicken stock

½ tsp chilli flakes (optional)

salt and freshly ground black pepper

2 tbsp crème fraîche, to garnish

1 Put a large saucepan over a medium heat, add the butter to the pan and allow to slowly melt. Add the chopped onion, garlic, leek, celery, carrots and potato to the pan, mix thoroughly and cook for 6–8 minutes, stirring continuously to prevent the vegetables sticking to the bottom. Allow them to roast off in the pan for a few minutes longer to infuse the garlic with the vegetables.

2 Pour in the cream and two-thirds of the stock, keeping the rest back in case you wish to adjust the consistency of the soup later. Bring the mixture to the boil and then reduce the heat to a constant simmer. Simmer for 15–20 minutes, or until all of the vegetables have softened.

3 Remove the pan from the heat and use a hand-held blender to blitz the soup until smooth, adjusting the consistency to your liking by adding more stock as required.

4 Taste the soup and season accordingly. If you wish, you may add some chilli flakes at this time to achieve a more daring flavour.

5 Serve the soup in bowls or teacups and garnish the top of each with a little dollop of crème fraîche.

Curried Sweet Potato and Coconut Soup

This punchy soup gives a good strong afterkick at the back of the throat. It's the perfect cure for the morning after the night before!!! My preferred curry pastes are by Mae Ploy or Thai Gold, but feel free to use whichever you like or have access to. This soup is also great made with pumpkin, parsnip or butternut squash instead of the sweet potato.

Vegetarian
Serves 8

butter, for cooking
½ medium onion, peeled and finely chopped
1 leek, trimmed and thinly sliced
2 celery sticks, chopped
2 carrots, peeled and cut into chunks
3 large sweet potatoes, peeled and cut into chunks
between 1 tsp and 1 tbsp green curry paste, amount depending on your taste
400ml/14fl oz/1¾ cups coconut milk
1.2 litres/2 pints/5 cups water
salt and freshly ground black pepper

1 Melt a knob of butter in a large saucepan over a medium heat. Add the onion, leek, celery, carrots and sweet potatoes and cook gently in the butter until the vegetables are beginning to soften and are just starting to brown.

2 Add the curry paste to the pan, mix to coat the vegetables and continue to cook over a medium heat until the mixture is coloured. Season lightly with salt and pepper.

3 Pour the coconut milk into the pan, along with 800ml/28fl oz of water, and bring to the boil, then reduce the heat and simmer for about 20 minutes.

4 Remove the pan from the heat and adjust the consistency of the soup to your liking by adding more water as required. Blitz well with a hand-held blender, then return to the heat briefly to warm through.

5 Add a little more salt and pepper to your taste just before serving, but be careful not to over-season, as coconut milk does tend to be a little salty. Serve the soup in bowls with crusty bread.

6 Alternatively, if you wish to freeze the soup, transfer into containers and put in the freezer until required. To defrost, thaw overnight in the refrigerator and reheat in a pan until hot. Adjust the seasoning to your taste when serving.

Chicken Noodle Soup

This is a warming, nourishing dish, which you can make as spicy or as mild as you like.

Serves 6–8

oil, for cooking

1 large red onion, peeled and diced

3 garlic cloves

1 red chilli, finely diced

2.5cm/1in piece of fresh root ginger, peeled and grated

3 chicken breasts, cut into very thin strips

1.2 litres /2 pints/5 cups well-flavoured chicken stock

150g/5oz broccoli, broken into small spears

75g/3oz sugar snap peas

50g/2oz frozen peas

75g/3oz dried medium egg noodles

juice of 1 lime

1 tbsp Thai fish sauce

4–5 tbsp soy sauce

2 tbsp chopped fresh coriander

75g/3oz baby spinach leaves

1 Heat a little oil in large saucepan and add the onion, garlic, chilli and ginger. Sauté gently until just softened. Add the chicken to the pan and cook for a moment or two until it is lightly glazed.

2 Pour in the stock and allow to come to the boil, then add the broccoli, sugar snaps and frozen peas and allow the contents of the pan to gently simmer for 3–4 minutes.

3 Gently break the noodles into the pan and allow them to cook for a few minutes until soft. Then adjust the flavour of the soup to your taste by adding some lime juice, Thai fish sauce and soy sauce. Finally, stir in the coriander and baby spinach leaves, transfer to bowls and serve.

Minestrone Soup

This is my all-time favourite soup to make at home, and Catherine and the children all love it. It requires a little bit of effort to make but, trust me, it's well worth it. The soup has a nice pronounced flavour and is wonderfully warm and nourishing.

Serves 6–8

oil, for cooking

3 garlic cloves, peeled and crushed

1 large onion, peeled and diced

2 celery sticks, chopped

1 leek, finely sliced

2 large carrots, peeled and diced

3 small potatoes, peeled and diced

75g/3oz smoked bacon, chopped

½ tsp tomato purée

1 x 400g/14oz tin of chopped tomatoes

2 fresh thyme sprigs, woody stems removed

1 rounded tsp chilli flakes (optional)

1–1.2 litres/1¾–2 pints/ 4–5 cups well-flavoured chicken or ham stock

110g/4oz spaghetti

2 tbsp natural yoghurt

salt and freshly ground black pepper

fresh flat-leaf parsley sprigs, to garnish

1 Gently heat a large saucepan with a drizzle of oil. Add in the crushed garlic, all the chopped and diced vegetables and the bacon pieces and sauté gently for 3–4 minutes. Then stir in the tomato purée and chopped tomatoes and drop in the thyme sprigs. The chilli flakes can also be added at this stage, if using.

2 Pour in three-quarters of the stock and bring the mixture gently to the boil. Then break the spaghetti into the soup, season with salt and pepper and reduce to a gentle simmer. Allow to cook until all of the vegetables are soft and tender. Correct the consistency as desired with the remaining stock.

3 Whisk in the natural yoghurt, transfer the soup into serving bowls and garnish with sprigs of flat-leaf parsley.

Mild Curried **Chickpeas**

Because chickpeas are such a good source of protein, I often incorporate them into our family meals in an attempt to keep us fit and raring to go. This dish is a favourite with the Dundons, as it is so simple and tasty.

Vegetarian
Serves 4

2 tbsp sunflower oil
1 red onion, peeled and chopped
1 red chilli, finely chopped
3 garlic cloves, peeled and crushed
2.5cm/1in piece of fresh root ginger, peeled and chopped or ½ level tsp ground ginger
1 green pepper, cored, deseeded and finely chopped
2 x 400g/14oz tins of chickpeas
½ tsp ground turmeric
1 tsp cumin seeds
½ tsp ground coriander
150ml/5fl oz/⅔ cup vegetable stock
1 x 400g/14oz tin of tomatoes
4 tbsp natural yoghurt
2 tbsp chopped fresh coriander
salt and freshly ground black pepper
boiled basmati rice, to serve

1 Gently heat the oil in a large wide-based saucepan. Add the onion, chilli, garlic and ginger and fry gently for 3–5 minutes, or until fragrant. This will produce an intense, spicy aroma in the kitchen. Add in the chopped green pepper and cook for a further 2–3 minutes.

2 Drain the chickpeas and rinse them under cold water, as sometimes the liquid can be very strong in taste. Add to the pan and stir to coat thoroughly with the vegetable mixture. Stir in the spices, then add the stock and tinned tomatoes and reduce the heat to very low. Cover the saucepan with a tightly fitting lid and simmer, very gently, for 15–20 minutes.

3 Remove the lid, gently stir in the yoghurt and season with a little salt and black pepper. Finally, mix in some chopped fresh coriander and serve immediately with boiled basmati rice.

Chilli con Carne

This chilli is ideal served with rice, crusty bread or jacket potatoes, and guacamole, sour cream and a big green salad. I've also included a non-meat alternative.

Serves 4–6

2 tbsp olive oil
2 onions, peeled and chopped
4 garlic cloves, peeled and crushed
900g/2lb minced lamb or soya mince
1 red pepper, cored, deseeded and chopped
50g/2oz sliced mushrooms
1 glass of red wine
2 x 400g/14oz tins of chopped tomatoes
3 tbsp tomato purée
2 red chillies, thinly sliced (and deseeded if you wish)
1 tsp dried chilli flakes
1 tsp ground cumin
1 tsp ground coriander
1 stick of cinnamon
good shake of Tabasco sauce
1 x 400g/14oz tin of red kidney beans, drained
1 large bunch of fresh coriander leaves, roughly chopped
salt and freshly ground black pepper
lime wedges, to serve

1 Heat the oil in a large, heavy-based saucepan and fry the onion and garlic until softened. Increase the heat and add the minced lamb or soya mince, red pepper and mushrooms, cooking quickly until browned and breaking down any chunks of soya with a wooden spoon. Pour in the red wine and boil for 2–3 minutes. While waiting, pour a glass for yourself!

2 Stir in the tinned tomatoes, tomato purée, fresh chilli and chilli flakes, cumin, ground coriander, cinnamon and Tabasco sauce. Season well with salt and pepper. Bring to a simmer, cover with a lid and cook over a gentle heat for 50–60 minutes, stirring occasionally, until the mixture is rich and thickened.

3 Add the kidney beans and fresh coriander. Cook for a further 10 minutes, uncovered. Remove from the heat, add extra seasoning if necessary and serve with lots of lime wedges.

Traditional **Risotto**

Risotto is a warming family favourite – nutritious and very filling. Use good-quality chicken stock to give the dish real depth and flavour. It's such a versatile meal, be sure to try the delicious variations below.

Serves 4

25g/1oz/¼ stick butter

2 shallots, peeled and finely chopped

½ tsp chopped fresh thyme,

3 garlic cloves, peeled and very finely chopped

350g/12oz/generous 2½ cups arborio rice

50ml/2fl oz/¼ cup dry white wine

1 litre/1¾ pints/4 cups boiling chicken stock

100ml/3½fl oz/scant ½ cup double cream (optional)

75g/3oz/¾ cup freshly grated Parmesan cheese, plus extra for serving (optional)

salt and freshly ground black pepper

1 On a low heat, slowly melt the butter in a wide saucepan with a thick base. Add the shallots, thyme and garlic and cook very gently until completely softened. Add the rice and mix in well to ensure that it does not stick to the base of the pan at this crucial time. Allow the rice to become glazed and cook without any liquid for 3–4 minutes while continuing to stir. Add the white wine and once again continue to stir the rice, as the wine will evaporate quite quickly.

2 Do not change the heat. Add the stock little by little into the rice mixture – don't add the next ladle until the previous one has evaporated. It is vitally important not to rush this process, but continue to add all the liquid until the rice is plump and tender.

3 Season this mixture and if you wish to obtain a nice creamy risotto you can add both the cream and Parmesan cheese. Adding just Parmesan will also make a great risotto.

4 Serve immediately with additional Parmesan cheese if desired.

Tip:
It is important that the chicken stock is hot before being added to the dish; otherwise it will cool the risotto down during cooking and make it very stodgy.

Variations:
All of the following are great added to your basic risotto mixture:
Roasted asparagus tips with Parmesan
Pan-fried wild mushrooms
Roasted pumpkin with chunks of goat's cheese
Cooked chicken breast and chorizo

Hot and Sour **Prawn** Broth

With its fragrant aroma of lemongrass and chilli, this is a lovely dish to serve as a starter at a dinner party or as a light lunch. Dublin Bay prawns (langoustines) are perfect in the spicy broth, which is also wonderful served chilled.

Serves 4

2 shallots, peeled and thinly
 sliced
3 garlic cloves, peeled and
 crushed
olive oil, for frying
2 lemongrass stalks, chopped
 into small pieces
850ml/1½ pints/3¾ cups light
 chicken stock, boiling
75g/3oz onoiki mushrooms
1 red chilli, very finely chopped
450g/1lb uncooked prawns,
 peeled
juice of 2 limes
2 tbsp dark soy sauce
2 tbsp chopped fresh coriander
salt and freshly ground black
 pepper

1 Sauté the shallots in a large pan with the garlic and olive oil for 2–3 minutes. Add the chopped lemongrass and cook for a couple of minutes.

2 Add the chicken stock and bring the mixture to the boil. Add in the mushrooms, the red chilli and the prawns. Continue to cook for 3–4 minutes, or until the prawns are lightly cooked.

3 Finally, add the lime juice, soy sauce and the chopped coriander. Correct the seasoning and serve.

Kevin's Irish **Paella**

This is great midweek supper, ideal if you've got guests popping in for a bite to eat. Although paella is a traditional Spanish dish, I have added a couple of quintessentially Irish ingredients to this version.

Serves 4

½ onion, peeled and sliced
2 garlic cloves, peeled and crushed
50g/2oz chorizo, chopped
6 rashers of smoked bacon, chopped
350g/12oz/1¾ cups paella rice (or basmati, if you are stuck)
90ml/3fl oz/⅓ cup white wine
½ tsp saffron strands
1.2 litres/2 pints/5 cups mild fish stock
450g/1lb selection of raw fish such as pollock or haddock, cubed
2 tbsp chopped fresh flat-leaf parsley
50g/2oz spinach
110g/4oz curly kale (optional)
12 large whole Dublin Bay prawns (langoustines)
lemon wedges or juice of 1 lemon
salt and freshly ground black pepper

1 Place the onion, garlic, chorizo and bacon in a large wok or wide-based saucepan and fry together over a gentle heat.

2 Add the rice and stir until completely combined with the onion mixture. Pour in the white wine and leave to reduce for a few minutes. Infuse the saffron strands in 100ml/3½fl oz/scant ½ cup boiling water and add to the pan – this will immediately colour the dish.

3 Add half the fish stock and mix thoroughly. Allow the liquid to come to the boil, then simmer gently until all the liquid has evaporated.

4 Add the cubed fish and the remainder of the fish stock. Cook gently on a low heat for 5–6 minutes, stirring occasionally.

5 When the fish is cooked through, add the parsley, spinach and kale, if using. Season to taste. Lay the prawns across the top and scatter over the lemon wedges or squeeze the juice directly onto the dish. Bring the saucepan to the table and allow people to help themselves.

Hearty Fish Stew

Tiger prawns, monkfish and mussels are gently simmered in a rich garlic and tomato sauce, bringing a real Mediterranean flavour to the table. The broth can be made in advance, so you can reheat it and add the fish just before serving.

Serves 4

1 large fennel bulb
2 tbsp olive oil
1 garlic clove, peeled and
    chopped
200ml/7fl oz/scant ¾ cup dry
    white wine
300ml/10fl oz/1¼ cups fresh
    fish stock
2 x 400g/14oz tins of chopped
    tomatoes
pinch of sugar
250g/9oz cherry tomatoes,
    halved
450g/1lb monkfish fillet, cut
    into 4cm/1½in chunks
12 large tiger prawns, heads
    removed
12 mussels, scrubbed clean
pimento paste (optional)
1 tbsp snipped garlic chives
1 tbsp chopped fresh lemon
    thyme
extra-virgin olive oil
salt and freshly ground black
    pepper

1 Remove the feathery tops from the fennel bulb, roughly chop and set aside to use as a garnish. Cut the remaining fennel bulb lengthways into quarters and finely chop, discarding the core.

2 Heat the oil in a large frying pan or wok, add the fennel and fry for 5 minutes. Add the garlic and fry for a further 1 minute. Stir in the wine, stock, tinned tomatoes and sugar, bring to the boil, then simmer gently for 5 minutes. Add the cherry tomatoes and cook for a further 5 minutes. Season well with salt and pepper.

3 Add the monkfish and bring back to a simmer. Stir in the prawns and mussels, cover and cook for approximately 5 minutes, or until the mussels have opened and the fish is cooked. Discard any mussels which have not opened. Mix in the pimento paste, if using, at this stage.

4 To serve, ladle the stew into 4 deep plates or bowls, scatter over the fennel tops, garlic chives and lemon thyme and drizzle with extra-virgin olive oil.

Seafood **Chowder**

With a large supply of seafood so readily available in Wexford, where I live, is it any wonder that fish features so much in this book? I often double the quantities in this recipe and use the leftovers to make fish pie (see page 139).

Serves 4

50g/2oz/½ stick butter

1 small onion, peeled and chopped

1 leek, trimmed and diced

1 small carrot, diced

1 potato, peeled and cubed

50g/2oz smoked salmon slices, cut into julienne (long thin strips)

125ml/4fl oz/½ cup dry white wine

425ml/15fl oz/generous 1¾ cups fish stock or water

275g/10oz mixed fresh fish fillets, skinned and cut into bite-sized pieces (such as cod, haddock, hake and salmon)

12 raw Dublin Bay prawns (langoustines), scrubbed clean

150g/5oz mussels, scrubbed clean

1 tbsp chopped fresh tarragon

200ml/7fl oz/generous ¾ cup pouring cream

salt and freshly ground black pepper

1 Heat a large pan over a medium heat. Add the butter and once it is foaming, tip in the onion, leek, carrot, potato and smoked salmon. Sauté for 2–3 minutes, or until softened.

2 Pour the wine into the pan and allow to reduce by half. Add the fish stock and bring to a simmer, then add the fresh fish and shellfish. Return the pan to a simmer and add the tarragon and cream, then season to taste. Cover with a lid and simmer gently for a further 2–3 minutes, or until the fish and prawns are tender and the mussels have opened (discard any that remain closed).

3 To serve, ladle the chowder into warmed serving bowls, piling plenty of the fish and shellfish into the centre of each one.

Chicken in Red Wine

At the end of a busy day, it's lovely to come home to a comforting stew. I usually buy a whole chicken and cut it into pieces (your butcher will happily do this for you or you could just use chicken legs). You can choose any red wine you like, but I prefer a full-bodied Burgundy. Goose fat adds real depth of flavour to this dish.

Serves 4

1 whole large chicken (1.3kg/3lb), cut into portions with skin on
50g/2oz/¼ cup butter or goose fat
200g/7oz button mushrooms, quartered or sliced
20 pearl onions, peeled but left whole
2 garlic cloves, peeled and chopped
4 rashers of back bacon, cut into strips (lardons)
1 tsp tomato purée
600ml/1 pint/2½ cups red wine
200ml/7fl oz/generous ¾ cup chicken stock
3–4 fresh thyme sprigs
2 bay leaves
salt and freshly ground black pepper
1 bunch of fresh parsley, to garnish

To Thicken:

25g/1oz/¼ stick butter, softened
50g/2oz/⅓ cup plain flour

1 Preheat the oven to 180°C/350°F/Gas Mark 4.

2 Place the chicken in a large bowl. Sprinkle with salt and black pepper and mix the chicken around to ensure that it is fully seasoned.

3 Heat the butter in a large pan. Pan-fry the chicken pieces for 2–3 minutes, or until they are golden brown all over. Take the chicken pieces out of the pan and transfer to a large casserole dish.

4 If required, add another teaspoon of butter to the pan and add the mushrooms, onions, chopped garlic and bacon. Cook for 4–5 minutes, or until glazed and golden brown. Add the tomato purée and whisk in the red wine together with the chicken stock. Bring the mixture to the boil, then add the fresh thyme sprigs and the bay leaves to the sauce. Pour the sauce over the chicken pieces in the casserole and place in the oven for 1–1¼ hours, or until the chicken is cooked through.

5 Remove the chicken from the sauce, place on a warmed plate, cover with foil and leave for a couple of minutes. Remove the thyme and bay leaves from the sauce. Return the casserole dish to the hob and bring the sauce to the boil.

6 Mix the softened butter with the flour into a soft dough. Break this into the boiling liquid (it is very important that the liquid is boiling at this stage; if not, it will make for a very lumpy sauce) and whisk rapidly, then allow the sauce to thicken for 8–10 minutes.

7 Put the chicken on a serving plate, pour over the sauce and garnish with the parsley. Serve with crusty bread and crisp green vegetables.

Beef and Black Bean stir-fry

Stir-fries are the ultimate one-pot meal, and this is a quick, healthy and very tasty dish. You don't have to use a wok – a large frying pan works just as well.

Serves 4

1 tbsp sunflower oil
500g/1lb 2oz beef fillet, sliced into very thin strips
250g/9oz green vegetables, sliced (such as broccoli, mangetout or French beans)
beef or vegetable stock (optional)
350g/12oz egg noodles
1 bunch of spring onions, trimmed and chopped
110g/4oz beansprouts
toasted sesame seeds, to garnish

Black Bean Sauce:

2 red chillies, roughly chopped and deseeded (unless you prefer a very hot dish)
2 garlic cloves, peeled
2.5cm/1in piece of fresh root ginger, peeled
100ml/3½fl oz/scant ½ cup soy sauce
100ml/3½fl oz/scant ½ cup beef stock
1 x 110g/4oz tin of black beans, drained
2 tsp sugar
2 tsp Thai fish sauce
juice of 1 lime
pinch of salt

1 Begin with the black bean sauce, which can be made up and stored in the refrigerator for up to 2 weeks. Place all of the ingredients for the sauce into a food processor and blitz at medium speed for 3–4 minutes, or until it is completely smooth.

2 Heat a large frying pan or wok, add the oil and fry off the meat until almost cooked. Add the vegetables and quickly fry them, using a little stock if the mixture gets too dry.

3 Bring a large pan of water to the boil. Add the noodles with a pinch of salt and cook according to the packet instructions, for around 6–8 minutes. Drain.

4 Pour half the black bean sauce into the beef mixture and bring the mixture to a rapid boil. The remaining sauce can be stored in the refrigerator for up to 2 weeks.

5 Add the chopped spring onions to the beef together with the beansprouts just before you serve the dish. Pile the beef and sauce on top of the noodles and serve immediately, garnished with toasted sesame seeds.

Traditional Beef Casserole with Herb Dumplings

A casserole makes a convenient and nourishing meal at any time of the year. You can pop it on top of the cooker or in the oven and just forget about it for an hour or two while it happily bubbles away. Here, I have added herb dumplings, which are a real family favourite.

Serves 6

1 tbsp sunflower oil
700g/1lb 8oz lean stewing beef, finely diced
1 onion, peeled and sliced
2 carrots, peeled and diced
½ turnip, peeled and finely diced
1 parsnip, peeled and chopped
2 celery sticks
1 large tsp tomato purée
25g/1oz/2½ tbsp plain flour
850ml/1½ pints/3¾ cups beef stock
salt and freshly ground black pepper

Herb Dumplings:

200g/7oz/1⅓ cups self-raising flour
50g/2oz/½ cup suet
pinch of salt
½ onion, peeled and very finely chopped
2 tsp chopped fresh parsley
50g/2oz/½ cup grated Cheddar cheese (optional)
about 5 tbsp soured milk

1 Heat the sunflower oil in a large saucepan. Add the diced stewing beef and fry quickly until coloured or sealed all over. Add the vegetables to the pan, mix around well and cook for 3–4 minutes, or until all the vegetables are sealed and glazed like the beef.

2 Next, add the tomato purée and a little salt and pepper and sprinkle the flour on top of the mixture. Mix in the flour (this will act as a thickening agent), ensuring that all the vegetables and meat are covered and lightly coated. Pour in the stock and mix it well to ensure that there are no lumps of flour stuck to the sides of the saucepan.

3 Allow the mixture to come to the boil, then reduce the heat to a gentle simmer, cover with a lid and cook for 1½–2 hours, or until the meat and vegetables are tender and the sauce is a nice consistency.

4 Meanwhile, make the dumplings. In a large bowl mix the flour, suet, salt, finely chopped onion, fresh parsley and Cheddar cheese, if using, together well. Gently stir in the soured milk a little at a time – do not add all the milk at once because you may not need all of the liquid. The mixture should resemble a soft dough (like a scone).

5 Turn out onto a floured work surface and knead the dough very gently, just until it comes together, then cut out the dumplings, using a cup or a scone cutter. They should be no thicker than 2cm/¾in.

6 About 30 minutes before the stew is ready, drop in the dumplings. These cook in the stew and take about 25–30 minutes. If you wish, at this stage you can finish the stew off in the oven by transferring it to a casserole dish with a lid and placing in an oven preheated to 150°C/ 300°F/Gas Mark 2.

Irish Stew with Pearl Barley

This is a real 'mammy' dish – all mums have their own special recipe. My recipe has a long-tailed history – it has satisfied several generations and will be passed on to future Dundons. This version uses diced lamb, but you could use mutton neck chops – a cheaper cut of meat, which benefits from the prolonged cooking time.

Serves 6

1 tbsp sunflower oil

1.1kg/2lb 8oz neck of lamb, diced

3 carrots, peeled and diced

1 onion, peeled and diced

225g/8oz turnip, peeled and chopped

5–6 fresh parsley sprigs, plus extra to garnish

600ml/1 pint/2½ cups lamb stock or water

2 large potatoes, peeled and diced

75g/3oz pearl barley

1 Heat a large saucepan with the sunflower oil, add the meat and quickly brown. Add the diced carrots, onion and turnip and fry off for 3–4 minutes. Add some parsley sprigs and the stock and allow the mixture to come to the boil, then reduce the heat to a very gentle simmer and cook, covered, for 1 hour.

2 Add the diced potatoes and pearl barley and stir to combine well. These two ingredients will both act as thickening agents, so you may need to add a little extra stock, depending on the consistency you like in your stew.

3 Allow the stew to cook gently for a further 1 hour – this will make the meat nice and tender and will ensure a great end result. If it begins to dry out, add a little more stock or water.

4 When the stew is cooked, sprinkle the dish with a little chopped parsley and serve immediately with some deliciously creamy mashed potatoes.

Braised **Beef** Short Ribs with **Horseradish** Mash

There is something truly delightful about the aroma of this dish wafting through the house. You can run out to the shops for a couple of hours while the ribs are cooking and come home to a beautiful slow-braised meal. If you can find them, Rooster potatoes are perfect for the mash; otherwise use King Edward, Golden Wonder or any other floury potato.

Serves 4

sunflower oil, for frying
16 short beef ribs
2 carrots, peeled and cut into chunks
1 large onion, peeled and sliced
5 garlic cloves, peeled
2–3 fresh thyme sprigs
1 x 400g/14oz tin of chopped tomatoes
350ml/12fl oz/1½ cups red wine
200ml/7fl oz/generous ¾ cup beef stock

Horseradish Mash:

6 large potatoes, peeled and cut into chunks
milk
50g/2oz/½ stick butter
1 tsp creamed horseradish
salt

1 Preheat the oven to 150ºC/300ºF/Gas Mark 2.

2 Heat a little oil in a large roasting tin and seal the short ribs on each side until they are nicely browned off. Add in the vegetables and garlic and stir to coat them lightly. Next, pop in the thyme sprigs and add the chopped tomatoes, red wine and beef stock. Bring the mixture to the boil, then transfer the tray to the oven for 2½ hours.

3 Boil the potatoes in salted water until they are tender. Drain off the water, return the saucepan to the hob and steam for a few minutes. Mash with a little milk and butter (add gradually as you do not want the mash to become sloppy) and mix in the creamed horseradish.

4 Remove the ribs from the oven and serve with the creamy horseradish mash.

quick & easy suppers

These days, everyone seems to be constantly on the run, trying to beat the clock at every turn. Here are some mouth-watering, time-saving recipes that are tasty, nutritious and ideal for all the family. Most importantly, they use ingredients that are readily available in your local shop or supermarket.

Baked Goat's Cheese, Beetroot, Orange and Walnut Salad

Each ingredient in this attractive salad has its own unique flavour, but they marry together extremely well. The sweetness of the orange contrasts beautifully with the strong and sometimes salty taste of the cheese.

Vegetarian
Serves 4

200g/7oz young baby beetroot
olive oil, for drizzling
350g/12oz young goat's
  cheese, cut into chunks
2 tbsp walnut oil
2 tbsp balsamic vinegar
juice of ½ orange
200g/7oz fresh rocket leaves
  (or any type of salad leaves)
3 large ripe oranges, peeled
  and segmented
75g/3oz/¾ cup walnuts
salt and freshly ground black
  pepper

1 Preheat the oven to 190ºC/375ºF/Gas Mark 5.

2 Cut the beetroot into large wedges and place on a baking tray. Drizzle with olive oil and season with the salt and pepper. Roast for 20–25 minutes, or until the wedges are just tender.

3 Line a baking tray with non-stick baking parchment. Arrange the cheese on top and place the tray in the oven for 5–6 minutes, or until the cheese is just beginning to melt.

4 While the goat's cheese is cooking, make the dressing by mixing together the walnut oil, balsamic vinegar and orange juice.

5 Arrange the rocket leaves in serving bowls or on plates. Divide the orange segments between the bowls. Scatter in the warm beetroot and the baked goat's cheese. Toss in the walnuts at the end and drizzle generously with the nutty dressing.

Roasted **Root Vegetable,**
Chilli and Pumpkin **Soup**

This is a delicious and really warming soup, and on cold days the girls often take it to school. Its beauty is that it can be made in advance and reheated as required, so why not make a double batch to keep out the winter chill?

Vegetarian
Serves 6–8

2 large carrots, peeled and cut into chunks

400g/14oz pumpkin, peeled and cut into chunks

2 celery sticks, sliced

1 parsnip, peeled and cut into chunks

2 sweet potatoes, peeled and cut into chunks

75g/3oz/¾ stick butter

½ onion, peeled and cut into chunks

1 leek, trimmed and sliced

2 garlic cloves, peeled and chopped

1 rounded tsp dried chilli flakes (optional)

1.5 litres/2½ pints/6¼ cups vegetable stock

200ml/7fl oz/generous ¾ cup double cream, plus extra for serving

salt and freshly ground black pepper

1 Preheat the oven to 190ºC/375ºF/Gas Mark 5.

2 Put the prepared carrots, pumpkin, celery, parsnip and sweet potatoes in a roasting tin, sprinkle with a little salt and pepper and roast in the oven for 15–20 minutes.

3 Meanwhile, gently heat the butter in a large saucepan. Add the onion, leek, garlic and chilli flakes, if using, and fry for 6–8 minutes. Add the roasted vegetables, pour in the vegetable stock and bring the mixture to the boil. Reduce the heat and simmer for 20 minutes, or until all the vegetables are fully softened. Remove the pan from the heat, add the cream, season with salt and pepper and blitz to a smooth purée using a hand-held blender.

4 Correct the consistency with additional stock if required. Return the pan to the heat and reheat gently. Serve steaming hot with a swirl of double cream, a twist of black pepper and buttered crusty brown bread.

Cream of Asparagus Soup

Asparagus is a wonderful spring vegetable, and this smooth and creamy soup is great for those days when there's still a chill in the air. It has the most delightful green colour, which is enhanced by the fragrant garlic leaves. For a lighter option, try using crème fraîche instead of cream.

Vegetarian
Serves 6–8

900g/2lb fresh asparagus
50g/2oz/½ stick butter
sunflower oil
1 onion, peeled and finely
    chopped
25g/1oz/2½ tbsp plain flour
1.2 litres/2 pints/5 cups
    boiling vegetable stock
125ml/4fl oz/½ cup double
    cream
50g/2oz wild garlic leaves, or
    chives, roughly chopped
salt and freshly ground black
    pepper

Croûtons:

3 slices of stale bread, cut into
    small dice
2 tsp sunflower oil

1 If you want to make your own croûtons, preheat the oven to 180°C/350°F/Gas Mark 4. Spread out the cubes of bread flat on a baking tray and drizzle with the oil. Bake for 10 minutes, or until golden brown. Cool on a rack, then store in an airtight container for 3–5 days. Alternatively, buy ready-made croûtons.

2 Prepare the asparagus by trimming off the tough outer stalks. These can be used for making stock.

3 Melt the butter in a large saucepan, adding just a little oil to help prevent burning. Add the chopped onion and fry gently for 6–8 minutes, or until soft but not brown.

4 Add the trimmed asparagus and cook with the onion for a further 10 minutes, or until it begins to soften. Mix in the flour and stir until the vegetables are completely coated with the flour. Pour in the boiling stock and stir for 2 minutes, making sure that none of the flour has stuck to the sides of the pan. Bring this mixture to the boil, then reduce the heat and simmer for 20 minutes.

5 Remove the pan from the heat and stir in the cream, wild garlic and seasoning. Using either a hand-held blender or a food processor, purée the soup in small batches. Return to the heat, correct the seasoning, warm through and serve with croûtons.

Spiced Marinated Salmon

This recipe is great, as it uses ingredients that you may already have in your larder. Because the marinade is quite strong, it takes only 30 minutes to infuse the fish with its piquant flavour.

Serves 6

6 salmon darnes or steaks
   (about 175g/6oz each)
sunflower oil, for frying

Marinade:

250ml/9fl oz/generous 1 cup
   soy sauce
scant 4 tbsp rice vinegar
1 tsp tomato purée
dash of Tabasco sauce
juice of 1 lemon
2 tsp sesame oil
1 red chilli, chopped
2.5cm/1in piece of fresh root
   ginger, peeled and chopped
2 tsp chopped fresh coriander

1 To make the marinade, put all the ingredients into a large bowl and whisk rapidly until thoroughly combined. Place the salmon darnes or steaks into the marinade and mix gently to ensure that the salmon is completely covered. Set aside in a cool place to marinate for 30 minutes.

2 When you are ready to cook the salmon, remove it from the marinade. Place a large frying pan drizzled with a little oil over a medium heat. Pan-fry the salmon on each side for 4 minutes (starting flesh-side down), then pour the remainder of the marinade into the pan and allow it to bubble up around the fish. Continue cooking on a medium heat for a further 5–6 minutes, depending on the thickness of the salmon. When the salmon is cooked, it should be firm to the touch.

3 Transfer to serving plates and spoon a little of the reduced syrupy marinade onto the top of the salmon. I like to serve this with boiled basmati rice and garden salad (see page 152).

Leek and Sweetcorn **Roulade**

This roulade looks amazing, but is really very simple to make and tastes delicious with a crisp glass of Chablis. I use leeks and sweetcorn for the filling, but you can try alternatives such as goat's cheese and roasted red peppers, chargrilled aubergine and courgettes or roasted cherry tomatoes and buffalo mozzarella.

Vegetarian
Serves 6

25g/1oz/¼ stick butter, plus extra for cooking the leeks
½ tsp ground nutmeg
600g/1lb 5oz baby spinach
4 free-range eggs, separated
75g/3oz/¾ cup grated Parmesan cheese
2 leeks, trimmed and thinly sliced
175g/6oz/¾ cup crème fraîche
1 x 275g/10oz tin of sweetcorn, drained
4 tsp chopped fresh parsley
salt and freshly ground black pepper

1 Preheat the oven to 190ºC/375ºF/Gas Mark 5. Line a 33 x 23cm/ 13 x 9in Swiss roll tin with baking parchment.

2 In a large saucepan, melt the butter, add the nutmeg and spinach and wilt the spinach for 3–4 minutes, or until it is completely cooked. Remove from the heat, squeeze dry, season with a little salt and pepper and allow to cool for 10 minutes.

3 Beat the egg yolks in a large bowl for 3–4 minutes, or until they are pale and creamy. Add the cooled and drained spinach.

4 Beat the egg whites in a separate bowl until they are stiff and full of air. Gently fold the egg whites into the spinach mixture and transfer to the prepared tin. Sprinkle the grated Parmesan on the top. Bake for 18–20 minutes, or until well risen and golden brown. Allow to cool completely in the tin.

5 Meanwhile, in a small pan, sweat the leeks in a little butter until they are completely soft. Allow to cool. Invert the roulade onto a large piece of baking parchment.

6 Mix the leeks, crème fraîche, sweetcorn and parsley together with some seasoning. Spread the creamy filling over the roulade and roll up tightly. Be warned – it does have a tendency to crack. Serve with a large salad or some minted baby potatoes.

Prawn Cocktail

Shallots, a sprinkling of paprika, a dash of Tabasco and brandy add a real twist to this classic starter.

Serves 4

16 Dublin Bay prawns
(langoustines)
1 bay leaf
5 lemon wedges
1 small head of iceberg lettuce,
   finely shredded
2 shallots, peeled and thinly
   sliced
salt
freshly snipped chives, to
   garnish

Marie-Rose Sauce:

150ml/5fl oz/²/₃ cup
   mayonnaise
4 tsp tomato ketchup
pinch of paprika, plus extra for
   dusting
dash of Tabasco sauce
2 tbsp brandy

1 To prepare the sauce, mix the mayonnaise, ketchup and paprika together until well combined. Stir in the Tabasco and brandy to suit your own taste. Proceed with caution with the Tabasco, as it can give excessive heat to the dish. Cover the bowl and store the sauce in the refrigerator until required – it will sit there happily for a couple of days.

2 Bring a large saucepan of salted water to the boil. Prepare the prawns by cracking them at the base and pulling off the tail and the shell as far as the head. Using a sharp knife, make a shallow cut down the middle of the outside vein and pull out the dark coloured vein. Alternatively, ask your friendly fishmonger to do this for you. I like to leave the head on, as it gives a nice finished look to the cocktail.

3 Add the bay leaf and a wedge of lemon to the boiling water and plunge in the prawns. The water will immediately cool down, so you must allow it to come back to the boil again. Once it reboils, cook the prawns for 60–90 seconds, or until they are firm to the touch.

4 Have a large bowl of iced water standing by. When the prawns are cooked, plunge them into the iced water for 4–5 minutes to cool them rapidly and prevent them overcooking. The boiled water in which you cooked the prawns can be chilled and/or frozen and used as a simple fish stock for other recipes.

5 Serve in large martini glasses for a bit of fun. Mix the shredded lettuce with the thinly sliced shallots and arrange it at the bottom of the bowl or glasses. Put four of the prawns on top of the lettuce (hanging slightly overboard) and add a large dollop of the chilled sauce on top. Dust with a little additional paprika and garnish with the remaining lemon wedges and fresh chives.

Mild **Monkfish Curry** with Coconut

Coconut milk, peppers and red curry paste turn this simple monkfish dish into a mouth-watering treat. Use the tender monkfish tail for this quick and easy recipe and serve with plain basmati rice.

Serves 6

1 tbsp sunflower oil

1 green pepper, cored, deseeded and thinly sliced

1 red pepper, cored, deseeded and thinly sliced

1 red onion, peeled and thinly sliced

1 bunch of spring onions, trimmed and chopped

7–8 mushrooms, sliced

2 tsp red curry paste

800ml/28fl oz/generous 3 cups coconut milk (2 tins)

1 monkfish tail (about 1kg/2^1/4lb) cut into 6 pieces

450g/1lb 2oz boiled basmati rice, to serve

fresh basil leaves, torn (optional)

1 Heat a deep wide-based pan with the sunflower oil. Quickly fry the vegetables over a high heat until just beginning to soften. Add the red curry paste and fry for 2–3 minutes, or until the vegetables are all fully coated with the paste.

2 Pour the coconut milk into the pan, making sure you scrape every last bit out of the tins. I usually rinse them out with a little water and add this to the pan as well to make sure I get all the goodness. Bring the mixture to the boil, then reduce the heat and place the pieces of monkfish in the broth. Cover the pan and gently simmer for 8–10 minutes over a very low heat, or until the fish is cooked. Baste the fish with the broth during cooking.

3 Remove the fish from the pan and place on top of softly boiled basmati rice and divide the remaining sauce among the plates. If the sauce has become too thick, add a little water, vegetable stock or even white wine if you are feeling indulgent and return to the boil. Freshly torn basil is also good mixed into the sauce.

Halibut en Papillotte

Serving this fish still in its wrapper means that each member of the family gets a full facial from all the steam escaping and it works very well as a quick meal. *En papillotte* is a French term that translates as 'cooked in paper'.

Serves 4

1 red pepper, cored, deseeded and thinly sliced
1 carrot, peeled and thinly sliced
1 red onion, peeled and thinly sliced
110g/4oz/¾ cup green beans, thinly sliced
50g/2oz/scant 1 cup fresh basil
4 halibut steaks (about 150g/5oz each)
1 lemon, thinly sliced
salt and freshly ground black pepper

1 Preheat the oven to 200ºC/400ºF/Gas Mark 6. Cut four sheets of baking parchment, A4 size, 30 x 20cm/12 x 8in.

2 Mix the vegetables together in a bowl. Divide the basil leaves among the four pieces of baking parchment, placing the basil in the centre of the paper. Neatly arrange the vegetables on top of the basil.

3 Gently place the fish steaks on top of the vegetable mixture. Place a slice or two of lemon on top of each fish. Season with a little salt and pepper.

4 Fold the baking parchment over from each side and twist both ends, much like a Christmas cracker, making sure that the fish is completely enclosed and sealed in.

5 Transfer to a baking sheet and bake for 10–15 minutes, depending on the thickness of the fish. Serve immediately, placing each paper parcel on the plates.

Tip:
It is important to cut the vegetables into thin slices, as the fish will cook quite quickly and you don't want the vegetables to remain too hard.

Linguine with Mushrooms and Seafood

Pasta is an obvious choice when you have one eye on the clock. This delicious recipe is laden with seafood – just pick and choose your favourite types. Firm fish gives the best result. Most good fishmongers and supermarkets now sell bags of ready-prepared frozen mixed seafood.

Serves 4–6

400g/14oz dry linguine
olive oil
1 fennel bulb, finely sliced
3 garlic cloves, peeled and
  crushed
110g/4oz mixed wild
  mushrooms (porcini and/or
  ceps)
350ml/12fl oz/1½ cups double
  cream
150ml/5fl oz/⅔ cup fish stock
2 tsp basil pesto (optional)
  (see page 11)
450g/1lb mixed seafood such
  as mussels, cockles, prawns,
  salmon, haddock and
  mackerel
3 large plum tomatoes, cut into
  small dice
75g/3oz/¾ cup grated
  Parmesan cheese
salt and freshly ground black
  pepper

1 Cook the pasta in a large pot of boiling salted water according to the packet instructions. When cooked, drain and toss in a little olive oil to prevent the strands from sticking together.

2 Meanwhile, heat a little oil in a large pan over a medium heat. Add the sliced fennel, crushed garlic and wild mushrooms. Sauté for 4–5 minutes, or until they are gently cooked but not browned. Add the cream, fish stock and pesto (if using) and allow the mixture to come to the boil.

3 Once it has reached boiling point, reduce the heat a little and add the seafood. Cook very gently for 5–6 minutes, or until the fish is just beginning to flake and the shellfish are fully opened. Discard any which do not open.

4 Taste the sauce and season with salt and pepper. Add the cooked pasta and stir gently to coat the pasta in the sauce, avoiding breaking up the pieces of fish. Just before serving, sprinkle the diced tomatoes and Parmesan cheese on top of the dish.

Pan-seared Pollock with Lemon-scented Potatoes

The lemon-scented potatoes flavoured with thyme make a perfect accompaniment to this delicious fish dish. Now that cod populations have been over-fished, pollock makes a good sustainable alternative.

Serves 4

30g/1½oz/generous ¼ stick butter

110g/4oz/generous ⅔ cup plain flour

4 fillets of pollock (about 150g/5oz each)

salt and freshly ground black pepper

Lemon-scented Potatoes:

50g/2oz/½ stick butter

2 tsp sunflower oil

12 baby potatoes, sliced 5mm/¼in thick

½ onion, peeled and thinly sliced

1 lemon, zested and cut into wedges

4–5 fresh thyme sprigs

1 Preheat the oven to 190ºC/375ºF/Gas Mark 5.

2 Heat the butter in a large ovenproof pan over a medium heat. Put the flour in a medium bowl and season with salt and pepper. Add a fish fillet to the bowl and turn in the flour until coated on all sides – this gives a nice crust to the fish at a later stage. Repeat with the other fillets. Put the coated fish in the hot pan and fry flesh-side down until sealed on each side, then transfer the pan to the oven for 10–12 minutes, depending on the thickness of the fish.

3 Meanwhile, prepare the potatoes. Heat the butter and oil in a large saucepan set over a medium heat, add the sliced potatoes and pan-fry gently on both sides, then reduce the heat to low. Add the onion, lemon wedges, zest and thyme and fry for 5–6 minutes, or until the potatoes are cooked and the onions have softened.

4 To serve, arrange the potatoes on a large serving platter, pile the fish pieces on top and place the pan-roasted lemon wedges beside the fish. This is great with buttered French beans.

Sea Bass Fillets stuffed with Salmon Mousse

These tasty fish rolls make an ideal dish for a dinner party – they look very impressive but are quite easy to make. A piping bag will give the filling a really professional finish, but a spoon works just as well. I like to serve these fillets with pasta and salsa verde (see page 157).

Serves 6

6 large fillets of sea bass
   (about 175g/6oz each),
   skinned
250g/9oz salmon, diced
2 tsp torn fresh basil
25g/1oz/½ cup fresh
   breadcrumbs
1 shallot, peeled and very
   finely chopped
1 large free-range egg white
2 tbsp pouring cream
salt and freshly ground black
   pepper

1 Place each fillet of sea bass between two sheets of clingfilm and use a rolling pin to flatten them out quite gently, making sure that you do not break the flesh of the fish; otherwise it will be difficult to stuff. Leave the flattened fish between the clingfilm and store in the refrigerator until required.

2 Meanwhile, prepare the salmon mousse. Place the diced salmon, torn basil, breadcrumbs, shallot, egg white, cream and seasoning in a food processor. Blitz for just over 1 minute, or until you have a puréed but still coarse consistency. Transfer the fish mousse to a piping bag in order to stuff the sea bass. If you don't have one, you can spoon the mixture instead.

3 Unwrap the sea bass, then lay each fillet flat on a fresh sheet of clingfilm. Season with salt and pepper. Pipe or spread the mousse evenly over the fillets, then carefully roll up or fold over (depending on the size of your fillets) to enclose the stuffing. Wrap up tightly in the clingfilm to make a sausage or cylindrical shape out of the fish. Tie the clingfilm at both ends to keep the cylindrical shape. Wrap the clingfilm parcel in a layer of foil and seal at both ends. Allow the fish parcels to rest in the refrigerator until required.

4 Bring a large saucepan of salted water to the boil. Drop the fish parcels into the boiling water and poach gently for 15 minutes, or until firm to the touch.

5 Once removed from boiling water, allow the parcels to rest for 2–3 minutes, then unwrap and cut each fish roll into two or three slices.

Grilled **Mackerel** with Sun-dried **Tomato** Butter

Mackerel are full of nutrients and this dish makes a very quick light meal, requiring little more than a big chunk of fresh bread and a green salad.

Serves 4

200g/7oz/1¾ sticks butter, slightly softened

50g/2oz/⅓ cup sun-dried tomatoes, finely chopped

3–4 fresh basil leaves, torn into very small pieces

8 whole mackerel

black pepper

1 To make the sun-dried tomato butter, place the softened butter in a large bowl. Add the tomatoes and basil, season with a little black pepper and mix together. Spoon the butter onto a piece of non-stick baking parchment and roll into a long, cylindrical shape. Wrap tightly in clingfilm and either freeze or refrigerate until firm.

2 Preheat the grill or barbecue to its highest heat and arrange the mackerel on a grill tray with a wire rack. I normally put some foil underneath the wire rack to catch any juices that overflow from the mackerel.

3 Place the mackerel under the grill or on the barbecue and cook for 2–3 minutes, then turn them over and cook for a further 2–3 minutes, or until the fish is firm and opaque.

4 Remove the flavoured butter from the refrigerator or freezer, unwrap and cut into thin slices. Put a slice on each mackerel to serve.

Crock of **Mussels** in Thai Cream Broth

There is something hugely satisfying about picking your own mussels on the seashore, ferrying them home, washing and cleaning them and serving them to the entire family. Even for those without the time or resources to hand-pick their dinner, the succulent mussels and delicate flavour of the curried broth will set your mouth watering.

Serves 6
1.8kg/4lb mussels
sunflower oil, for frying
1 onion, peeled and roughly
   chopped
2 garlic cloves, peeled and
   roughly chopped
2 lemongrass sticks, crushed
   and chopped
2.5cm/1in piece of fresh root
   ginger, peeled and chopped
2 tsp red curry paste
50ml/2fl oz/¼ cup white wine
400ml/14fl oz/1¾ cups
   coconut milk
juice of 1 lime
4 tsp chopped fresh coriander

1 Scrub the mussels to ensure that all beards and dirt particles are removed. Place the mussels in a large bowl and cover with a cold, damp cloth and store in the refrigerator until required.

2 Heat a little oil in a large wok or wide-based frying saucepan. Add the chopped onion, garlic, lemongrass and ginger and fry on a gentle heat for 4–5 minutes, or until the vegetables have softened but not coloured. Add the red curry paste and increase the heat. Stir briskly to colour the vegetable mixture.

3 Add the mussels, making sure that they are tightly closed. If they are not, give them a sharp tap on the work surface – if they close immediately, continue to use them; if they don't, discard them, as they are dead and not suitable for consumption. Stir the mussels for a moment or two, then add the wine. Allow the wine to come to the boil, then pour in the coconut milk and bring the mixture back to the boil.

4 Cook until the majority of mussels have opened. (Discard any that remaining resolutely closed, as they are unsafe to eat.) Drizzle over the lime juice and sprinkle with chopped coriander just before serving.

5 This is a great dish for bringing to the table in the pot or in a large earthenware dish and allowing people to help themselves.

Fish and Chips with Pea Purée

This is my take on the classic dish with a shot glass of green pea purée served alongside the beer-battered fish and chips. I cook this dish when I am having people round for drinks, as it leaves little washing up to do afterwards. I like to use a variety of fish. Cod (from a sustainable source), lemon sole and haddock are my personal favourites.

Serves 4

4 large Maris Piper potatoes
600ml/1 pint/2½ cups
　　sunflower oil for deep-frying
200g/7oz/1⅓ cups plain flour,
　　plus extra for dusting
50g/2oz/⅓ cup cornflour
250ml/9fl oz/generous 1 cup
　　lager
4 portions of fish such as cod,
　　lemon sole or haddock
　　(about 250g/9oz each), cut
　　into thin strips

Pea Purée:

200g/7oz/2 cups frozen peas
300ml/10fl oz/1¼ cups chicken
　　stock
50ml/2fl oz/¼ cup double
　　cream
4 tsp snipped fresh chives (or
　　any mild bright green herb)
salt and freshly ground black
　　pepper

1 Preheat the oven to 190ºC/375ºF/Gas Mark 5.

2 Peel the potatoes, cut into thick chips and put on a baking tray. Drizzle with a little sunflower oil and bake for 30 minutes, or until completely soft.

3 To make the beer batter, sift the flour and cornflour into a bowl. Make a well in the centre and add the lager. Gradually whisk the lager into the flour mixture until you have achieved a smooth batter and store in the refrigerator until required.

4 To make the pea purée, put the frozen peas and chicken stock in a medium-sized saucepan and bring gently to the boil. Boil for 5–6 minutes, or until the peas have softened and cooked. Add the cream, chives and seasoning, then blitz with a hand-held blender until a soup consistency has been achieved.

5 Heat the oil in a deep-fat fryer or large saucepan to 180ºC/350ºF, or until a small piece of white bread turns golden brown in about 30 seconds. If using a saucepan, be very careful and do not fill the oil to the brim – leave a 4–6 cm/1½–2½ in gap at the top.

6 Dust the strips of fish in a light coating of flour, then dredge in the batter, shaking off any excess. Deep-fry for about 5 minutes, or until cooked through and golden brown. You may have to do this in batches, depending on the size of your fryer. If you are cooking larger pieces of fish, start cooking in the fryer and then transfer to the oven to finish.

7 For a bit of fun, serve the fish and chips in little newspaper cones and place a shot glass of the hot pea soup beside the fish.

Grilled Cod with Minted New Potato Salad

This is my favourite type of quick supper. The potato salad with sun-dried tomatoes is a Mediterranean-style variation on the classic. Garlic butter adds the perfect finishing touch to this dish. If I use cod, I always make sure it's from a sustainable source. Otherwise, sea bass and pollock are excellent alternatives.

Serves 4

50g/2oz/½ stick butter
4 pieces of cod (about 175g/ 6oz each)
salt and freshly ground black pepper

Minted New Potato Salad:

16 new potatoes
4 tsp chopped fresh mint
1 bunch of spring onions, trimmed and chopped
2 tbsp mayonnaise
50g/2oz/1 cup sun-dried tomatoes

Garlic Butter:

75g/3oz/¾ stick butter, softened
2 garlic cloves, peeled and crushed
2 tsp freshly snipped chives

1 First make the potato salad. Boil the potatoes in a large pan of salted water until they are just tender, then drain off all the water. Allow them to cool down naturally (which will further soften the potatoes without over-cooking them). When cool, sprinkle the mint and spring onions over the potatoes. Season the potatoes well with salt and a good crack of black pepper. Add the mayonnaise and stir well so all the potatoes are coated, then scatter the sun-dried tomatoes over the top. Transfer to a medium bowl, cover with clingfilm and store the salad in the refrigerator until required.

2 Gently melt the butter in a large frying pan over a low heat, then increase the heat under the pan to medium. Season the fish with a little salt and pepper on both sides and place flesh-side down in the hot pan. Seal for 3 minutes on each side to generate a nice crust. Ensure that the fish is fully cooked before serving – it should feel firm to the touch. Thicker pieces of fish may take a minute or two longer.

3 To make the garlic butter, simply combine all the ingredients together.

4 Serve the fish with a spoon of the garlic butter generously smothered over and with the new potato salad on the side.

Herb Pancakes with Smoked Salmon and Lemon-scented Crème Fraîche

This is a really simple dish, but can easily be transformed from starter to main course by doubling the quantities. For an extravagant flourish, garnish the salmon with a tiny amount of caviar.

Serves 6

Pancakes:
250g/9oz/1²/₃ cups plain flour
pinch of salt
2 large free-range eggs
400ml/14fl oz/1³/₄ cups milk
1 bunch of **spring onions**,
    trimmed and finely sliced
4 tsp finely chopped fresh
    parsley
sunflower oil, for frying

**Lemon-scented Crème
    Fraîche:**
225g/8oz/1 cup crème fraîche
2 tsp chopped fresh parsley
zest of 1 lemon
6–12 slices of smoked salmon
freshly ground black pepper
lemon wedges, to garnish
caviar (optional), to garnish

1 Begin by making the pancake batter. Sift the flour into a large mixing bowl. Add the salt and mix well. Crack the eggs into the flour mixture, add the milk and use a large whisk to incorporate the egg and milk into the flour. Add the spring onions and parsley to the batter. Mix well, cover the bowl with clingfilm or a dry cloth and allow the batter to rest in the refrigerator for at least 1 hour.

2 Meanwhile, put the crème fraîche into a mixing bowl and whisk for a moment or two to soften it a little. Add the chopped parsley, lemon zest and black pepper and mix well. Transfer to a clean bowl and store in the refrigerator until required.

3 To cook the pancakes, heat a large frying pan on a gentle heat. Add a little sunflower oil to the pan and, using a dessertspoon, spoon small amounts of the pancake batter into the pan, keeping them separate. I tend to cook no more than six at a time. Pan-fry the tiny pancakes for 2–3 minutes on each side, or until golden brown.

4 Serve the pancakes either hot or cold, piled high with smoked salmon and the flavoured crème fraîche. Garnish with lemon wedges and caviar as required.

Trout with Toasted Almonds and Lemon-infused Olive Oil

I take the girls fishing in picturesque Dunmore East in Waterford and bring home some of the most beautiful–tasting trout. My philosophy here is to let good-quality ingredients speak for themselves and not over-complicate the flavours.

Serves 4

50g/2oz/½ stick butter
50g/2oz/⅓ cup plain flour
8 boneless fillets of trout (about 110g/4oz each)
75g/3oz/¾ cup flaked almonds
salt and freshly ground black pepper

Lemon-infused Olive Oil:

150ml/5fl oz/⅔ cup olive oil
zest and juice of 1 unwaxed lemon

1 Begin by making the lemon-infused olive oil. Pour the olive oil into a small saucepan. Add the zest and juice of the lemon. Heat very gently for 10 minutes, then set aside to rest for a couple of minutes, but do not allow to cool completely.

2 Over a medium heat, gently melt the butter in a large frying pan. Add a tiny amount of the lemon oil to prevent the butter from burning.

3 Put the flour in a bowl and season with a little salt and pepper. Dip the flesh side of the trout in the seasoned flour and pan-fry in the butter on a medium heat for 3–4 minutes on each side. When the fish is cooked, turn off the heat, scatter the flaked almonds over the fish and allow them to warm up in the heat of the pan.

4 To serve, transfer two fillets of the fish onto each plate, scatter any rogue almonds on top and drizzle lightly with the warmed lemon-infused olive oil. Serve simply with minted peas (see page 157) and a few boiled potatoes or a large chunk of bread.

Crunchy Chicken and Bacon Bun

This is great for the barbecue. If you have young children, you can hold back a little on the marinade to make the chicken less spicy – familiarize them with spices little by little, and they will quickly get used to the flavours. If you like, use tortilla wrap or pitta bread instead of burger buns.

Serves 4

4 chicken fillets
   (about 225g/8oz each)
scant 3 tbsp mayonnaise
4 tsp sweet chilli jam (see
   page 137)
sunflower oil, for brushing
4 slices of smoked bacon
4 bread rolls or burger buns
4 slices of Cheddar cheese
lettuce, chopped onion and
   sliced tomato, to serve

Marinade:

½ tsp cayenne pepper
½ tsp dried chilli flakes
2 garlic cloves, chopped and
   crushed
4 tsp olive oil
juice of 1 orange

1 Mix the marinade ingredients together in a large non-metallic bowl. Slice the chicken fillets in half, add to the bowl and leave to marinate in a cool place for at least 1 hour.

2 Mix the mayonnaise and sweet chilli jam together and chill until required.

3 Oil the grill or your barbecue and grill the chicken for 5–6 minutes on each side, depending on its size. Make sure it is thoroughly cooked by piercing with a knife to see if the juices run clear. Grill the bacon until crisp.

4 Cut the rolls or buns in half and grill on the inside to warm them up a little. Lay the slices of cheese on top of the cooked chicken on the barbecue or grill and allow the cheese to melt for a minute or two.

5 Spread some sweet chilli mayonnaise on each side of the toasted rolls and garnish with some lettuce leaves, chopped onion and the sliced tomato. Carefully arrange the bacon on top of the salad. Add the hot chicken and cheese combination and top with the remaining half of the roll. Secure with a cocktail stick and serve.

Pan-fried Breast of Chicken with Wild Mushroom and Spinach

Make sure that the the chicken skin is smooth, without cracks and coats the entire breast. You can also use cooked, chopped chicken in this recipe, serving the whole thing as a sauce over freshly boiled pasta.

Serves 4

50g/2oz/⅓ cup plain flour
4 chicken breasts (about 250g/9oz each), skin and wing still attached (see above)
sunflower oil, for frying
salt and freshly ground black pepper

Wild Mushroom and Spinach Sauce:

25g/1oz/¼ stick butter
200g/7oz wild mushrooms (such as oyster, shiitake, chanterelle, etc)
5 tbsp white wine
350ml/12fl oz/1½ cups double cream
75g/3oz/¾ cup freshly grated Parmesan cheese
175g/6oz spinach
2 tbsp chopped fresh parsley

1 Preheat the oven to 180°C/350°F/Gas Mark 4.

2 Season the flour with salt and pepper and place in a shallow dish. Dip the chicken breasts in the flour to coat on both sides.

3 Heat a large frying pan with a little drizzle of oil over a low heat. Pan-fry the chicken on each side for 3–4 minutes, or until nicely browned (but not too dark). Transfer to a baking tray and place in the oven for a further 15–20 minutes, depending on the size of the breasts. Make sure they are thoroughly cooked – cut into the centre with a knife just to be sure the juices run clear.

4 Meanwhile, reheat the pan in which you cooked the chicken. Melt the butter over a low heat and gently fry the mushrooms. Season as required – sometimes I just put a little salt on the mushrooms at this stage. Pour in the white wine and allow to reduce slightly. Add the cream and Parmesan cheese and allow the mixture to come to the boil. Next, add the spinach leaves and chopped parsley and simmer for 2–3 minutes, or until the spinach is cooked. Taste the sauce and correct the seasoning.

5 Slice the chicken breasts in half lengthways and arrange them in the centre of serving plates. Spoon the mushroom and spinach sauce over the chicken and around the side of the plate. Serve with baby roasted potatoes.

Pan-fried Duck with Spiced Noodle Stir-fry

Teaming duck with a noodle stir-fry is a great way to introduce your family to this meat. If you want to stretch the duck further, you could shred it into very thin strips and incorporate it into the actual stir-fry rather than serving it on top.

Serves 4

4 duck breasts (about 250g/9oz each)
2 tsp coriander seeds
1 tsp sea salt
3 black peppercorns
1 fresh thyme sprig
sunflower oil, for frying
2–3 tbsp honey
4 portions of egg noodles
1 onion, peeled and thinly sliced
1 green pepper, cored, deseeded and thinly sliced
125ml/4fl oz/½ cup soy sauce
juice of 1 orange
salt and freshly ground black pepper

1 Prick the duck breasts all over with a fork. Put the coriander seeds, salt, peppercorns and thyme into a food processor and blitz to a coarse consistency. Rub this spice mixture all over the duck breasts and leave to rest in a cool place for about 20 minutes.

2 Preheat the oven to 190ºC/375ºF/Gas Mark 5.

3 Heat a large frying pan with a little oil over a medium heat. Seal the duck breasts, skin side down first, on each side for 2–3 minutes, then drizzle the honey over the duck. Transfer to a baking tray and bake in the oven for a further 10–12 minutes, depending on whether you like your duck pink or well done.

4 Cook the egg noodles according to the packet instructions in boiling salted water.

5 Using the same pan in which you cooked the duck, quickly fry the vegetables in a little oil over a medium heat. Add the noodles, followed by the soy sauce and orange juice. Season to taste and divide the mixture among serving bowls. Slice the duck breasts and arrange on top of the noodles.

Spicy Chicken **Fajitas**

This delicious recipe is suitable for family and friends alike. When I'm entertaining, I prefer just to put all the components of the meal in the middle of the table and allow my guests to help themselves. Building your own fajita can be both fun and messy in equal measure! The stir-fry part of this recipe can also be made with pork, duck or beef.

Serves 6

1 tbsp honey

3 tbsp soy sauce

sunflower oil, for cooking

2 garlic cloves, peeled and chopped

½ red chilli, very finely chopped

5–6 chicken fillets, cut into very thin strips

1 medium red or white onion, peeled and thinly sliced

1½ mixed peppers, thinly sliced

5–6 mushrooms, sliced

½ tsp ground cumin

8–12 medium flour tortillas

200g/7oz/2 cups grated red Cheddar cheese, or other hard cheese

salt and freshly ground black pepper

Citrus Crème Fraîche:

200ml/7fl oz/generous ¾ cup crème fraîche

juice and zest of 1 lime

1 tbsp chopped fresh parsley

cracked black pepper

1 Combine all the ingredients for the citrus crème fraîche together in a bowl and mix well. Chill in the refrigerator until required.

2 Mix the honey and soy sauce together in a small bowl and set aside until needed.

3 Set a large frying pan or wok over a very high heat and have the prepared meat and vegetables close to hand. Add a little oil to the pan or wok, then add the garlic, chilli and chicken pieces. Stir-fry the chicken quite quickly until the edges are all sealed. Next, add the sliced onion, peppers and mushrooms to the pan and allow these to cook.

4 When the chicken and vegetables are almost fully cooked (after about 8–9 minutes), add the honey and soy sauce mixture and stir to coat well. Cook for a further minute or two and then season the stir-fry with salt and pepper, being careful not to add too much as the soy sauce can be quite salty. Sprinkle with the ground cumin.

5 Spoon the stir-fry mixture on to the tortillas, top with the citrus crème fraîche, sprinkle with grated cheese and roll up. Serve immediately. Cajun potato wedges are a delicious accompaniment.

Kevin's **Club Sandwich**

A club sandwich makes a great midnight feast or a fantastic option when you come in after a busy day at work. Vary the fillings to suit yourself – it's a good way of using up leftover cold meat.

Serves 1
2 bacon rashers
oil, for cooking
1 egg
3 slices of bread
½ tbsp mayonnaise
handful of mixed lettuce
  leaves, shredded
1 tomato, sliced
5 slices cooked chicken, sliced
  (use poached or leftover
  roast chicken)
thick-cut chips (see page 142),
  to serve

1 Cook the bacon under a preheated grill until it is really nice and crispy. Set a frying pan over a medium heat, add a little oil and fry the egg. Toast the slices of bread under the grill or in a toaster.

2 To build the sandwich, lay a slice of toasted bread on a chopping board. Spread lightly with a little mayonnaise, then put some shredded lettuce and slices of tomato on top. Arrange one piece of bacon and two slices of chicken above the lettuce and tomato. Top with a second slice of crisp toast.

3 Spread the second piece of toast with mayonnaise and repeat the previous step with the rest of the lettuce, tomato, bacon and chicken. Then put the fried egg on top of the stack before finishing off the sandwich with the final slice of toast.

4 Cut the sandwich in half and secure each half with a cocktail stick. Serve with some homemade thick-cut chips.

Lamb Cutlets with Herb Crust and White Wine Sauce

This is a delicious way of cooking lamb, in which the crust helps to keep all the moisture in the meat. A perfect dish for a romantic night in.

Serves 2

1 tbsp chopped fresh parsley
3 fresh rosemary sprigs, woody stems removed, leaves chopped
1½ tbsp chopped fresh mint
1 rack of lamb (about 6–8 cutlets)
butter or oil, for cooking
salt and freshly ground black pepper
mashed potato, to serve

White Wine Sauce:

100ml/3½fl oz/scant ½ cup white wine
200ml/7fl oz/generous ¾ cup pouring cream
extra handful of chopped parsley and chives (optional)

1 Mix the chopped parsley, rosemary and mint together in a bowl with a little salt and pepper. Divide the rack of lamb into individual cutlets and dip each cutlet into the herb mixture, turning to coat.

2 Heat a little butter or oil in a large non-stick frying pan, add the herb-coated lamb cutlets and seal on both sides until golden brown and cooked to your liking – this should take about 3–4 minutes on each side. If you like your meat more well done, you could then transfer the lamb on to a baking tray and finish cooking it in the oven (preheated to 190ºC/375ºF/Gas Mark 5) for a further 5–6 minutes.

3 Remove the pan from the heat or remove the baking tray from the oven, transfer the lamb to a plate and allow to rest while you make the sauce.

4 Discard the majority of the fat (and any charred herb residue) from the pan, then pour in the white wine and return to a medium heat. Bring to a gentle boil and allow to bubble until reduced by half.

5 Once the wine has reduced, pour in the cream, turn the heat down to low and allow the sauce to reduce again for 8–10 minutes, during which time it will thicken. Add some chopped fresh parsley or chives to the sauce just before serving, if you wish. Transfer the sauce into a separate sauceboat or jug to serve.

6 The herb-crusted lamb cutlets are delicious served on top of some creamy mashed potato – try flavouring it with roasted garlic or fresh basil pesto (see page 11).

Mini Spiced **Lamb Burgers**

These mini burgers are perfect as a tasty snack, quirky canapés when you've invited a few family and friends round for a glass of wine or for kids' parties.

Serves 6–8

450g/1lb minced lamb
50g/2oz/1 cup fresh
    breadcrumbs
½ tsp ground coriander
½ tsp ground cumin
1 red onion, peeled and finely
    chopped
1 free-range egg
2 tsp chopped fresh coriander
plain flour, for dusting
small bread rolls, mayonnaise,
    sliced tomatoes and lettuce,
    to serve

Tomato Chutney:

6 ripe plum tomatoes, diced
½ red onion, peeled and
    chopped
50g/2oz/¼ cup (solidly packed)
    soft brown sugar
½ tsp dried red chilli flakes
3 tbsp white wine vinegar
pinch of ground cinnamon

1 Place all the chutney ingredients in a medium-sized saucepan. Bring to the boil, then reduce the heat and simmer for 20–30 minutes, or until all the vegetables are softened and the liquid has reduced. Allow to cool thoroughly. Tip into a bowl or jar, cover and store in the refrigerator for up to 8 weeks.

2 Preheat the oven to 180ºC/350ºF/Gas Mark 4.

3 Place all the burger ingredients in a large mixing bowl. Mix together, then take golf-ball-sized amounts (approximately 60g/2½oz) and shape into burgers, using a little flour on your hands to prevent the burgers from sticking.

4 Heat a large frying pan, add the burgers and seal on each side, then transfer to a baking tray and cook in the oven for 10–12 minutes, or until all the juices run clear and the meat is thoroughly cooked.

5 Serve the burgers in small bread rolls with mayonnaise, sliced tomatoes, lettuce and tiny spoonfuls of tomato chutney.

Parmesan Pork with Mint-infused Mangetout

The delicious Parmesan cheese crust helps retain the pork's moisture, preventing the meat from drying out during cooking. Mangetout and mint make a fresh and light accompaniment.

Serves 6

110g/4oz/generous ⅔ cup plain flour
2 free-range eggs
200ml/7fl oz/generous ¾ cup milk
200g/7oz/scant 4 cups fine fresh breadcrumbs
75g/3oz/¾ cup grated Parmesan cheese
4 tsp chopped fresh parsley
6 pork escalopes (about 150g/5oz each)
sunflower oil, for cooking
salt and freshly ground black pepper

Mint-infused Mangetout:

225g/8oz/1½ cups **mangetout**
50g/2oz/½ stick butter
2 tsp finely chopped fresh mint

1 Preheat the oven to 190ºC/375ºF/Gas Mark 5.

2 You will need three bowls. Tip the flour into the first bowl and season with a little salt and pepper. In another bowl, mix the two eggs with the milk. In the third bowl, mix together the breadcrumbs, Parmesan cheese and chopped parsley.

3 Place each escalope between two pieces of clingfilm and, using a meat hammer or large rolling pin, batter the meat until it is very thin (about 1cm/½in thick).

4 Dip each piece of pork first in the seasoned flour, then in the egg wash mixture and finally in the Parmesan breadcrumbs.

5 Heat a little oil in a large ovenproof frying pan. Fry the pork on each side for 3–4 minutes, or until golden brown, then transfer the pan to the oven for 10–12 minutes, or until the pork is cooked though.

6 To prepare the mint-infused mangetout, bring a large saucepan of salted water to the boil. Plunge the mangetout into the pan and boil for 3–4 minutes, or until they are just about to soften. Strain off the water and season with a little black pepper. Add the butter and chopped mint and serve immediately with the pork.

Egg and Bacon Beef Burger

I simply adore homemade burgers – I tend to make them at least once a week. With so many different possible flavourings, you can try a different one every time you indulge. The recipe below will make 6–7 substantial burgers, so if you don't need them all at once, you can wrap the extras in clingfilm and freeze until required.

Serves 6

Burgers:

700g/1lb 8oz lean minced beef
1 bunch spring onions (about 6 stems), thinly sliced
50g/2oz/½ cup breadcrumbs
50g/2oz/½ cup blue cheese, crumbled
2 tbsp sweet chilli jam (see page 137)
1 tbsp chopped fresh parsley
pinch of ground cinnamon
1 large egg
plain flour, for dusting,
sunflower oil, for brushing and cooking
salt and freshly ground black pepper

To Serve:

6 round bread rolls or burger buns, sliced in half
3 tbsp mayonnaise
1 tbsp sweet chilli jam
6 bacon rashers
6 eggs
handful of lettuce leaves

1 Put the minced beef in a large mixing bowl with the sliced spring onion, breadcrumbs, cheese, chilli jam and chopped parsley. Mix together well. Season the mixture with a little salt and pepper and some ground cinnamon.

2 Break the egg into the bowl and mix with the meat using your hands until it all binds together well. Divide the mixture into 6–7 pieces, dust with a little plain flour and shape each piece into a burger about 1cm/½in thick. Allow the uncooked burgers to rest in the refrigerator for at least 30 minutes.

3 You can cook the burgers on a barbecue or in the oven. If cooking on the barbecue, light the coals. If using the oven, preheat to 180°C/350°F/Gas Mark 4. Brush the burgers all over with a little oil to prevent them from sticking to the grill, then barbecue for 4–5 minutes on each side or cook in the oven for 20 minutes. Alternatively, you could start them off on the barbecue until the meat is sealed all over, then transfer to a baking sheet and put in the oven for 10–12 minutes, or until completely cooked.

4 Meanwhile, grill the sliced bread rolls or burger buns lightly on the barbecue or under the grill. Mix the mayonnaise in a bowl with the sweet chilli jam and spread on to the toasted bread.

5 Grill the bacon rashers on the barbecue or under the grill until crispy. Heat a little oil in a frying pan, either on the hob or placed directly on the bars of the barbecue. Crack 2–3 eggs into the pan, or however many will fit comfortably without touching, and fry gently. When cooked to your liking, remove from the pan and repeat with the remaining eggs.

6 When the cooking time for the burgers is up, cut through the centre of one burger to check if it is cooked, as it's risky to serve undercooked mince. If still pink in the centre, return to the barbecue or oven for a couple more minutes.

7 To serve, place each burger on one half of a bun, and top with some lettuce, a rasher of crispy bacon and a softly fried egg. Put the remaining part of the bun on top or serve alongside.

Classic Italian Meatballs
with Spaghetti and Tomato Sauce

This is a firm favourite in the Dundon household. Whenever it is served, we end up with clean plates – which, from a parent's point of view, is always good news. My secret ingredient is the cinnamon, which gives these meatballs that extra edge. You can also use this basic mince mixture to make burgers.

Serves 4–6

sunflower oil, for frying
350g/12oz dry spaghetti
freshly grated Parmesan cheese, to serve

Meatballs:

½ onion, peeled and finely chopped
1 garlic clove, peeled and finely chopped
700g/1lb 8oz lean minced beef
50g/2oz/1 cup fine fresh white breadcrumbs
2 tsp grated Parmesan cheese
chopped fresh parsley
½ tsp ground cinnamon
1 free-range egg
plain flour, for dusting

Tomato Sauce:

½ onion, peeled and chopped
4–5 mushrooms, thinly sliced
2 garlic cloves, peeled and chopped
1 tsp dried mixed herbs
1 x 400g/14oz tin of chopped tomatoes
125ml/4fl oz/½ cup double cream (optional)
salt and freshly ground black pepper

1 Preheat the oven to 180ºC/350ºF/Gas Mark 4.

2 The meatballs are very simple to make and will be ready in no time. In a large bowl, mix the onion and garlic in with the meat. Add all the other ingredients, using the egg to bind them together. Flour your hands and mould the mixture into meatballs – they should weigh about 75g/3oz each or be about the same size as a golf ball.

3 Heat a large pan with a little oil, add the meatballs and cook over a medium heat for 3–4 minutes, then transfer to an ovenproof dish and cook in the oven for an additional 12–15 minutes to ensure that they are thoroughly cooked.

4 Meanwhile, make the tomato sauce in the same pan used for the meatballs. Fry the onion, mushrooms and garlic over a medium heat until soft. Stir in the mixed herbs and chopped tomatoes. Allow the mixture to bubble for about 10 minutes. Add the cream, if using, and adjust the seasoning. When the meatballs are cooked, add them to the sauce.

5 Meanwhile, cook and drain the spaghetti following the packet instructions.

6 Serve the meatballs on top of spaghetti, sprinkled with freshly grated Parmesan cheese.

roasts & family meals

When I was a child, I woke up every Sunday morning to the wonderful aroma of a joint roasting in the oven. Even now, when I cook roast beef, I recall those early days.

Nowadays, we try to cook a roast at weekends, then use up the leftovers during the week in many creative ways. But roasts and joints aren't just for lazy Sundays and holidays. They also make easy midweek meals because once they're in the oven, you can sit back and relax.

Vegetarian **Moussaka**

This is a fantastic hearty vegetarian recipe to keep up your sleeve for a special occasion.

Vegetarian
Serves 4–6

3 large aubergines, trimmed and sliced
200g/7oz/1 cup green lentils
600ml/1 pint/2½ cups vegetable stock
sunflower oil, for cooking
1 red onion, peeled and thinly sliced
2 garlic cloves, peeled and crushed
8–10 button mushrooms, sliced
1 x 400g/14oz tin of chickpeas, rinsed
1 x 400g/14oz tin of chopped tomatoes
1 tsp tomato purée
½ tsp dried mixed herbs
300ml/10fl oz/1¼ cups natural yoghurt
75ml/2½fl oz/scant ⅓ cup milk
110g/4oz/1 cup grated Cheddar or mozzarella cheese
3 eggs
salt and freshly ground black pepper
salad and crusty bread, to serve

1 Place the aubergine slices in a colander and sprinkle generously with salt. Leave for 20 minutes.

2 Put the green lentils in a large saucepan with the vegetable stock. Set over a medium heat, bring to the boil and simmer for 20 minutes, until tender. Drain and keep warm.

3 Heat some oil in another large saucepan over a medium heat and cook the red onion and garlic until soft. Stir in the cooked lentils along with the mushrooms, chickpeas, chopped tomatoes, tomato purée, herbs and 100ml/3½fl oz/½ cup of water. Bring to the boil, then reduce the heat and simmer for 10 minutes, stirring occasionally. Season with salt and pepper.

4 Preheat the oven to 180°C/350°F/Gas Mark 4. Rinse the aubergine slices and dry well, then fry in a little oil until brown on both sides. Place a layer of the slices in the bottom of a 25cm/10in square ovenproof dish, then top with some of the cooked lentil mixture. Continue to layer up all of the aubergine and lentils (much like a lasagne), finishing with a layer of aubergine.

5 Beat together the yoghurt, milk, cheese and eggs and season with salt and pepper. Pour this over the vegetable mixture in the dish, then bake the moussaka in the oven for 45 minutes, or until golden brown and bubbling. Serve with salad and crusty bread.

Smoked **Haddock** and **Rocket** Tart

This recipe does require a little extra work, but it looks sophisticated and tastes great.

Serves 8–10

Pastry:

225g/8oz/1½ cups plain flour, plus extra for dusting
½ tsp salt
110g/4oz/1 stick butter, cut into pieces
1 tsp fennel seeds
ice cold water, about 4–5 tbsp

Filling:

400g/14oz smoked haddock
6–8 mushrooms, thinly sliced
½ medium onion, peeled and diced
350ml/12fl oz/1½ cups milk
4 eggs
1 small bunch fresh rocket, washed and chopped
110g/4oz/1 cup grated hard cheese (optional)
salt and freshly ground black pepper

1 To make the pastry, sift the flour and salt into a large bowl, then rub in the butter until the mixture resembles very fine breadcrumbs. Stir in the fennel seeds, then pour in the ice cold water and knead until the pastry comes together into a ball. Rest for at least 40 minutes, then roll out on a lightly floured board and use to line a 23cm/9in fluted flan dish.

2 You need to blind bake the pastry case before adding the filling. Preheat the oven to 180°C/350°F/Gas Mark 4. Line the pastry with a circle of baking parchment and fill with ceramic baking beans or uncooked rice, lentils or coffee beans. (Alternatively, you could line with strips of clingfilm – three going left to right, three top to bottom – but if so, only use rice, lentils or coffee beans to fill it, not baking beans.) Bake in the preheated oven for 15 minutes, then remove the beans and parchment or clingfilm, and return the tin to the oven for another 6–7 minutes to crisp up the pastry. Remove from the oven and allow to cool. Leave the oven turned on.

3 Meanwhile, prepare the filling. Put the smoked haddock, mushrooms and onion in a saucepan with the milk and gently poach over a medium heat for 6–7 minutes. Strain off the milk but retain.

4 Whisk the eggs with the poaching milk and salt and pepper. Mix in the chopped rocket.

5 Spoon the haddock mixture into the blind-baked pastry case. Pour the egg and rocket mixture on top. Bake in the oven for 30–40 minutes, or until the filling is well set – give the tart a gentle shake to check. Sprinkle with the grated cheese, if using, and pop the tart back in the oven for 4–5 minutes to melt the cheese.

Baked Salmon Fillet

The children love baked salmon, and if Catherine and I have been working all day, this is a quick and easy evening meal. Do try to obtain the best quality fish you can, as it really makes a huge difference to the flavour.

Serves 6

1 side of salmon (about
    1.6kg/3lb 8oz)
1 lemon
2 tbsp chopped fresh parsley
75g/3oz/1½ cups fine fresh
    white breadcrumbs
75g/3oz/¾ cup grated
    Parmesan cheese
2 garlic cloves, peeled and
    finely chopped
50g/2oz/½ stick butter
freshly ground black pepper

1 Preheat the oven to 200°C/400°F/Gas Mark 6.

2 Line a large flat baking tray with a piece of baking parchment and lay the salmon (either whole or in pieces) flat out on the paper.

3 Finely grate the zest of the lemon into a bowl and add the chopped parsley, breadcrumbs and Parmesan cheese. Mix in the finely chopped garlic and black pepper. Scatter this crumb mixture over the top of the salmon fillet and press it gently into the flesh to secure it.

4 Chop the butter into very small pieces and dot these along the top of the salmon. This will help to hold the breadcrumb mixture in place.

5 Bake the salmon for 25–30 minutes, or until the salmon is firm to the touch. The crust should be nice and crunchy.

6 This fish is beautiful eaten either hot or cold. I love to serve it cold on homemade brown bread, with a large green salad on the side.

Pan-fried Turbot
with Roasted Sweet Potatoes

This is a perfect dish for family cooking, but it still has a touch of special occasion about it. The sweet potatoes are baked in goose fat, which gives them a mouth-watering flavour that marries beautifully with the delicate turbot.

Serves 6

4 large sweet potatoes, peeled and cut into slices about 3cm/1¼in thick
400g/14oz/1 cup goose fat
2 tsp sunflower oil
1 piece of turbot (about 1kg/2¼lb)
plain flour, for dusting
225g/8oz/2 cups frozen garden peas
50g/2oz/½ stick butter
1 tbsp chopped fresh mint, plus extra to garnish
salt and freshly ground black pepper

Lemon Butter:

110g/4oz/1 stick butter
zest of 1 lemon
2 tbsp chopped fresh parsley

1 Preheat the oven to 150ºC/300ºF/Gas Mark 2.

2 Place the sweet potato slices in a deep roasting tin.

3 Gently melt the goose fat in a saucepan, then pour it over the potatoes until they are covered about halfway up their sides. Transfer to the oven and bake for 1 hour, turning them over halfway throughout the cooking time. Be careful – the fat will be extremely hot.

4 To make the lemon butter, mix all ingredients together and chill in the refrigerator.

5 Meanwhile, heat the oil in a large frying pan. Dust the turbot with flour, then pan-fry the turbot, flesh-side down first, for about 2–3 minutes on each side. Place in a roasting tin and roast for around 12 minutes, or until the fish flakes easily when tested with a fork.

6 Boil the peas for 2–3 minutes in a small pan of boiling salted water. Remove from the water and place in a large bowl with the butter and chopped mint and toss together.

7 To serve, remove the sweet potatoes from the roasting tin and allow them to drain on kitchen paper for a minute or two. Divide the sweet potato slices among four plates. Scatter the buttered peas next to the potatoes. Arrange the turbot beside the potatoes and on top of the buttered garden peas. Dot with a little lemon butter and garnish with fresh mint.

Roasted Lemon Chicken
with Bread Sauce

My ideal Sunday is a lazy morning with the papers, a leisurely lunch of roast chicken, bread sauce, crisp broccoli and roast potatoes, then off for a long walk with the children.

Serves 4–6

1 large lemon
3–4 fresh thyme sprigs, plus a
    couple extra to put inside the
    chicken
75g/3oz/¾ stick butter, at
    room temperature
1 large free-range chicken
    (about 1.3kg/3lb)
1 whole bulb of garlic
**salt and freshly ground black
    pepper**

Bread Sauce:

1 small onion, peeled
4 cloves
2 bay leaves
425ml/15fl oz/generous
    1¾ cups milk
110g/4oz/2 cups fresh white
    breadcrumbs
½ tsp freshly grated nutmeg
50g/2oz/½ stick butter
4 tsp double cream

1 Preheat the oven to 170ºC/325ºF/Gas Mark 3. Finely grate the zest of the lemon. Chop the thyme and add to the butter with the lemon zest.

2 Wipe out the cavity of the chicken with kitchen paper. Loosen the skin around the chicken and, using your fingers, spread some of the lemon butter under the skin (directly onto the flesh) and gently massage into the breasts – this will make the chicken nicely fragrant. Return the skin to its original position.

3 The remainder of the whole lemon can be pushed into the cavity of the chicken with one or two extra sprigs of thyme and the entire bulb of garlic. This will add extra flavour. Season the skin with salt and pepper. Weight the chicken and calculate the cooking time, allowing 15 minutes per 450g/1lb plus 20 minutes.

4 Season the chicken, then transfer it to a roasting tray and bake for 1 hour 20 minutes, or until the chicken is thoroughly cooked. Insert a skewer into the thigh and check that the juices run clear; if they don't, continue to cook for a little longer. Once cooked, removed from the oven, cover with foil and allow to rest for a further 10–15 minutes before carving.

5 To make the bread sauce, stud the onion with the cloves, then place in a large saucepan with the bay leaves. Pour in the milk and bring gently to the boil. When the milk has come to the boil, remove the studded onion and bay leaves. Sprinkle in the breadcrumbs and allow to cook over a very gentle heat for 8–10 minutes. Stir in the nutmeg, butter and cream, which will flavour and enrich the sauce even further, and cook for another 5–10 minutes. Transfer to a warmed sauceboat to serve with the chicken.

Spatchcock Chicken

The butcher can prepare the chicken for you, so this is quite simple. Basically, the entire chicken is opened out, split down the middle and flattened in order to cut down on cooking time. Be patient and leave the marinade for a full 12 hours – the result will be well worth the wait!

Serves 4–6

1 oven-ready spatchcock chicken (1.5kg/3lb 5oz)
4 tsp sunflower oil

Marinade:

1 tsp paprika
½ tsp cayenne pepper
2 red chillies, chopped (deseeded if you wish)
2–3 black peppercorns
2–3 fresh thyme sprigs
zest of 1 orange
zest of 1 lemon
2 garlic cloves, peeled and finely chopped
250ml/9fl oz/generous 1 cup lager (purely for cooking purposes!)

1 Mix all the ingredients for the marinade together and blend in the food processor. Place the chicken in a non-metallic dish, pour over the marinade and leave for up to 12 hours prior to cooking it.

2 Preheat the barbecue and get it nicely hot. I try to brush the bars of the grill lightly with oil, as this helps to stop the meat sticking. Alternatively, preheat the oven to 180ºC/350ºF/Gas Mark 4 and roast the chicken for 1¼ hours (see step 4).

3 Cook the chicken for 7–10 minutes on each side on the hottest part of the barbecue, then transfer it to the outer side of the barbecue where it can cook over a more gentle heat for a further 30–40 minutes. This time will depend largely on the heat of your own barbecue as they are all different. Baste the chicken with additional marinade during the cooking process (see tip below).

4 The flesh of the chicken should be soft and ready to come away from the bone easily and the juices should run clear. Sometimes if the chicken is a little larger or the barbecue too hot, I transfer it to a hot oven for the last few minutes to ensure it is fully cooked.

5 Serve with a tomato and shallot salad (see page 152).

Tip:
If you wish to baste the partially cooked meat with additional marinade, bring the marinade to a gentle boil for 4–5 minutes first, to kill off any bacteria it may harbour.

Perfect Christmas Turkey with Sage and Onion Stuffing

There is something wonderfully satisfying about placing a beautiful turkey in the middle of the dinner table on Christmas day. If cooked properly, turkey can be a deliciously moist bird, which everyone, including the cook, will enjoy.

Serves 6–8

6.5kg/14lb turkey
7–8 rashers of streaky bacon

Stuffing:

175g/6oz/1½ sticks butter
1 onion, peeled and finely chopped
225g/8oz/2 cups sausagemeat
4 tsp chopped fresh parsley
2 tsp chopped fresh sage
450g/1lb/8 cups fresh white breadcrumbs
salt and freshly ground black pepper

1 To make the stuffing, melt the butter in a pan over a very gentle heat. Add the onion and cook until softened but not coloured. Take off the heat, allow to cool slightly, then add the sausagemeat, chopped herbs and breadcrumbs. The mixture should not be too dry, as this will result in a dry stuffing. Season the stuffing and allow to cool completely. The stuffing can be made a couple of days in advance if you wish and chilled in the refrigerator until required.

2 On Christmas morning, preheat the oven to 200°C/400°F/Gas Mark 6.

3 Wipe out the cavity of the turkey with kitchen paper, then line the cavity with foil and loosely pack the stuffing into the bird. Don't forget to weigh the turkey again with the stuffing enclosed.

4 Place the turkey in a large roasting tin and lay the bacon across the breast to protect the meat and prevent it from drying out. Put the turkey in the oven. To calculate the cooking time, allow 20 minutes per 450g/1lb plus an additional 20–30 minutes. In total, a turkey of this size should take about 4½ hours. It is cooked if the juices run completely clear when a skewer is inserted into the leg. After the first hour, turn down the oven to 150°C/300°F/Gas Mark 2. If you feel the turkey is browning too quickly, cover it with foil for the first 2 hours.

5 Allow the meat to rest for 20–30 minutes, covered with foil, when it comes out of the oven, then carve as required. Remove the foil packet of stuffing from the cavity and serve with the turkey. Enjoy the turkey and the day!

Traditional Roast Goose
with Cranberry Stuffing

We normally wait until New Year's Day to have goose
for a long extended family lunch that lingers late into
the evening. If Catherine has cooked for Christmas,
I usually do the works on New Year's Day. This is what
life should be about – good food in good company.

Serves 8–10

6.5kg/14lb goose
1 orange
butter, oil, vegetables
    (optional)
8 rashers of streaky bacon
salt and freshly ground black
    pepper

Cranberry Stuffing:

110g/4oz/1 cup fresh
    cranberries
50ml/2fl oz/¼ cup port
150g/5oz/1¼ sticks butter
½ onion, peeled and finely
    chopped
2 garlic cloves, peeled and
    crushed
2 tbsp chopped fresh herbs
    (such as parsley, thyme,
    sage)
450g/1lb/4 cups sausagemeat
450g/1lb/8 cups fresh white
    breadcrumbs

1 Soak the cranberries in the port for up to 1 hour. Preheat the oven to
200°C/400°F/Gas Mark 6. Melt the butter in a frying pan and gently fry
the onion and garlic until soft but not coloured. Tip into a bowl and
allow to cool a little. Add in the remaining stuffing ingredients, mix well
and season with salt and pepper.

2 Clean the cavity of the bird with dry kitchen paper and stuff with an
orange. This will give a beautiful flavour to the bird. Roll the stuffing
mixture up tightly in foil and stuff it into the neck of the goose. Close
the gap using the flap of skin.

3 Place the goose in a roasting tray and prick all over with a fork. Season
well. Add a little butter or oil to the tray and some vegetables if you wish
for additional flavour. Cover the goose with the rashers of bacon.

4 Don't forget to re-weigh the bird after the stuffing is added, as this
will make a difference to the cooking time of around 15 minutes per
450g/1lb plus 15 minutes over. Roast a 4kg/9lb goose for 3 hours,
a 4.5–5kg/10–11lb goose for 3½ hours and a 6.5kg/14lb goose for
4½ hours. After the first 40 minutes, turn down the oven to 170°C/
325°F/Gas Mark 3 and cover the goose with foil.

5 Remove the foil 30–40 minutes before the end of the cooking time so
that the skin can brown and crisp. To test whether the goose is cooked,
pierce the fattest part of the thigh with a skewer. If the juices run clear,
the bird is done. Rest for 20–30 minutes, covered with foil, before carving.
(Save the meat juices to make delicious gravy to accompany the meat. See
page 107.) Serve slices of the goose on top of a generous amount of the
cranberry stuffing.

Orange-**Roasted Duck**
with Spiced Plum Compote

Duck is one of those meats that goes particularly well with fruit compote or chutney. This plum sauce is a delicious accompaniment and will last for up to 1 week in the refrigerator.

Serves 6–8

1.5kg/3lb 5oz whole free-range duck

sunflower oil, for rubbing

1 large orange

salt and freshly ground black pepper

Plum Sauce:

125ml/4fl oz/½ cup red wine

125ml/4fl oz/½ cup red wine vinegar

75g/3oz brown sugar

2 bay leaves

½ cinnamon stick

½ tsp mixed spice

pinch of ground nutmeg

4 fresh plums, stoned and cut into 6 wedges each

1 Preheat the oven to 180ºC/350ºF/Gas Mark 4.

2 Place the duck on a wire rack set over a deep roasting tin and make a number of incisions in the flesh with a sharp knife. Boil a kettle of water and carefully pour the boiling water over the duck. This will help to achieve a crispy skin later on. Carefully discard the water in the tin. Rub a little of the sunflower oil into the skin of the duck and season with salt and pepper.

3 Place the duck into a dry roasting tin. Insert a whole orange into the cavity of the bird and roast for 1½ hours. Cover loosely with foil if it's cooking too quickly. When cooked, remove from the oven and rest, covered in foil, for 10 minutes before carving.

4 Meanwhile, heat the red wine, vinegar and brown sugar together in a large saucepan. Add the bay leaves, cinnamon stick and spices. Bring to the boil and then reduce the heat to a simmer. Add the plum wedges to the syrup. Cook for a further 5–8 minutes, or until the plums have softened down a little. Place in a warmed sauceboat.

5 Carve the duck and serve with your choice of vegetables and the sauce.

Roasted Saddle of **Rabbit** with Chicken and Mushroom Filling

Once a so-called 'peasant' food, rabbit has now become a real delicacy. This Italian-style recipe is wonderful for a fancy dinner party or a special occasion.

Serves 6

6 saddles of rabbit (allow 175g/6oz per portion)
110g/4oz wild mushroom selection
butter, for frying
50ml/2fl oz/¼ cup double cream
1 chicken breast (225g/8oz)
2 tsp chopped fresh parsley
12 slices of Parma ham
salt and freshly ground black pepper

1 Preheat the oven to 200ºC/400ºF/Gas Mark 6.

2 Ask the butcher to prepare the saddles of rabbit for you. Make sure there is a piece opened out to allow you to spoon in the savoury stuffing.

3 Pan-fry the wild mushrooms in butter over a medium heat, season and set aside to cool, then place in the refrigerator. When chilled, place in a small blender or food processor with the cream and chicken and blend to a smooth purée. Season the mixture lightly, bearing in mind that the mushrooms have already been seasoned. Mix in the chopped parsley.

4 Spread out two slices of Parma ham on the work surface, place one of the saddles of rabbit on top and pipe or carefully spread the chicken mixture on top. Fold over the rabbit and encase in the Parma ham. Repeat with the remaining ham and rabbit.

5 Pan-fry the 'parcels' in a large ovenproof pan on all sides until the rabbit is sealed, then finish off in the oven for about 10–12 minutes.

6 Transfer the rabbit to a plate. If you wish, deglaze the pan with some chopped garlic, shallots and red wine for a very simple but tasty sauce to accompany the rabbit.

7 To serve, slice the rabbit into thin slices to reveal the glorious stuffing on the inside. Serve the sauce separately.

Roasted Leg of Lamb
with Orange Marmalade Crust

I just adore lamb – it has such a deliciously delicate flavour and this marmalade crust gives an unusual tangy twist. You can use bought marmalade, but I prefer to make my own (see recipe on page 154).

Serves 6

3 carrots, peeled and cut into large chunks

1 whole bulb of garlic, halved horizontally

3 celery sticks, chopped into large chunks

1 leg of lamb (about 2kg/ 4lb 8oz)

2–3 fresh rosemary sprigs

sunflower oil, for drizzling

2 tbsp orange marmalade (see page 154)

salt and freshly ground black pepper

Sauce:

25g/1oz/2½ tbsp plain flour

½ tsp tomato purée

100ml/3½fl oz/scant ½ cup red wine

300ml/10fl oz/1¼ cups good-quality meat stock

½ tsp chopped fresh rosemary

1 Preheat the oven to 200°C/400°F/Gas Mark 6.

2 Arrange large chunks of the carrots, garlic and celery in a large roasting tin to form a trivet to raise the meat off the base of the tin. Lay the leg of lamb on top of the vegetables. Using a sharp knife, make a number of incisions in the fat of the lamb and push pieces of the rosemary into the slits. Season lightly with a little salt and pepper and drizzle with a little oil. Roast in the oven for 1–1½ hours (15 minutes per 450g/1lb for rare and 20 minutes for medium), turning over halfway through the cooking time.

3 About 20 minutes before the cooking time is up, remove from the oven and spread the marmalade over the crust and return to bake for the remaining cooking time.

4 Allow the meat to rest for at least 15 minutes before carving to allow the juices to soak into the flesh.

5 To make the sauce, drain most of the fat from the roasting tin and discard the vegetables. Place the tin on the hob over a gentle heat. Sprinkle in the flour, add the tomato purée and stir with a whisk until well coloured. Gradually pour in the red wine and stock and continue to whisk until the mixture comes to the boil. Sieve into a clean saucepan to remove any impurities. Add the chopped rosemary and boil for 4–5 minutes, or until reduced and thickened. Adjust the seasoning and pour into a warmed sauceboat to accompany the lamb.

6 Serve with baby boiled potatoes dressed with mint and butter.

Crown of Lamb
and Roasted Root Vegetables

I love spring for so many reasons, but what I look forward to most is the return of lamb. A crown is just two racks tied together in a circular shape, and the beauty of this dish is that the butcher will do all the preparation for you.

Serves 6

Roasted Lamb:

1 crown of lamb (you will need about 15–18 bones)
fresh rosemary sprigs
4 garlic cloves, peeled and chopped
2 tsp sunflower oil

Roasted Root Vegetables:

2 carrots, 2 parsnips and 1 turnip, peeled and cut into large chunks
sunflower oil, for drizzling
4 tsp honey
chopped fresh herbs

Classic Roast Potatoes:

4 tsp sunflower oil or goose fat
2–3 floury potatoes (Rooster are ideal), peeled and cut into large chunks
sea salt

1 Preheat the oven to 190°C/375°F/Gas Mark 5.

2 Put the lamb crown into the roasting tin bone side up. (Sometimes I slot a small ovenproof glass bowl in the centre to keep the crown rounded during the cooking process.) Cover the top of each bone with foil to prevent them becoming overcooked and burnt. Make sharp incisions in the fat of the lamb and stud with some rosemary and chopped garlic. Drizzle the oil over the top of the lamb and roast in the oven for 45–60 minutes.

3 Take out of the oven and allow to rest for 10–15 minutes before serving. If you prefer your meat well done, allow an additional 10–15 minutes cooking time before resting.

4 To roast the root vegetables, place the chopped vegetables in a roasting tin and drizzle with oil. Roast in the oven for up to 45 minutes, or until the vegetables are well cooked. About 10 minutes before they are ready, drizzle them with honey and return to the oven. When the vegetables are cooked, sprinkle with the chopped herbs.

5 For the roast potatoes, heat the oil or fat in a roasting tray in the oven. Place the potatoes in a large saucepan of cold water and bring to the boil. Allow them to boil for 9 minutes, then strain off all the water, cover the saucepan with its lid and allow the potatoes to dry out.

6 When the oil is very hot, slide the tin out of the oven, being careful not to spill the hot fat. Shake the potatoes gently in the saucepan to ruffle up their sides. Place the potatoes in the hot fat, sprinkle with sea salt, return to the oven and roast for about 30 minutes, or until they are soft on the inside but golden and crispy on the outside.

Redcurrant **Gravy**

Redcurrant Gravy:

50g/2oz/⅓ cup plain flour
1 tsp tomato purée
100ml/3½fl oz/scant ½ cup
  red wine
425ml/15fl oz/generous
  1¾ cups homemade stock
110g/4oz/½ cup fresh
  redcurrants
½ tsp chopped fresh rosemary
salt and freshly ground black
  pepper

1 To make the redcurrant gravy, remove the meat from the roasting tin and drain off any excess fat. Place the roasting tin on the hob and allow to sizzle a little. Sprinkle in the flour and, using a whisk, rub in the flour, removing all the sediment from the bottom of the tray. Gently whisk in the tomato purée, red wine and homemade stock and bring to the boil. Sieve the sauce into a large saucepan and continue to boil and reduce rapidly for 10 minutes. Add the fresh redcurrants and the chopped rosemary. Correct the seasoning and set aside until you are ready to serve.

2 To serve, remove the foil from around the bones and replace with the little paper cutlet frills you can get in the supermarket. Arrange the lamb crown on a large serving platter.

3 Pile the roasted root vegetables into the centre of the crown. Scatter the roast potatoes around the outside. Serve a sauceboat of the redcurrant gravy separately.

Venison Loin with Roasted Root Vegetables

Venison is low in fat, high in protein and iron and makes a healthy and appetizing addition to your family's diet. In this recipe I use a loin, which is far superior to other cuts. Rump or topside could be substituted, but are not so tender and require longer cooking times.

Serves 6

6 tbsp olive oil

1 long red chilli, deseeded and finely chopped (optional)

1 heaped tsp fresh thyme

4 large garlic cloves, peeled

8 small carrots, peeled and halved lengthways

4 small parsnips, peeled and halved

12 large shallots, peeled and trimmed

1 small butternut squash, peeled, deseeded and cut into wedges

1 venison loin (about 750g/ 1lb 10oz)

salt and freshly ground black pepper

1 Preheat the oven to 190ºC/375ºF/Gas Mark 5.

2 To cook the roasted root vegetables, place 4 tablespoons of the olive oil in a large roasting tin and add the chilli, if using, thyme, garlic and all the vegetables except the squash. Toss well to combine.

3 Season generously and roast for 40 minutes, or until almost tender and lightly golden, tossing from time to time to ensure the vegetables caramelize evenly. Add the butternut squash to the tin and toss to combine, then roast for another 20–30 minutes, or until all the vegetables are tender and caramelized. Remove from the oven and keep warm. Reduce the oven to 180ºC/350ºF/Gas Mark 4.

4 Heat a large heavy-based frying pan until very hot. Rub the remaining oil all over the venison and season to taste. Add to the heated pan and sear for 2–3 minutes, then turn over and sear for another 2–3 minutes.

5 Place in a roasting pan and roast for 30–35 minutes. Remove from the oven and set the venison aside in a warm place to rest for a few minutes. Carve the loin into 12 slices and arrange them on warmed serving plates on a pile of the roasted root vegetables. Serve immediately.

Tip

Roasting is a great way to cook root vegetables, as they're robust enough to cope with the intense heat, and this method of cooking draws out the most wonderful flavours. Try using any root vegetable combination you fancy; just make sure they are are cut into chunks roughly the same size to ensure even cooking.

Glazed Loin of Bacon

This is one of those quintessentially Irish dishes that has been around for years, and every cook will have developed their own version. I like to use the loin of bacon, which is quite tender and tasty and easy to carve and serve.

Serves 4–6

1.3kg/3lb loin of bacon (back bacon)

12–15 cloves

2 tbsp honey

110g/4oz/½ cup (solidly packed) demerara sugar

100ml/3½fl oz/scant ½ cup water

1 Place the loin of bacon in a large pan and cover with cold water. Bring to the boil, then reduce the heat and simmer for 1¼ hours, or until completely tender. Remove the bacon from the water and allow to cool for 15–20 minutes.

2 Preheat the oven to 180ºC/350ºF/Gas Mark 4.

3 Transfer the bacon to a roasting tin. Using a sharp knife, make some incisions in the fat of the bacon in a criss-cross pattern – this will give an attractive finish to the dish. Push the cloves into the slits in the bacon in a uniform pattern.

4 Place the honey and demerara sugar in a small saucepan with the water and allow to come gently to the boil, then pour over the clove-studded loin of bacon. Transfer to the oven for 15–20 minutes, or until the bacon has acquired a nice crunchy crust.

Pot-roasted Pork
with Apples

The entire family really loves this dish. Prepare it the night before so you can just pop it into the oven whenever you wish. The flavour of the meat naturally infuses the sauce, giving it real depth and subtlety.

Serves 6

sunflower oil, for frying

2kg/4lb 8oz loin of pork, boned and rolled, skin removed

3 garlic cloves, peeled and chopped

2 carrots, peeled and cut into chunks

3 celery sticks, chopped

2 bay leaves

4 black peppercorns

12 baby onions, peeled and left whole

50g/2oz/$\frac{1}{3}$ cup plain flour

300ml/10fl oz/1$\frac{1}{4}$ cups red wine

300ml/10fl oz/1$\frac{1}{4}$ cups chicken stock

2 large cooking apples, peeled, cored and cut into chunky wedges

3–4 fresh thyme sprigs

salt and freshly ground black pepper

1 Preheat the oven to 150°C/300°F/Gas Mark 2.

2 Heat a little oil in a large frying pan over a medium heat. Seal the pork in the hot pan on all sides, ensuring that it gets browned all over. This should take no more than 8–10 minutes. Keep the pork tied with the string, as this will help the joint keep its shape. Transfer the pork to a large casserole dish with a tightly fitting lid.

3 Meanwhile, add the garlic, carrots, celery, bay leaves, peppercorns and peeled baby onions to the pan used to brown the meat. Toss those around on the pan for a few minutes until they begin to turn a nice golden brown colour, then add in the flour and use the flour to dry up the vegetables slightly.

4 Finally, pour the red wine and chicken stock into the frying pan. Bring this mixture to the boil and pour over the pork in the casserole dish. Toss the apple wedges in on top of the pork mixture. Season the mixture with salt and pepper and add in the thyme sprigs. Cover with the lid and place in the oven for 2$\frac{1}{2}$ hours.

5 Serve piping hot with roasted garlic mashed potatoes (see page 161).

Roasted Loin of Pork
with Apple and Cider Sauce

Pork is excellent served with this delicious, creamy sauce to enhance its flavour. There is no need to baste the pork during cooking, as it has a thick layer of fat that will keep it moist. If you wish, you can substitute the cider with apple juice.

Serves 6

3–4 unpeeled carrots
2kg/4lb 8oz loin of pork, with skin attached
2 tsp sunflower oil
2 tsp rock salt

Apple and Cider Sauce:

25g/1oz/¼ stick butter
1 small onion, peeled and chopped
7–8 mushrooms, thinly sliced
25g/1oz/2½ tbsp plain flour
300ml/10fl oz/1¼ cups good-quality cider or apple juice
200ml/7fl oz/generous ¾ cup pouring cream
2 tsp wholegrain mustard
1 dessert apple, cored and cut into small dice
salt and freshly ground black pepper

1 Preheat the oven to 200°C/400°F/Gas Mark 6.

2 Lay the carrots across the base of a large roasting tin. Score the fat on the pork in a criss-cross pattern with a very sharp knife. Drizzle with a little oil and rub with the rock salt. Place on top of the carrots.

3 Roast for 20 minutes, then reduce the heat to 170°C/325°F/Gas Mark 3. Continue to roast for a further 1¼ hours, by which stage the juices of the meat should run clear and the skin should be crisp.

4 Transfer the meat to a carving board and allow it to rest for 10 minutes, or until you are ready to carve.

5 To make the sauce, melt the butter over a low heat in a large pan and gently fry the onion and sliced mushrooms for 4–5 minutes, or until lightly cooked. Scatter the plain flour into the pan and use it to coat the onions and mushrooms and dry up the pan.

6 Add the cider and cream together and whisk continuously to ensure that the flour does not stay in lumps. Mix in the wholegrain mustard. Allow the sauce to come to the boil, then reduce the heat to a simmer for 5–6 minutes, or until it has reduced sufficiently and coats the back of a spoon. Finally, add the diced apple and allow it to warm through.

7 Check the seasoning of the sauce and serve alongside slices of the roasted loin of pork. A mixture of steamed green vegetables works well with this dish.

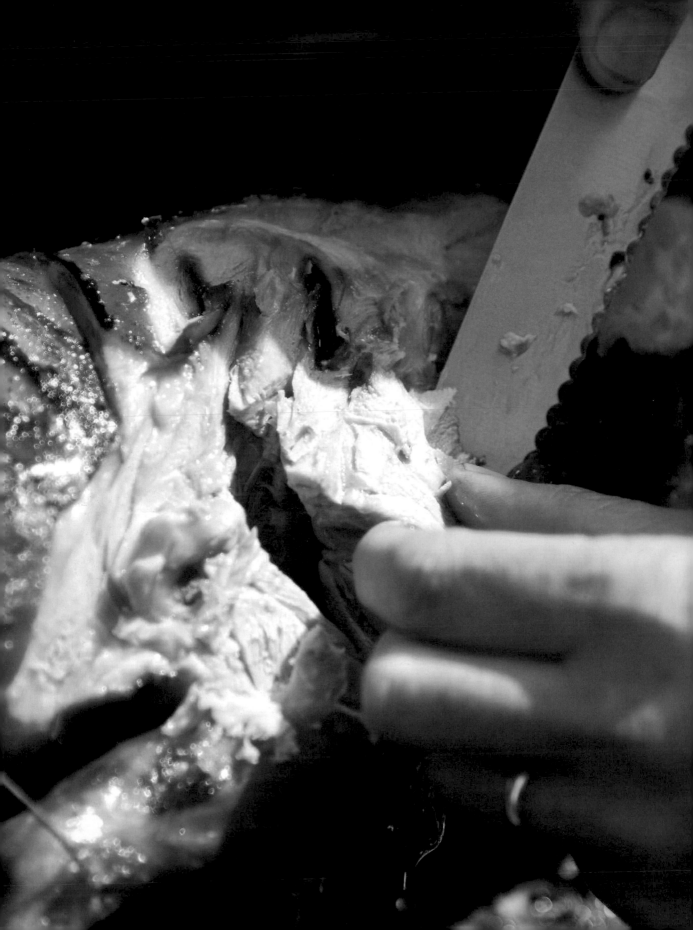

Suckling Pig

This is a real show-off recipe that always generates attention at a barbecue. Always give the butcher your order in advance and make sure that the pig is oven-ready when collected from your butcher. Pigs less than 9kg/20lb will fit comfortably into a domestic oven.

Serves 10–12

whole suckling pig (about
    6.9kg/16lb)
1 orange
about 3 tbsp honey
4 aubergines, peeled and thinly
    sliced

1 Preheat the oven to 170ºC/325ºF/Gas Mark 3.

2 Prick the skin of the pig all over to prevent it bursting later. Carefully place the orange in the pig's mouth. Put the meat in a large, deep roasting tin and roast in the oven for 2½ hours. Calculate cooking times for other weights of meat based on 20 minutes per 450g/1lb.

3 Meanwhile, light the barbecue and heat it to very hot – they tend to cool down quite quickly. After the pig comes out of the oven, baste it with the fat from the roasting tin and drizzle the honey over the top. Place it on the cooler part of the barbecue and cover with a lid to prevent it drying out. Be very careful as the pig is quite hot. I normally use a couple of fish slices to manoeuvre the pig off the roasting tray and onto the barbecue. Glaze on the barbecue for 20–25 minutes, or until the skin is nice and crunchy.

4 Meanwhile, place the aubergines lengthways on the barbecue and griddle both sides for 5 minutes.

5 Transfer the pig from the barbecue to a very large serving platter and arrange the aubergine slices around the side. Be as imaginative as you like in the presentation!

Tip
You can also use the spit attachment of your barbecue to cook the pig. However, I prefer to always cook in the oven first as cooking entirely on the barbecue tends to burn the meat.

Paddy's Pork with Sausagemeat Stuffing

This is a very popular dish on the menu at Raglan Road Pub & Restaurant in Orlando, Florida, with which I'm involved. It's a traditional Irish pub that serves great food and drinks to many tourists who are visiting DisneyWorld. Paddy's pork is named after Patrick Kavanagh, the author of the well-known poem 'Raglan Road'.

Serves 4

1 large pork fillet
3 rashers of bacon (optional)
oil, for drizzling
6 potatoes, peeled and halved
2 fresh rosemary sprigs, woody
    stems removed

Stuffing:

225g/8oz/generous 3½ cups
    white breadcrumbs
½ medium onion, peeled and
    finely diced
grated zest of 1 orange
75g/3oz sausagemeat
50g/2oz/⅓ cup sultanas
1 eating apple, peeled and
    grated
2 tbsp in total of fresh chopped
    parsley, thyme and chives
175g/6oz/1½ sticks butter,
    melted
sea salt and freshly ground
    black pepper

Apple Compote:

5 large cooking apples
50g/2oz/¼ cup granulated
    sugar
4–5 tbsp water

1 To make the stuffing, put the breadcrumbs, onion, orange zest, sausagemeat, sultanas, grated apple, chopped herbs and seasoning in a large bowl and mix together. Add the melted butter and stir well. The stuffing should be soft and well bound together without being wet.

2 Preheat the oven to 190°C/375°F/Gas Mark 5. Clean the pork fillet well, removing all sinew and fat. Cut horizontally through the fillet, making sure not to cut all the way through, then open out the two halves like a butterfly and lay flat. Cover the butterflied pork with clingfilm and use a rolling pin to flatten it.

3 Remove the clingfilm and spoon a long strip of stuffing on to the flattened pork fillet. Roll the meat up tightly around it. If necessary, secure with string or cocktail sticks, or wrap with three rashers of bacon, if using. Place the rolled meat in a roasting tray, drizzle with a tiny bit of oil and cover loosely with foil. Add the potatoes to the tray and sprinkle with rosemary. Roast in the oven for 45–60 minutes, removing the foil for the last 15 minutes of cooking, until the pork is firm to the touch and well browned. Remove from the oven and allow the meat to rest for at least 10–15 minutes before slicing.

4 To make the apple compote, peel, core and dice the apples and put in a saucepan with the sugar and water. Set over a low heat and cook for 5–6 minutes, then turn off the heat. Leave the apples to rest in the pan for a further 10 minutes, then mash them roughly.

Cottage Pie

This is yet another classic recipe that has been adapted and changed a lot over the years. It's one which I use extensively in casa Dundon, for good reason – everyone loves it.

Serves 4–6

450g/1lb potatoes, peeled
1 tbsp olive oil
1 small onion, peeled and finely chopped
1 small leek, trimmed and finely sliced
1 small carrot, peeled and finely chopped
1 garlic clove, peeled and crushed
700g/1½lb lean minced beef
1 tbsp tomato purée
1 x 200g/7oz tin of chopped tomatoes
100ml/3½fl oz/scant ½ cup beef stock
3 tbsp milk
25g/1oz/¼ stick butter
salt and freshly ground black pepper

1 Put the peeled potatoes in a saucepan, cover with cold water and add a pinch of salt. Bring to the boil, then simmer for 15–20 minutes, or until completely tender when pierced with the tip of a sharp knife. Drain in a colander.

2 Meanwhile, heat the olive oil in a saucepan. Add the onion, leek, carrot and garlic and sauté for 3–4 minutes until just beginning to soften but not to brown. Stir in the mince and cook for 2–3 minutes until browned, breaking up any lumps with a wooden spoon. Stir in the tomato purée, chopped tomatoes and beef stock and cook gently for another 10 minutes until the vegetables are completely tender. Season to taste with salt and pepper and keep warm or reheat as needed.

3 Preheat the oven to 180°C/350°F/Gas Mark 4. Pour the milk into a saucepan and set on the hob to heat. Push the cooked peeled potatoes through a potato ricer or use a spatula to push them through a sieve. Beat the butter into the warm mashed potato and then add enough warm milk to make a smooth purée. Season with salt and pepper to taste.

4 Transfer the meat mixture into an ovenproof dish, top with the mashed potato purée and bake in the oven for about 30 minutes until piping hot and bubbling.

Fillet of Beef with
Cauliflower and Thyme Purée

Buy your meat from a good butcher to ensure that it is well hung and wonderfully flavoursome. This is a perfect meal to have on a Friday night with a nice bottle of red wine after a hectic week at work. Wilted spinach works well with this dish.

Serves 4
775g/1½lb fillet of beef, well hung
2 tsp sunflower oil
1 head of cauliflower
4–5 fresh thyme sprigs, chopped
350ml/12fl oz/1½ cups milk
salt and freshly ground black pepper

1 Heat an ovenproof griddle pan until very hot. Season the beef fillet. Add the oil to the pan and then add the beef and brown well for 10 minutes on all sides until you have achieved a nice, thick crust. Remove from the heat and leave to stand in a warm place until the beef has relaxed. This will take at least 10 minutes. If you prefer your beef well done, transfer it to the oven preheated to 180°C/350°F/Gas Mark 4 for a further 10 minutes prior to resting.

2 To make the cauliflower purée, chop the cauliflower up into chunks and place in a large saucepan with the chopped thyme. Cover with the milk and bring to the boil. Allow to simmer until the cauliflower is very soft. Strain off the majority of the cooking liquor, leaving just a little to make the purée nice and creamy. Season the mixture well and transfer to a food processor or use a hand-held blender to purée the mixture. Correct the seasoning.

3 If you are not serving the cauliflower immediately, transfer it to a clean ovenproof bowl for up to 1 hour. To reheat it, stir in 2 tablespoons of double cream and warm through in a low oven for 4–5 minutes. Alternatively, reheat it gently on the hob.

4 Place the meat on a platter and carve into 2cm/¾in slices, then serve with the cauliflower purée.

Roasted Sirloin of Beef
with Yorkshire Puddings

There is something very special about this traditional roast dinner and every household has their own way of serving it. It is good, wholesome, no-nonsense family food – I love it!

Serves 6
3 carrots, peeled and cut into
    large chunks
1 large onion, peeled and cut
    into large chunks
1 whole bulb of garlic
4–5kg/8–10lb sirloin of beef
sunflower oil
cracked black pepper

Yorkshire Puddings:
110g/4oz/generous ⅔ cup
    plain flour
pinch of salt
2 large free-range eggs
225ml/8fl oz/1 cup milk

Gravy:
50g/2oz/⅓ cup plain flour
600ml/1 pint/2½ cups beef
    stock
chopped fresh herbs

1 Preheat the oven to 200ºC/400ºF/Gas Mark 6.

2 Arrange the carrots, onion and garlic on the base of a large deep roasting tin and sit the sirloin of beef on top of the vegetables. Score the fat of the beef in a criss-cross pattern. Sprinkle generously with cracked black pepper and drizzle with a couple of dessertspoons of sunflower oil. Place in the oven.

3 After 30 minutes, reduce the heat to 170ºC/325ºF/Gas Mark 3. Baste the joint with the beef's fat and continue to cook, allowing 15 minutes per 450g/1lb plus an extra 15 minutes. Once the joint is cooked, allow a further 20–30 minutes resting time in a warm place, covered with foil, before carving.

4 Meanwhile, prepare the batter for the Yorkshire puddings. Sift the flour and salt into a large mixing bowl. Add the eggs and milk and mix until a nice smooth batter is achieved.

5 Increase oven temperature to 200ºC/400ºF/Gas Mark 6. Put one dessertspoon of sunflower oil into each cup of a 12-cup muffin tray and heat in the oven until the oil is very hot and spitting. Being very careful, remove the tray from the oven and divide the batter among the cups of hot oil. Return to the oven for 20–25 minutes, or until the batter has become puffed up and golden brown.

6 To make the gravy, add the flour to the cooking juices in the roasting tin and stir over a direct heat. Whisk in the beef stock and chopped herbs. Boil for 6–7 minutes to reduce, then pour into a warmed sauceboat. Carve the beef and serve with the puddings and gravy.

Salt Beef and Cabbage

This is called corned beef in Ireland and is another wonderful example of typical Irish cuisine. I often had this as a child and now, years later, my own children are enjoying it as much as I once did. The beef dish acquired the 'corned' name from the 'corns', or grains, of salt that were once used to cure it.

Serves 6

2kg/4lb 8oz piece of salt beef (preferably the top rib, but silverside is good too)
2 onions, peeled
2 carrots, peeled
2 fresh parsley sprigs
2 bay leaves
3–4 black peppercorns
1 medium cabbage, chopped

Parsley Sauce:

4–5 cloves
1 small onion, peeled
600ml/1 pint/2½ cups milk
50g/2oz/½ stick butter
50g/2oz/⅓ cup plain flour
2 tsp chopped fresh parsley
salt and freshly ground black pepper

1 Rinse the beef well to get rid of any brine that it may contain, then place in a large saucepan. Add the onions, carrots, parsley, bay leaves and peppercorns. Cover the meat with cold water, ensuring that all the meat is covered.

2 Bring to the boil, skimming off any scum that may rise to the surface. Cover and simmer for 2 hours, or until the meat is tender. Remove from the pan and allow to rest for 10 minutes before carving.

3 Meanwhile, make the parsley sauce to accompany the corned beef. Stud the cloves into the onion. Put the milk in a saucepan with the studded onion and bring to the boil.

4 Melt the butter slowly in another small saucepan. Add in the flour and mix until combined. Cook this mixture over a low heat for a few minutes to take the taste of the flour away. Gradually whisk in the boiling milk and continue to stir, especially around the edges, until it comes to the boil again, then turn the heat right down and cook over a very low heat for 10–15 minutes. Add the chopped parsley and season.

5 If you would like to thin the sauce a little further, whisk in a little of the water/stock in which you boiled the corned beef – this will also add to the flavour of the sauce.

6 About 25 minutes before the corned beef is ready, I like to add some chopped cabbage. Serve the corned beef in slices with the sauce and the cabbage.

leftovers

I hate eating reheated dinners, so I've had to come up
with ways of using leftovers to create totally different
meals. Vegetables can be turned into stir-fries or
lasagnes, and meat can be the basis of pies and good
old-fashioned bakes. With a bit of imagination,
Monday's dinner will never be the same again!

Green Vegetable Stir-fry with Garlic and Chilli

When we do our weekend shopping, we are overly ambitious about what we will eat, so normally on a Wednesday or Thursday evening we go vegetarian and throw together a big stir-fry.

Vegetarian
Serves 4

1 head of broccoli
110g/4oz/¾ cup green beans
110g/4oz/¾ cup mangetout
2 small shallots, peeled
2 garlic cloves, peeled
1 red chilli, deseeded if you
  wish
sunflower oil, for frying
75g/3oz/½ cup whole cashew
  nuts
100ml/3½fl oz/scant ½ cup
  soy sauce
50ml/2fl oz/¼ cup medium
  sherry
salt and freshly ground black
  pepper

1 Prepare all of the vegetables. Cut the broccoli into small florets. Slice the green beans and mangetout at an angle. Thinly slice the shallots. Chop the garlic and chilli into small pieces.

2 Heat a little oil in a large wok or frying pan to quite a hot temperature. Add the shallots and green vegetables and stir fry for 3–4 minutes. Add the chilli and garlic and stir to coat and seal the green vegetables and infuse them with flavour. Throw in the cashew nuts. Next, add in the soy sauce and the sherry. Season the mixture, allow the sauce to come to the boil, then serve immediately.

3 This is delicious with boiled basmati rice, and also makes a healthy accompaniment to grilled chicken.

Savoury Bread and Butter Pudding

The savoury version of this classic pudding is flavoured with spinach, wild mushrooms, goat's cheese and shallots and is ideal for using up bread that's past its best.

Vegetarian
Serves 4–6

1 loaf of bread
110g/4oz/1 stick butter
200g/7oz wild mushrooms (porcini and/or ceps)
sunflower oil, for frying
2 shallots, peeled and finely chopped
2 garlic cloves, peeled and finely chopped
75g/3oz spinach
½ tsp ground nutmeg
225g/8oz goat's cheese, thinly sliced
6 large free-range eggs
400ml/14fl oz/1¾ cups milk
salt and freshly ground black pepper

1 Preheat the oven to 180°C/350°F/Gas Mark 4.

2 Remove the crusts from the bread and butter each slice lightly. Tear the wild mushrooms roughly.

3 Heat a little oil in a large pan over a medium heat and quickly fry the shallots, garlic and wild mushrooms for 3–4 minutes. Add the spinach and cook for another 1–2 minutes. Sprinkle in the nutmeg and turn off the heat.

4 Arrange a layer of the bread in a casserole dish. Divide the spinach and mushroom filling over the first layer and add some slices of goat's cheese. Season and continue this process until the bread and spinach filling are all used up. The top layer of the pie should be just plain buttered bread.

5 Mix the eggs in a large bowl. Put the milk into a saucepan and bring slowly to the boil. Pour the boiled milk over the eggs, then pour this egg custard mixture over the bread pudding. Leave it to soak in for 10 minutes and then bake in the oven for 35–40 minutes.

6 If you wish, you can sprinkle a little extra cheese on the top of the pudding for the last 10 minutes of cooking. Serve immediately with a large salad.

Savoury **Quiche**

This is my version of the classic dish. Serve it plain, or you can add any leftover vegetables such as broccoli, carrots or spinach to the filling. Skip the pastry recipe and use ready-made if you're in a hurry.

Serves 10

sunflower oil, for frying
1 onion, peeled and sliced
6 mushrooms, thinly sliced
150g/5oz cooked bacon
10 cherry tomatoes
6 large free-range eggs
50ml/2fl oz/¼ cup double
  cream
300ml/10fl oz/1¼ cups milk
200g/7oz cooked vegetables
  such as broccoli, carrots or
  spinach (optional)
110g/4oz/1 cup grated Cheddar
  or mozzarella cheese
salt and freshly ground black
  pepper

Pastry:

200g/7oz/1⅓ cups plain flour,
  plus extra for dusting
pinch of salt
100g/3½ oz/scant 1 stick hard
  butter
2 tsp poppy seeds
about 4 tbsp ice-cold water

1 To make the pastry, sift the plain flour into a large mixing bowl. Add the salt. Rub the butter into the flour until the mixture resembles fine breadcrumbs and add the poppy seeds. Mix in enough cold water to bind the pastry together. Cover with clingfilm and rest in a cool place until required.

2 Preheat the oven to 180°C/350°F/Gas Mark 4.

3 Roll out the pastry on a lightly floured surface and line a 23cm/9in quiche dish. Fill with baking beans or dried pulses and blind-bake the pastry shell for 15–18 minutes, or until the pastry is lightly browned. Remove from the oven. Alternatively, you can use a ready-prepared pastry case.

4 Meanwhile, prepare the filling. Add a little oil to a small pan and fry the sliced onion and mushrooms over a gentle heat for 4–5 minutes, or until they are just softened. Spread the mushroom and onion filling over the base of the quiche dish. Finely chop the bacon and spread it over the onion mixture. Dot the cherry tomatoes on top, so they will appear roughly one in each slice. Season the filling.

5 Mix the eggs, cream and milk together in a jug and pour over the top of the quiche. Add the cooked vegetables, if using. Sprinkle with the grated cheese and bake in the oven for 30–35 minutes.

Vegetarian **Lasagne**

There's usually no shortage of leftover vegetables in our house, so we normally prepare this for family occasions or when we have a crowd around to the house for a main course and a glass of wine. It's also the perfect dish to prepare in advance.

Vegetarian
Serves 6

2 red onions, peeled
3 garlic cloves, peeled and crushed
2 carrots, peeled
1 large aubergine
2 large sweet potatoes, peeled
3 peppers, cored and deseeded
10 mushrooms, sliced
sunflower oil, for frying
1 rounded tsp tomato purée
1 glass of red wine
2 x 400g/14oz tins of tomatoes, roughly chopped
300ml/10fl oz/1¼ cups vegetable stock
½ tsp dried mixed herbs
100ml/3½fl oz/scant ½ cup double cream
about 20 no-cook lasagne sheets
150g/5oz/1¼ cups grated mozzarella cheese
salt and freshly ground black pepper

Béchamel sauce:

25g/1oz/¼ stick butter
25g/1oz/2½ tbsp plain flour
600ml/1 pint/2½ cups milk
150g/5oz/1¼ cups grated mozzarella cheese

1 Preheat the oven to 180ºC/350ºF/Gas Mark 4.

2 Chop all the vegetables into bite-sized portions. Heat a little oil in a large frying pan over a medium heat and sauté the onions and garlic for 2 minutes, or until cooked but not too soft. Add the remainder of the vegetables and mix thoroughly. Cook gently for 5–6 minutes. Mix in the tomato purée. Add in the red wine and allow the mixture to cook gently.

3 Add the chopped tomatoes, vegetable stock and mixed herbs and cook for 20–30 minutes, or until the majority of the liquid has reduced and the vegetables have softened. Season the vegetables. Stir in the cream and allow the mixture to cool down.

4 To make the béchamel sauce, melt the butter in a small pan and add the flour, stirring constantly to achieve a soft roux. Gently whisk in the milk little by little to achieve the required consistency. Mix in the cheese. Cook for 10–12 minutes over a very gentle heat, being careful not to burn the sauce.

5 Place a layer of the lasagne sheets on the base of a roasting tin. Spoon some of the vegetable mixture on top, then some cheese sauce. Repeat this process to build up the lasagne, ending with a layer of the pasta covered in the cheese sauce. Sprinkle the grated mozzarella on the top and bake for 30–40 minutes, or until it is steaming hot.

6 Serve with a crisp green salad and garlic bread.

Tip:
Lasagne sheets can be quite hard, but running hot water over them or soaking them for 2 minutes in a bowl of hot water will soften them.

Wild Mushroom, Spinach and Smoked Cheese Parcels

This is a great combination of textures and flavours. Don't be put off by the slightly longer method – it's easy to follow and absolutely worth it.

**Vegetarian
Serves 6**

oil, for oiling
450g/1lb puff pastry
plain flour, for dusting
25g/1oz/¼ stick butter
½ medium onion, peeled and
   finely chopped
2 garlic cloves, crushed
200g/7oz wild mushrooms,
   roughly torn
30ml/1fl oz/2 tbsp white wine
50g/2oz/½ cup fresh
   cranberries
80ml/3fl oz/¹⁄₃ cup double
   cream
75g/3oz/¾ cup grated smoked
   cheese
50g/2oz baby spinach
25g/1oz/1 cup chopped fresh
   flat-leaf parsley
egg wash (1 egg mixed with
   1 tbsp milk), to glaze
salt and cracked black pepper

1 Preheat the oven to 180°C/350°F/Gas Mark 4. Oil six 10cm/4in tartlet tins or moulds.

2 Roll out the puff pastry on a lightly floured surface. Place a tartlet tin (or use a regular food tin) on to the pastry as a guide to cut round. With a sharp knife, cut a disc twice as large as the tin. Repeat so that you have 12 pastry discs. Use six of them to line the well-oiled tartlet tins, pushing the pastry well into the base and against the sides with your fingers to secure it in place. Set aside the remaining six discs to use later as lids.

3 Melt the butter in a large saucepan over a low heat, add the onion and garlic and cook gently, not allowing them to brown. Add the torn wild mushrooms, along with half of the white wine, and allow to cook for 5 minutes. Season with salt and cracked black pepper, toss in the cranberries and mix thoroughly. Cook for a further 3–4 minutes.

4 Once the vegetables are cooked, gently increase the heat and pour in the remaining wine and the cream. Bring the liquid to a rapid boil and add the grated cheese, which will thicken the liquid and bind everything together. Finally, stir in the baby spinach and chopped parsley, remove the pan from the heat and allow the mixture to cool slightly.

5 Fill the pastry-lined tins with the cooled mushroom mixture. Brush a little egg wash around the pastry rims and put a second pastry disc on top of each tartlet to encase the filling. Press the edges of the pastry together to seal and cut some incisions in the top of each tartlet so that the steam can escape while cooking. Brush the entire tartlet with egg wash and bake for 18–20 minutes until golden brown. Serve with a green salad or some crisp green vegetables and baby boiled potatoes.

Cheddar and Bacon Omelette

An omelette is one of those fail-safe recipes for when you're short on ideas, ingredients or time. It's the perfect way of using up the leftovers from your refrigerator.

Serves 1

3 large free-range eggs
2 tbsp pouring cream
1 tsp chopped fresh parsley
oil or butter, for cooking
50g/2oz cooked bacon or ham, diced
50g/2oz/½ cup grated Cheddar cheese
salt and freshly ground black pepper

1 In a mixing bowl, whisk the eggs with the cream, chopped parsley and a little salt and pepper. Set aside until needed.

2 Heat a little oil or butter in an ovenproof frying pan, then add the diced bacon or ham. Cook the meat until it is golden brown, then pour in the egg and cream mixture.

3 Cook over a high heat, whisking the mixture continuously until it begins to set slightly. Leave to set for a moment, cover with half of the cheese, then fold the omelette over in half and sprinkle with the remaining cheese.

4 Preheat the grill to its highest setting and pop the omelette under it, still in the pan, for 30 seconds to melt the cheese, then serve immediately.

Bubble and Squeak
Potato Cakes

This is a great way of re-using the leftovers from that most traditional Irish dinner – bacon and cabbage and mash. We often have these for Sunday morning breakfast, topped with poached eggs. It lifts the hearts of a nation and is the perfect hangover cure – try it!

Serves 6

150g/5oz leftover cooked spring cabbage

150g/5oz/²/₃ cup leftover chopped cooked bacon or ham

4 tsp chopped fresh parsley

1 bunch of spring onions, trimmed and chopped

450g/1lb leftover mashed potatoes

1 free-range egg yolk

plain flour, for dusting

sunflower oil or butter, for frying

salt and freshly ground black pepper

6 poached eggs

garden salad, to serve (page 152)

1 Mix the cabbage, bacon or ham, chopped parsley and spring onions into the mashed potatoes. Mix in the egg yolk and seasoning. Divide the mixture into six portions and, using a little flour, shape them into burger shapes. Allow to set in the refrigerator for an hour or so (or as much time as you can afford).

2 Heat a large frying pan with a little oil or butter. Pan-fry the potato cakes on each side for 4–5 minutes, or until they are piping hot. The cakes are delicious with softly poached eggs or garden salad (see page 152).

Smoked Haddock Fish Cakes

Potatoes and haddock are the basic ingredients in this delicious supper dish. Add coriander or parsley for extra flavour and serve with the chilli sauce and a fresh green salad.

Serves 4–6

1 tsp wholegrain mustard
450g/1lb leftover mashed potatoes
1 bunch of spring onions, trimmed and chopped
4 tsp chopped fresh coriander or parsley
1 free-range egg
450g/1lb leftover cooked smoked haddock, flaked
plain flour, for dusting
sunflower oil, for frying
salt and freshly ground black pepper
garden salad, to serve (page 152)

Sweet Chilli Jam:

2 mild red chillies, deseeded and cut into julienne (long, thin strips)
200g/7oz/1 cup caster sugar
225ml/8fl oz/1 cup white wine vinegar

1 First, make the sweet chilli jam. Place the chillies in a small pan with the sugar and vinegar and bring to the boil, stirring until the sugar has dissolved. Reduce the heat and simmer for about 10 minutes, or until reduced by half. Remove from the heat and allow to cool completely, then transfer to a bowl and cover with clingfilm. Place in the refrigerator and use as required. It will keep for up to 6 months.

2 Preheat the oven to 180°C/350°F/Gas Mark 4.

3 Mix the wholegrain mustard in with the potatoes. Add the chopped spring onions, chopped coriander or parsley and the egg and mix well in. Season the mixture.

4 Gently incorporate the fish into the potato mixture and, using a little flour to dust your hands, gently mould the mixture into the patty shapes. You should aim to make 6–8 substantial fish cakes.

5 Pan-fry the fish cakes in a little oil until golden on each side, then transfer to a baking tray and place in the oven for a further 5–10 minutes, or until piping hot.

6 Serve with garden salad and the sweet chilli jam.

Bacon and Cheddar Cheese
Scones

We love to have a selection of scones in our larder, both sweet and savoury. Bacon, left over from breakfast, and cheese is a great combination and I always use buttermilk, which adds a rich, creamy flavour.

Makes 12

450g/1lb/3 cups plain flour, plus extra for dusting
1 tsp baking powder
pinch of salt
110g/4oz/1 stick butter, chilled
110g/4oz/1 cup grated Cheddar cheese
75g/3oz/⅓ cup leftover chopped cooked bacon
2 free-range eggs
200ml/7fl oz/generous ¾ cup buttermilk
milk, to glaze
handful of pumpkin seeds

1 Preheat the oven to 200ºC/400ºF/Gas Mark 6.

2 Sift the flour and the baking powder into a large bowl. Add the salt and mix in well. Cut the butter into cubes, add to the flour mixture and rub in until the mixture resembles fine breadcrumbs. Add 75g/3oz/ ¾ cup of the grated cheese and the chopped bacon.

3 In a separate small bowl, lightly beat one of the eggs with a fork and add to the dry ingredients. Mix in enough buttermilk to achieve a soft dough.

4 Transfer the mixture to a lightly floured work surface, knead gently and roll the mixture out to a thickness of 2cm/¾in. Using a scone cutter, cut out 12 scones and place on a lightly floured baking tray.

5 In a cup, mix the remaining egg with a little milk and, using a soft pastry brush, brush lightly over the top of the scones. Scatter some pumpkin seeds and the remainder of the grated Cheddar cheese on top of the scones.

6 Bake for 15–20 minutes, or until well risen and golden brown. Serve with lashings of butter and steaming hot soup.

Chicken and Broccoli
Tagliatelle

Personally, I prefer my pasta with a good, creamy sauce, like this one, but it also works well with tomato-based flavours, too. Whenever you are using leftover chicken, always ensure that the meat is piping hot before you serve the dish.

Serves 6
olive oil
350g/12oz dry tagliatelle
25g/1oz/¼ stick butter
2 garlic cloves, peeled and chopped
½ onion, peeled and chopped
10 button mushrooms, sliced
300ml/10fl oz/1¼ cups double cream
75g/3oz/¾ cup grated Parmesan cheese, plus extra to serve (optional)
1 large head of broccoli, cut into small spears
350g/12oz cooked chicken, cut into cubes
salt and freshly ground black pepper

1 Fill a large saucepan with water and bring it to the boil. Add a little salt and a drizzle of olive oil. Cook the tagliatelle in the water for 7–10 minutes, or until soft. Drain off the water and stir in the butter.

2 Meanwhile, in a medium pan, fry the garlic, onion and mushrooms very gently in a little oil over a low heat for 6–8 minutes, or until they are fully softened but not yet coloured. Stir in the cream and grated Parmesan cheese.

3 Bring another large pan of salted water quickly to the boil. Add the broccoli spears and cook for 2–3 minutes. Do not overcook the broccoli because it will lose its vivid colour.

4 Add the broccoli and cooked chicken to the cream sauce. Correct the seasoning and heat through until the chicken is fully reheated. Mix in the cooked pasta and serve immediately, with additional grated Parmesan, if you wish. Garlic bread works wonderfully with this dish.

Chicken Curry

Turn leftover roast chicken into this spicy dish, which makes a great hangover cure – served with soft boiled rice and thick-cut homemade chips, it's guaranteed to get you back on your feet!

Serves 4

sunflower oil, for frying

1 onion, peeled and roughly chopped

2 garlic cloves, crushed and finely chopped

2.5cm/1in piece of fresh root ginger, peeled and finely chopped

½ tsp turmeric

½ tsp cayenne pepper

1 tsp chilli powder

½ tsp ground cumin

1 apple, peeled, cored and diced

1 green pepper, cored, deseeded and chopped

2 medium potatoes, peeled and diced

1 tsp tomato purée

700ml/1¼ pints/3 cups hot chicken stock

100ml/3½fl oz/scant ½ cup pouring cream or coconut milk

400g/14oz cooked chicken, chopped

1 Heat a little oil in a large pan over a low heat. Add the onion, garlic and ginger and fry gently for 4–5 minutes to infuse the flavour of the ginger. Stir the spices into the onion mixture over a higher heat. You should get a fantastic fragrance at this stage. Cook this spiced onion mixture for a further 2 minutes, then add in the diced apple, green pepper, potatoes and tomato purée and cook for a further 2 minutes.

2 Pour in the chicken stock and cream and bring the mixture to the boil. Once it boils, reduce the heat and stir the cooked chicken into the curried sauce. Simmer for 20 minutes, or until the mixture has thickened slightly and the apple and potatoes are cooked.

3 Serve with the curry with a side portion of boiled basmati rice and chips (see below).

Thick-cut Chips:
Preheat the oven to 200ºC/400ºF/Gas Mark 6. Cut some potatoes (Rooster or Maris Piper) into thick chip shapes. Put onto a baking tray with some salt and pepper. Drizzle with a little oil and roast in the oven for 20–30 minutes, depending on the size of the chips.

Turkey and Mushroom Pie

Perfect for St. Stephen's Day (Boxing Day) when you just can't face cold turkey with reheated vegetables! This dish freezes exceptionally well, so you can make a double batch and freeze ahead for the more frugal days of early January.

Serves 6–8

50g/2oz/½ stick butter
50g/2oz/⅓ cup plain flour
600ml/1 pint/2½ cups milk
50ml/2fl oz/¼ cup white wine (optional)
90ml/3fl oz/⅓ cup double cream
50g/2oz/½ cup grated Parmesan cheese (optional)
1 small onion, peeled and chopped
2 garlic cloves, peeled and chopped
6–8 mushrooms, sliced
sunflower oil, for frying
500g/1lb 2oz cooked turkey, chopped
400g/14oz mix of carrots, turnips, parsnips, etc, fresh or cooked (if leftover)
salt and freshly ground black pepper

Topping:

75g/3oz/¾ stick butter
175g/6oz/generous 3 cups fine fresh white breadcrumbs
4 tsp chopped fresh parsley
25g/1oz/¼ cup grated Parmesan cheese

1 Preheat the oven to 180°C/350°F/Gas Mark 4.

2 First, make a white sauce. Melt the butter in a small pan, then stir in the flour to make a paste. Cook this mixture for about 90 seconds, just to take out the sharp taste of flour. Slowly whisk in the milk, then continue to stir using a wooden spoon until the mixture thickens. Make sure you stir in all the paste from around the sides of the pan. If you wish, pour in a little white wine and then add the cream to enrich the sauce. Grated Parmesan can be added at this time as well. Cook slowly for about 5–8 minutes, stirring the sauce all the time. Season the sauce to taste.

3 Pan-fry the onion, garlic and mushrooms in a little oil and add them to the sauce, together with the chopped turkey and vegetables. Stir well, then tip this mixture into a casserole dish or individual dishes and set aside.

4 To make the topping, melt the butter slowly in a saucepan on a low heat. Add the breadcrumbs, parsley and Parmesan cheese and mix thoroughly. The mixture should resemble a relatively dry stuffing.

5 Spoon the crumble mixture over the top of the turkey mixture. Bake for 30 minutes, or until piping hot. Serve immediately with a crisp green salad.

Crispy Duck Spring Rolls

Spring rolls are great as a simple starter or as party snacks. I normally make batches of up to 8 and freeze them until required. In this recipe I use the leftover duck from a weekend roast, but you can substitute pork, crabmeat, prawns, chicken or beef instead. The spring roll pastry is now easily available in most supermarkets.

Serves 8

1½ mixed peppers (½ each of red, green and yellow), cored and deseeded
2 celery sticks
1 leek (white part only) trimmed
1 carrot, peeled
1 red onion, peeled
sunflower oil, for frying
175g/6oz leftover cooked duck breast, finely shredded
4 tsp oyster sauce
8 sheets of spring roll pastry
egg wash (1 egg mixed with milk)
salt and freshly ground black pepper

1 Slice all of the vegetables into thin strips, each about 5cm/2in in length. Heat a little oil in a large wok, add the vegetables and stir-fry for 3–4 minutes, or until they are beginning to soften. Add the cooked duck breast and heat through, then mix in the oyster sauce and allow this to bind the mixture together.

2 Transfer the mixture to a clean bowl, season and allow it to cool down completely.

3 Lay one individual sheet of the spring roll pastry on the work surface so that one of the corners points towards you. Brush around the edges with egg wash, then spoon about 1 tablespoon of the duck and vegetable filling in a line near the top corner. Fold over to enclose and then roll it towards you a little. Fold in the sides and continue to roll up into a cylinder shape. Place on a non-stick baking tray and repeat with the remaining ingredients. Lightly brush with the remaining egg wash and chill for 30 minutes.

4 When ready to serve, pour oil into a deep-fat fryer or deep-sided pan to a depth of 6–7.5cm/2½–3in and heat to 180°C/350°F, or until a small piece of white bread turns golden brown in about 30 seconds. Deep-fry the spring rolls for 3–4 minutes, or until crisp on all sides and lightly golden. Drain well on kitchen paper.

5 To serve, using a sharp knife, cut off the very ends of each spring roll, then cut each one in half on the diagonal. They are delicious served with sweet chilli jam (see page 137).

Lamb and Rosemary Pie

We love roast leg of lamb for Sunday lunch and on Monday often transform the leftover chunks into a glorious lamb pie. I've used mashed potato for an easy topping, but pastry is also delicious.

Serves 6

sunflower oil, for frying
1 onion, peeled and chopped
175g/6oz mushrooms, sliced
1 carrot, peeled and diced
½ turnip, peeled and diced
2 small fresh rosemary sprigs
1 tsp tomato purée
4 tsp plain flour
300ml/10fl oz/1¼ cups red wine
450ml/16fl oz/2 cups chicken stock
700g/1lb 8oz cooked leg or shoulder of lamb, cut into chunks
salt and freshly ground black pepper

Topping:

6–7 large potatoes, peeled and boiled
25g/1oz/¼ stick butter
1 free-range egg yolk

1 Heat the oil in large pan over a gentle heat and fry the onion, mushrooms, carrot and turnip for 4–5 minutes – this will give a nice roasted flavour to the vegetables. Add the rosemary sprigs and a little seasoning.

2 Mix in the tomato purée to coat all of the vegetables. Sprinkle in the flour – this will coat the vegetables and also act as the main thickening agent in the sauce. Carefully pour the red wine and the stock into the pan and allow the mixture to come to the boil. Add the cooked lamb pieces, reduce the heat and simmer for 25 minutes on a very low heat. Transfer the mixture to a casserole dish and allow to cool slightly.

3 Preheat the oven to 200ºC/400ºF/Gas Mark 6.

4 Mash the potatoes with a little salt and pepper and the butter. Mix in the egg yolk and spoon on top of the lamb casserole, then use a fork to create an attractive pattern. Transfer to the oven and bake for 25–30 minutes, or until the lamb is piping hot. Serve immediately.

Stuffed Pork Slices

Pork can be one of the most difficult meats to use up, as reheating can dry it out. The apple and prunes in this stuffing really perk it up, adding moisture to make sure the slices are lovely and succulent.

Serves 4

75g/3oz/¾ stick butter

½ onion, peeled and finely chopped

1 dessert apple, peeled, cored and roughly chopped

6 dried prunes, finely chopped

4 tsp chopped fresh parsley

2 tsp chopped fresh sage

150g/5oz/2 generous cups fresh white breadcrumbs

50g/2oz/¼ cup leftover mashed potato

12 slices leftover pork loin

5 tbsp water or chicken stock

salt and freshly ground black pepper

1 Preheat the oven to 170ºC/325ºF/Gas Mark 3.

2 Begin by making the stuffing. Melt the butter in a medium saucepan over a low heat and add the onion, allowing it to cook gently for 4–5 minutes, or until it has softened but not coloured. Add in the chopped fruits, herbs, breadcrumbs and mashed potato and mix thoroughly. Season with salt and pepper and allow the stuffing to cool slightly.

3 Meanwhile, line the base of the roasting tin with a piece of baking parchment. Put one slice of meat down flat on the tin and tightly press one spoon of the stuffing mixture on top of the meat. Fan two more slices of meat on top of the stuffing and press down to secure. Repeat this process until all the remaining meat has been used up.

4 Pour the water or stock over the pork. Cover the roasting tin with foil and bake for 15 minutes, or until the meat and stuffing mixture are piping hot. Serve immediately with braised fennel (see page 160) and garlic mashed potatoes (page 161).

accompaniments

Vegetable side dishes are often just as delicious as the main course! I've included my favourites, as well as light and fresh salads, inspired by my garden at Dunbrody, plus compotes and fruit sauces that are wonderful served with roasted meats.

Garden Salad

We have a very extensive selection of lettuces in our garden at Dunbrody and often make a light lunch from just leaves with a very simple dressing and a large chunk of crusty bread. A glass of wine makes the perfect accompaniment!

**Vegetarian
Serves 6**

mixed lettuce leaves, such as cos, endive, red chard, rocket, lollo rossa and butterhead
1 cucumber
75g/3oz/²/₃ cup sun-dried tomatoes
2 radishes, thinly sliced
juice of 1 lemon
2 tbsp olive oil
4 tsp balsamic vinegar

1 Arrange the lettuce leaves in a large serving bowl or on a platter. Using a vegetable peeler, cut long strips of cucumber and place them gently on top of the salad leaves. Scatter in the sun-dried tomatoes and sliced radishes.

2 Mix the lemon juice, olive oil and balsamic vinegar together in a mixing bowl and when you are ready to eat, dress the leaves with the tangy dressing and serve immediately.

Tomato and Shallot Salad

Keeping it simple is often the key to a tasty salad. Here, the sweetness of the plum tomatoes complements the peppery flavour of the rocket.

**Vegetarian
Serves 4–6**

6 large plum tomatoes
110g/4oz fresh rocket
3 shallots, peeled and very thinly sliced
5 tbsp olive oil
freshly ground black pepper

1 Cut the tomatoes into wedges and mix with the rocket leaves in a large serving bowl. Scatter the thinly sliced shallots on the top and season with black pepper. Drizzle with the olive oil and rest for a few minutes before serving – this will allow the olive oil to take on the flavours of the tomatoes.

2 This is also great piled on top of a piece of toast and served as a chunky bruschetta.

Orange **Marmalade**

This is the marmalade we serve at Dunbrody House, based on a recipe passed down from my mother. It is infused with the ingredient that every Irish cook loves – whiskey!

Vegetarian
Makes 2 x 450g/1lb jars
4 oranges
225g/8oz/scant 1¼ cups caster
    sugar
50ml/2fl oz/¼ cup Irish whiskey
juice of ½ lemon

1 Chop the oranges into small chunks, leaving the peel intact. Put the oranges into a food processor and blitz to make smooth pulp. Place the pulp in a saucepan with the sugar, whiskey and lemon juice. Bring the mixture to the boil, then simmer gently for about 15 minutes. To test whether the marmalade is ready, place a teaspoon of it on a chilled saucer and see if it sets after 4–5 minutes in the refrigerator. If it doesn't, continue to cook for a few more minutes. Transfer to clean, sterilized jars and seal.

Cranberry **Sauce**

A Dundon kitchen staple – no turkey is complete without it (see page 99). Because it is so simple to make, there is no excuse for buying it ready-made.

Vegetarian
Makes 1 x 450g/1lb jar
350g/12oz/3 cups cranberries
150g/5oz/¾ cup caster sugar
½ tsp ground ginger
5 tbsp water

1 Put all the ingredients into a medium saucepan and bring the water to the boil. Reduce the heat and allow the cranberries to cook down gently. This will probably take 10–15 minutes on a very low heat. Tip into a bowl, allow to cool and store, covered with clingfilm, in the refrigerator for up to 6 weeks.

Pear and Clove **Chutney**

This chutney is delicious with a variety of cooked meats, but my preference is roast duck. If bottled in a pretty jar, this makes a great gift as part of an edible gift hamper.

Vegetarian
Makes 2 x 450g/1lb jars
25g/1oz/¼ stick butter
8 large firm pears, cored
1 onion, peeled and roughly chopped
175g/6oz/1 cup sultanas
12–14 cloves
1 level tsp mixed spice
150g/5oz/¾ cup (solidly packed) light brown sugar
175ml/6fl oz/¾ cup white wine vinegar

1 Gently melt the butter in a large saucepan over a low heat.

2 Dice the pears (there's no need to peel them) and add to the pan with the onion. Sauté them gently in the butter for 3–4 minutes. Add in the sultanas, cloves and mixed spice. Toss these around in the pan for a few minutes until the pears are coated with a film of spice.

3 Next, add the brown sugar and vinegar and bring this mixture to the boil. Be careful because it does have a tendency to burn, so do keep an eye on it. Simmer for a further 30 minutes, or until the liquid has reduced and thickened.

4 Transfer to hot sterilized jars and seal with a circle of baking parchment securely fastened with an elastic band. Refrigerate until required (this chutney will keep for about 8 weeks in the refrigerator).

Apple and Vanilla **Compote**

The vanilla seeds give the apple extra sweetness. We often enjoy this with homemade pancakes.

Vegetarian
Serves 8–12
1 vanilla pod
4 large cooking apples, peeled, cored and thinly sliced
110g/4oz/½ cup caster sugar
50ml/2fl oz/¼ cup water

1 Using a sharp knife, split the vanilla pod lengthways and collect all the seeds. Pop the apple slices into a large saucepan with the sugar, water and vanilla seeds. Bring to the boil, then reduce the heat and simmer for 10–12 minutes, or until the apples have softened completely. Mash with a hand-held potato masher or purée in a small food processor. Allow to cool and store, covered, in the refrigerator.

Zesty Corn-on-the-Cob

Grilled corn-on-the-cob is a great summer choice, and this recipe is really simple. So light up the barbecue and get going!

Vegetarian
Serves 4

4 ears of corn-on-the-cob, cleaned
zest of 1 lime
110g/4oz/1 stick butter
salt and freshly ground black pepper

1 Preheat the barbecue until it is quite hot.

2 Place each cob on a large piece of foil. Mix the lime zest with the butter and dot a piece of the lime butter on top of each cob. Season with a little salt and pepper. Wrap each piece up quite tightly in the foil and sit the covered package on the side of the barbecue for about 30 minutes, or until the corn is cooked all the way through.

3 Try to eat it as elegantly as possible – it's difficult!

Horseradish Sauce

This is great in mashed potatoes and a perfect partner for braised ribs or roast beef (see pages 38 and 120).

Vegetarian
Makes 1 x 450g/1lb jar

4 tsp grated horseradish
4 tsp white wine vinegar
1/2 tsp Dijon mustard
pinch of caster sugar
225ml/8fl oz/1 cup double cream, lightly whipped
salt and freshly ground black pepper

1 Very simple! Just mix all the ingredients together and tip into a clean jar or serving bowl. Store in the refrigerator for up to 2 weeks.

Minted Peas

Mint and peas make a perfect combination and this tasty relish is delicious served with pan-fried fish.

Serves 4

½ onion, peeled and chopped
2 garlic cloves, peeled and crushed
sunflower oil, for frying
275g/10oz/2½ cups frozen peas (you can use fresh if desired)
250ml/9fl oz/generous 1 cup chicken stock
4 tsp chopped fresh mint or 1 tsp mint sauce
50g/2oz/½ stick butter
salt and freshly ground black pepper
sesame seeds, to garnish (optional)

1 Using a large saucepan, quickly fry the onion and garlic in a little oil until browned. Add the peas and stir to coat with onion and garlic mixture. Pour in the chicken stock and boil for 4–5 minutes, or until the peas have softened.

2 When the peas are cooked, drain them and mix in the seasoning and chopped mint. Add the butter and stir to glaze the peas. Serve immediately. Scatter some sesame seeds on the top, if you like.

Salsa Verde

This tangy sauce is beautiful over fish or served with a simple plate of fresh pasta.

Serves 4–6

1 bunch of fresh parsley
1 handful each of fresh mint and basil leaves
4 tinned anchovy fillets
2 tbsp capers, rinsed, (optional)
3 garlic cloves, peeled and roughly chopped
150–250ml/6–9fl oz/²⁄₃–1 cup extra-virgin olive oil
1–2 tbsp white wine vinegar
1 tbsp caster sugar
salt and freshly ground black pepper

1 Tear or finely shred the parsley, mint and basil and place in a medium bowl.

2 Chop the anchovies and capers, if using, and add them with the garlic.

3 In a separate bowl mix together the olive oil, vinegar, sugar and seasoning. Pour over the herb mixture and allow to rest for at least 30 minutes. Store in the refrigerator for up to 3 days.

Braised **Red Cabbage**

This is a delicious accompaniment and has become synonymous with Christmas in our house. We normally host a festive dinner party where we serve venison fillets, wholegrain mashed potato and braised red cabbage – it always goes down a treat.

Vegetarian
Serves 6

1 medium head of red cabbage, thinly shredded
2 red onions, peeled and thinly sliced
1 large cooking apple, peeled, cored and cut into chunks
75g/3oz/½ cup sultanas
5 whole cloves
75g/3oz/½ cup demerara sugar
300ml/10fl oz/1¼ cups red wine
5 tbsp red wine vinegar

1 Preheat the oven to 180ºC/350ºF/Gas Mark 4.

2 Mix all the dry ingredients (cabbage, red onions, apples, sultanas, cloves and sugar) together thoroughly and tip into a large roasting tin. Pour in the red wine and vinegar and cover the roasting tin tightly with foil.

3 Bake for 1–1¼ hours, or until the cabbage is completely soft and juicy, stirring two or three times during cooking.

Spring Cabbage Stir-fry

This is a far better way to cook cabbage than the traditional excessive boiling it sometimes receives. This stir-fry is particularly delicious served with spring lamb and crisp roast potatoes.

Vegetarian
Serves 4–6

2 tsp sesame oil
1 head of spring cabbage
2 garlic cloves, peeled and
  crushed
2 tbsp dark soy sauce
1 tbsp sesame seeds

1 Heat the sesame oil in a large wok.

2 Shred the cabbage very finely, making sure that you remove the stalks from the outer leaves. Fry the crushed garlic in the wok for 1 minute, then add the cabbage. Stir-fry quickly for 4–5 minutes, or until the cabbage is cooked but still retaining a little crunch.

3 Pour in the soy sauce and gently heat it through. Sprinkle with the sesame seeds and serve immediately.

Traditional **Champ**

All the chefs that I speak to (both professional and domestic) have their own recipe for champ. For me, it conjures up delightful childhood memories when I first discovered my ongoing passion for food and cooking.

Vegetarian
Serves 4–6
6 large potatoes, peeled and
    cut into chunks
25g/1oz/¼ stick butter
50ml/2fl oz/¼ cup milk
4 tsp snipped fresh chives
1 bunch of spring onions,
    trimmed and chopped
salt and freshly ground black
    pepper

1 Boil the potatoes in a medium pan of salted water until soft and tender. Once the potatoes are cooked, drain off the water and leave the potatoes in the pan to steam for a few minutes.

2 Meanwhile, heat the butter and milk together in a small saucepan. Add this to the cooked potatoes and mash until completely smooth. Mix in the chives and spring onions and adjust the seasoning. Serve immediately.

Braised **Fennel**

Fennel is either loved or loathed. But this cooking method brings out its delicacy of flavour and will be enjoyed by everyone! This recipe is cooked in the oven, so you don't need to stand over it. Just leave it to happily bubble away!

Serves 6
6 fennel bulbs
1 carrot, peeled and cut
    lengthways
½ onion, peeled and sliced
2 bay leaves
1 whole bulb of garlic
350ml/12fl oz/1½ cups boiling
    chicken stock

1 Preheat the oven to 170ºC/325ºF/Gas Mark 3.

2 Remove all the leafy fronds from the fennel bulbs. Arrange the bulbs in a large roasting tin with the carrot and the onion. Scatter in the bay leaves and break in an entire unpeeled bulb of garlic.

3 Pour the chicken stock into the roasting tin and cover with foil. Bake in the oven for 1 hour, or until the fennel is soft and tender. Drain off the cooking liquor and serve immediately.

Boulangère **Potatoes**

This variation is a lighter alternative to gratin potatoes and goes particularly well with a good steak.

Serves 6

7–8 large potatoes
110g/4oz/1 stick butter
1 large onion, peeled and thinly sliced
4 garlic cloves, peeled and chopped (optional)
425ml/15fl oz/generous 1¾ cups boiling chicken stock

1 Preheat the oven to 170ºC/325ºF/Gas Mark 3.

2 Peel and thinly slice the potatoes, using either a sharp knife or a food processor. Melt half the butter in a large pan and quickly fry the onion and garlic, if using, for 3–4 minutes but without colouring them.

3 Begin to layer the potatoes in a large ovenproof dish. Divide the onion mixture between the layers of potatoes, finishing with a layer of potatoes. Pour the boiling stock over the potatoes until they are two-thirds covered. Brush with the remaining melted butter.

4 Bake uncovered for about 1 hour, or until the potatoes are tender.

Roasted **Garlic** Mashed **Potatoes**

Here's a very easy way of jazzing up a simple dish like mashed potatoes.

**Vegetarian
Serves 6**

1 whole bulb of garlic
7 large potatoes, peeled and cut into chunks
2 tbsp double cream
25g/1oz/¼ stick butter
2 tsp chopped fresh flat-leaf parsley
salt and freshly ground black pepper

1 Preheat the oven to 180ºC/350ºF/Gas Mark 4.

2 Place the bulb of garlic in a small roasting tin and bake in the oven for 40 minutes, or until soft. If you find it more convenient, you can break the bulb up into individual unpeeled cloves before roasting.

3 Cook the potatoes in a large saucepan of boiling water until soft and tender, then drain and mash them with the cream and butter (I like to heat the cream and butter gently in a small saucepan before adding it to the potatoes, as this prevents them developing a gluelike consistency).

4 Squeeze the roasted garlic cloves between your fingers to reveal the gloriously fragrant roasted flesh, add this to the mashed potatoes and mix well. Season with salt and pepper and stir in the flat-leaf parsley just before serving.

Honey-glazed Carrots
with Sesame Seeds

Honey is a magical ingredient that has an amazing affinity with root vegetables. This sticky glaze works wonderfully with the carrots, and the sesame seeds add extra flavour.

Vegetarian
Serves 4–6

4 large carrots, peeled and cut lengthways
25g/1oz/¼ stick butter
juice of ½ orange
4 tsp honey
2 tsp sesame seeds
chopped fresh parsley
salt and freshly ground black pepper

1 Bring the carrots to the boil in a medium pan of lightly salted water. When the carrots have softened, drain off the water and add the butter, orange juice, honey and seasoning. Place on a gentle heat for a further 1–2 minutes, or until the glazed carrots are piping hot.

2 Meanwhile, place a large frying pan on a high heat. Do not add any oil or butter to the pan. Dry-fry the sesame seeds for 1–2 minutes, or until they turn golden brown and start to pop.

3 Tip the carrots into a large serving bowl and sprinkle with the toasted sesame seeds and chopped parsley.

desserts

Fruit desserts, creamy desserts, indulgent desserts, healthy desserts... no meal would be complete without a happy ending.

Dessert for us often include cupcakes that Catherine and the children have made. Everyone has their own tasks – Catherine weighs out the ingredients, Emily mixes them together, while Sophie decorates each one with icing and feeds them to Tom, who looks on in total amazement. Invariably the kitchen will resemble a bomb site, but the cupcakes are delicious.

Of all the desserts that follow, my favourite is plum pudding. This is a very old recipe, which has stood the test of time for me and previous Dundon generations.

Classic Sherry **Trifle**

After all the hard work that Christmas involves for us in the restaurant and as a family, Catherine and I love to relax on Christmas night after the children have gone to bed and indulge in a glass of mulled wine and a heaped bowl of sherry trifle with freshly whipped cream. Heaven!

Serves 4

225g/8oz/1¾ cups fresh
   berries (such as raspberries,
   strawberries, blackcurrants)
100ml/3½fl oz/scant ½ cup
   good-quality sherry
250ml/9fl oz/generous 1 cup
   freshly whipped cream
50g/2oz/½ cup flaked
   almonds, toasted (optional)

Jam Swiss Roll:

4 free-range eggs
110g/4oz/½ cup caster sugar,
   plus extra for dusting
110g/4oz/generous ⅔ cup
   self-raising flour, sifted
scant 3 tbsp good-quality
   raspberry jam

Fresh Egg Custard:

½ vanilla pod
450ml/16fl oz/2 cups milk
150ml/5fl oz/⅔ cup double
   cream
6 free-range egg yolks
75g/3oz/scant ½ cup caster
   sugar
2 tsp cornflour

1 To make the jam Swiss roll, preheat the oven to 180°C/350°F/Gas Mark 4. Grease and line a 33 x 23cm/13 x 9in Swiss roll tin with baking parchment.

2 In a mixing bowl, whisk the 4 whole eggs with the sugar until very light and fluffy. The whisk should leave a figure-of-eight on the surface of the mixture when lifted out of it. Gently fold in the sifted flour with a metal spoon. Be very gentle to avoid knocking any air out of the sponge base, but do ensure that all the flour is incorporated. Pour the mixture into the prepared Swiss roll tin. Bake for 20 minutes, or until well risen and golden brown.

3 Before the sponge is fully cooled, invert it onto a sheet of baking parchment dusted with the caster sugar. Spread the sponge with a thin layer of raspberry jam. Carefully roll the Swiss roll up from the longest side rather than from the shortest. Cut into thin slices and arrange in individual glasses or a large bowl, making sure that the glass or bowl is fully lined all the way around (keep back a little of the Swiss roll for the middle if you wish). Sprinkle with the fresh berries, additional jam if desired, and sprinkle over a generous helping of sherry. Add any reserved slices of Swiss roll to the centre of the trifle.

4 To make the custard, split the vanilla pod lengthways and use a small sharp knife to scrape out the seeds from one half of the pod. Put the seeds and the half pod into a large saucepan with the milk and cream. (Wrap the remainder of the vanilla pod in clingfilm and retain for later use.) Bring the milk, cream and vanilla pod to the boil.

continued overleaf

5 Using a large, spotlessly clean bowl and a whisk, beat the egg yolks, sugar and cornflour together until light and creamy.

6 Spend about 2 minutes doing this, then pour the boiled milk and cream mixture onto the eggs and mix well. Return the mixture to the pan and cook until the mixture coats the back of a wooden spoon. It is important to stir the mixture at all times to prevent it from curdling. This should take no more than 2 minutes on a very gentle heat. Do not allow the mixture to boil. Taste the custard at this stage to make sure you cannot taste the cornflour. If you can, return to the heat and stir continuously on a low heat for another 1–2 minutes.

7 Pour the custard over the sponge mixture and allow to cool for a couple of hours or overnight. Cover with a disc of baking parchment or clingfilm to prevent a skin forming.

8 To serve, spoon some whipped cream on the top and decorate with a little more fresh fruit. Sprinkle, if desired, with some flaked and toasted almonds.

Tips:
If you wish, you can put a spoon or two of sherry into the custard for increased flavour. Sometimes I add 200g/7oz/1 cup melted white chocolate to the egg yolks and sugar before adding the boiled milk, and the result is very creamy white chocolate custard.

Steamed **Lemon Curd** Pudding

When it's cold outside, this pudding is a perfect
pick-me-up. You can experiment with different
flavours, such as raspberry jam or orange marmalade
instead of the lemon. If you want to cheat and use
ready-made marmalade, jam or curd, make sure
it's top quality.

Serves 6–8
Lemon Pudding:
225g/8oz/1½ cups plain flour
2 level tsp baking powder
225g/8oz/2 sticks butter, plus
    extra for greasing
225g/8oz/scant 1¼ cups caster
    sugar
4 large free-range eggs
zest and juice of 2 lemons
a little milk, to slacken (if
    required)
225g/8oz/1 cup lemon curd
    (see below)
raspberries and fresh mint or
    lemon balm, to decorate

Lemon Curd:
4 large free-range eggs
150g/5oz/¾ cup caster sugar
zest and juice of 2 lemons
150g/5oz/1¼ sticks butter,
    chopped into small cubes

1 To make the lemon curd, place a large glass bowl over a saucepan
of simmering water. Put the eggs, sugar, lemon zest and juice in the
bowl and whisk continuously until the mixture has thickened and
almost doubled in size. This will take about 10 minutes. Gradually add
the butter, beating well between each addition to ensure the mixture
does not split. When all the butter has been added, whisk for another
3–4 minutes, then take the bowl off the pan. Transfer to a storage
container and allow to cool. It can be kept refrigerated for 2–3 weeks.

2 To make the pudding, sift the flour and the baking powder together.
Cream the butter and sugar together in a large mixing bowl until light
and fluffy. Add the eggs and mix gently. Stir in the lemon zest and juice,
then mix in the flour and baking powder. If the mixture is a little stiff,
you can add a couple of dessertspoons of milk to loosen it up.

3 Grease a 1.3-litre/2-pint/5-cup capacity pudding basin with a lid or
individual pudding basins with butter, then spread a layer of lemon curd
in the base. Pour the sponge mixture on top and cook as required.

4 To oven bake (ideal for individual puddings), preheat the oven to
180°C/350°F/Gas Mark 4. Place the pudding basins in a deep roasting
tray. Pour in cold water to come one-third of the way up the side of
the basins. Cover with baking parchment and a sheet of foil and bake
for 1¼ hours.

5 To steam on the hob (ideal for larger puddings), cover the pudding
with a circle of baking parchment, fit the basin lid on top and put in
a large saucepan. Pour in water to come halfway up the side of the
basin. Bring to the boil, then reduce to a simmer for 1 hour 40 minutes.
Allow to cool for about 5 minutes, then invert onto a serving platter
and decorate.

Caramelized Pear Tarte Tatin

My famous no-hassle dessert! The washing up takes seconds, as the tarte is prepared, cooked and served in just one dish. If you prefer, you can use little individual dishes and make small tarts – just place the fruit into each dish and press a disc of puff pastry on top.

Serves 6–8

75g/3oz/1¾ sticks butter

175g/6oz/scant 1 cup (solidly packed) soft brown sugar

6 firm pears, peeled and cored

juice of ½ lemon

1 sheet of frozen puff pastry (thawed)

plain flour, for dusting

vanilla ice cream and ½ tsp ground cinnamon, to serve

1 Preheat the oven to 200ºC/400ºF/Gas Mark 6.

2 Gently melt the butter in a medium ovenproof frying pan over a low heat. Add the sugar and stir continuously until the mixture begins to bubble and all the sugar has dissolved.

3 Cut each pear into 6 wedges. Squeeze a little lemon juice on the pears to prevent them going brown. Add the pears to the pan and cook gently for 8–10 minutes, or until they begin to soften and are coated in a nice golden-brown caramel. Remove from the heat and allow to cool in the pan for a further 8–10 minutes.

4 Meanwhile, roll out the puff pastry on a lightly floured surface and cut out a disc to fit the top of the frying pan. When the pears have cooled slightly, fit the disc of pastry onto the top of the caramelized pear mixture. Secure it in place by pressing down on the sides, tucking it in. Transfer the pan to the oven and bake for 12–15 minutes, or until the pastry is golden brown. Remove from the oven and allow to set for 10 minutes.

5 Place a large serving platter on top of the pan and turn it over to reveal a glorious pastry case laden with caramelized pears. Serve with oodles of vanilla ice cream, laced with the ground cinnamon.

Lemon Drizzle Cake

This wonderful cake is very versatile – it can be served warm or stored for a few days in an airtight tin. I like to have this bake on standby to enjoy over coffee and a chat with friends.

Serves 8

225g/8oz/2 sticks butter, softened, plus extra for greasing
225g/8oz/scant 1¼ cups caster sugar
zest of 2 lemons
4 large or 5 small free-range eggs
225g/8oz/1½ cups self-raising flour (or plain flour with 1 tsp baking powder)
a little milk, to slacken (if required)

Topping:

zest and juice of 1 lemon
150g/5oz/1½ cups icing sugar

1 Preheat the oven to 180ºC/350ºF/Gas Mark 4. Grease a deep 20cm/8in cake tin or two sandwich tins or a 900g/2lb loaf tin.

2 Beat the softened butter in a large mixing bowl with the sugar. Stir in the lemon zest. When this mixture is creamy and fluffy, add in the eggs and then the flour. If you find the mixture is a little tight, you can add a dessertspoon of milk to loosen it up. Transfer to the prepared tin and bake for 30–40 minutes, or until a skewer inserted in the centre comes out clean. If you are using the sandwich tins, you will need a slightly shorter cooking time as the cake will be thinner. Allow to cool on a wire rack.

3 To make the topping, mix the lemon zest and juice with the icing sugar and drizzle over the top of the cake. If the drizzle is not loose enough in consistency, add a tiny amount of hot water and beat that into the mixture to achieve a running consistency.

Trio of **Pannacotta**

Raspberry, rhubarb and plum compotes are topped
with a smooth and creamy pannacotta in this distinctly
different dessert. The fruits can be varied depending
on the seasons or your own preference or you can keep
it simple and use just one fruit.

Serves 6

Fruit Compotes:

110g/4oz/generous ²/₃ cup
   frozen raspberries
110g/4oz rhubarb, chopped
   into small pieces
110g/4oz plums, stoned and
   roughly chopped
350g/12oz/1³/₄ cups caster
   sugar

Pannacotta:

700ml/1¹/₄ pints/3 cups double
   cream
150g/5oz/³/₄ cup caster sugar
2 leaves of gelatine
fresh fruit, to decorate

1 You will need 18 mini shot glasses or similar, or six ramekins if using
just one fruit. To make the fruit compote, place the three fruits, if
using, in separate medium saucepans. Divide the sugar equally among
the pans and cook over a gentle heat for 10–12 minutes, or until the
fruit has softened completely. Allow the fruit to cool slightly, then
divide each of the compotes among 6 glasses, or ramekins. You should
end up with 18 glasses in total – 6 glasses of each flavour.

2 To make the pannacotta, put the cream and sugar into a pan and
bring slowly to the boil. Place the leaves of gelatine in a bowl of cold
water to soften them, immersing them for 8–10 minutes.

3 Strain the gelatine through a fine sieve to remove excess moisture.
Take the cream off the heat and whisk in the gelatine. Allow the
mixture to cool slightly before pouring it over the fruit mixtures.
Transfer to the refrigerator for 3–4 hours to set.

4 To serve, place three glasses of pannacotta (each with a different
variety of compote) on each serving plate, or just one ramekin if using
one fruit, and decorate with a small piece of fresh fruit.

Summer Berry Pudding

A beautifully light dessert, which makes the most of all the delicious summer berries and also uses up bread that is past its best. You can use frozen berries if you fancy an out-of-season treat.

Serves 4

450g/1lb fresh berries
  (strawberries (quartered)
  redcurrants, blueberries,
  raspberries, etc)
150g/5oz/³⁄₄ cup caster sugar
juice of 1 lemon
50ml/2fl oz/¹⁄₄ cup water
1 shot of Grand Marnier
¹⁄₂ cinnamon stick
1 loaf of day-old bread, sliced
  1cm/¹⁄₂in thick and crusts
  removed
yoghurt or clotted cream, to
  serve

1 Place all the berries in a large saucepan. Scatter the sugar and lemon juice on top of the fruits and add the water, Grand Marnier and cinnamon stick. Heat very gently to allow the fruits to soften and to generate a little fruity syrup.

2 Meanwhile, line a large glass basin with a double layer of clingfilm, ensuring it covers the entire interior without any gaps. Allow the clingfilm to hang over the sides (you'll need to wrap it over the top of the basin later).

3 Cut out two bread circles to fit the top and the bottom of the basin. Cut the remaining bread into strips about 2cm/³⁄₄in wide.

4 Dip the smaller circle in the fruit mixture to coat with a little syrup and gently lay at the bottom of the basin, coated side facing outwards. Repeat this dipping process with the bread strips to cover the sides of the basin overlapping them. Dip the remaining upper circle of bread in the fruit compote and set aside.

5 Discard the cinnamon stick and spoon the fruit compote into the pudding basin. Place the remaining circle of bread on top. Using the palm of your hand, press the mixture down and wrap with the clingfilm over the top of the pudding. Rest the basin in the refrigerator for 3–4 hours, or preferably overnight. I like to put a plate on top, weighed down with a can of food, to keep the pudding in shape.

6 To serve the pudding, peel back the clingfilm from the base and then turn out onto a serving plate. Serve with yoghurt or clotted cream.

Baked Pumpkin Cheesecake

This recipe is a delicious way to use up any pumpkin flesh left after carving lanterns for Hallowe'en and makes a wonderful alternative to the more traditional pie. The sweet pumpkin flavour is enhanced by aromatic spices and the finished cake is drizzled with honey for a very sweet ending.

Serves 12

Crust:

550g/1lb 4oz digestive biscuits
225g/8oz/2 sticks butter, melted

Spiced Topping:

1 medium pumpkin
   (350g/12oz/3 cups of
   pumpkin flesh peeled,
   deseeded and chopped)
½ tsp ground cinnamon
½ tsp ground cloves
½ tsp ground nutmeg
½ tsp ground ginger
375g/13oz/generous 1½ cups
   cream cheese
225g/8oz/scant 1¼ cups
   (solidly packed) demerara
   sugar
3 large free-range eggs
½ tsp vanilla extract
50ml/2fl oz/¼ cup Baileys
   cream liqueur
honey, for drizzling
icing sugar, for dusting
fresh mint sprig, to decorate

1 Preheat the oven to 170°C/325°F/Gas Mark 3. Break the biscuits up into a crumblike consistency in the food processor or by placing them in a freezer bag and bashing them with a rolling pin. Tip into a bowl and mix in the melted butter. Using a large spoon or a potato masher, press the mixture onto the base of a 20cm/8in loose-bottomed springform tin. Bake in the oven for 8–10 minutes, or until just firm. Remove from the oven and allow the mixture to cool down.

2 Place the pumpkin chunks on a baking tray and bake in the oven for 35–45 minutes, or until they have softened completely. Transfer to a food processor or blender, then add the spices and blend until completely smooth – leave the blender running for at least 3 minutes. Allow to cool thoroughly.

3 In a large mixing bowl, cream the cream cheese with the sugar until light and fluffy. Mix in the eggs, spiced pumpkin purée, vanilla extract and Baileys. Make sure the mixture is completely blended together. Pour the mixture on top of the biscuit base and transfer to the oven for 40–45 minutes, or until the mixture is set around the edges but still slightly wobbly in the centre. Allow to cool slightly, then refrigerate for at least 3 hours but preferably overnight.

4 Drizzle with just a little honey if you like and slice with a hot sharp knife. A shake of icing sugar and a sprig of fresh mint on each slice will finish it perfectly.

Raspberry Parfait

Parfait means 'perfect' in French and, after you have tasted this, you will know just why this wonderful mousse merited its name. For the best results, prepare the day before and leave the dessert to freeze overnight.

Serves 8–10

150g/5oz/³/₄ cup caster sugar
50ml/2fl oz/¹/₄ cup liquid
  glucose
5 tbsp water
4 free-range egg yolks
700ml/1¹/₄ pints/3 cups double
  cream, lightly whipped

Raspberry Compote:

175g/6oz/scant 1¹/₄ cups frozen
  raspberries
110g/4oz/¹/₂ cup caster sugar
50ml/2fl oz/¹/₄ cup water

1 Line a 900g/2lb loaf tin with a double layer of clingfilm, ensuring that both the base and sides are covered.

2 To make the compote, place the frozen raspberries, sugar and water in a medium saucepan and cook gently over a low heat for 10–12 minutes, or until the raspberries have softened and generated a light syrup. Allow to cool slightly.

3 Meanwhile, place the sugar, liquid glucose and water in a small saucepan and bring to the boil, then reduce the heat and simmer for 2–3 minutes, or until the mixture thickens slightly.

4 At the same time, place the egg yolks in the bowl of a mixer and whip for 4–5 minutes, or until very pale and creamy. Reduce the speed of the machine to low, slowly pour in the simmering sugar mixture and beat for 8–10 minutes, or until the mixture has cooled down completely. Add the raspberry compote and gently fold in the whipped cream. Do not overmix at this stage.

5 Transfer the mixture to the prepared loaf tin and then place in the freezer for up to 12 hours or overnight.

6 To serve, tip out of the tin, remove the clingfilm and slice the loaf in its frozen state. Serve with a sharp fruit compote or homemade shortbread biscuits.

Health note
Elderly people, babies, toddlers, pregnant women and people who are already unwell should avoid eating uncooked egg yolks.

My Favourite Cupcakes

This is a simple recipe to get the children involved in cooking. Our girls love helping with the icing and decoration, but we never have much time to admire them, as they're usually eaten straight away and only occasionally make it to next day's lunch boxes! See below for recipe variation.

Makes 12 large or 24 small cupcakes

Basic recipe (to be flavoured):
450g/1lb/3 cups plain flour
1 rounded tsp baking powder
225g/8oz/1¼ cups caster sugar
75g/3oz/¾ stick butter
2 large free-range eggs
200ml/7fl oz/generous ¾ cup milk

Toppings:
melted chocolate
lemon curd (see page 176)
glacé icing (150g/5oz/1½ cups icing sugar mixed with hot water to make a stiff paste)
buttercream (see Easter Bunny Gâteau on page 210)
icing sugar, for dusting

1 Preheat the oven to 170°C/325°F/Gas Mark 3. Line a 12-cup muffin tin or a 24-cup mini-muffin tin with paper cases.

2 Sift the flour and baking powder together in a large bowl.

3 Fold in the caster sugar and rub in the butter until the mixture is soft and crumbly.

4 Break in the eggs, then add the milk and mix thoroughly.

5 Add the required flavouring, then spoon into the paper cases and bake for 20–25 minutes, or until well risen.

Variations:
(do not add more than 150g/5oz flavouring in total):
Triple chocolate: add a cup of dark, milk and white chocolate chips
Dark chocolate: melt 6 squares of dark chocolate and stir into the basic mixture
White chocolate and raspberry: frozen raspberries (no need to thaw first) and melted white chocolate
Banana: add 2 mashed bananas
Apple and cinnamon: add stewed apple and a sprinkling of cinnamon
Mixed frozen berries: add 200g/7oz/1 cup frozen berries (no need to thaw first)
Lemon and blueberry: add zest of 1 lemon and 150g/5oz/½ cup blueberries
Stewed rhubarb and natural yoghurt: add stewed rhubarb and replace 75ml/3fl oz/5 tbsp milk with yoghurt

Dark Chocolate **Marquise**

If this mousse is death by chocolate, I can't think of a better way to go! I have chosen dark chocolate here, but you could make a white chocolate variation by leaving out the cocoa and adding 75g/3oz white chocolate.

Serves 8

550ml/18fl oz/2¼ cups double cream
75g/3oz/⅔ cup icing sugar, plus extra for dusting
8 free-range egg yolks
225g/8oz/scant 1¼ cups caster sugar
400g/14oz/3½ sticks butter
150g/5oz/1½ cups cocoa powder
150g/5oz good-quality dark chocolate, melted
mascarpone cheese, to decorate
fresh mint sprigs, to decorate

1 Line a 900g/2lb loaf tin with a double layer of clingfilm.

2 Gently whip the cream with the icing sugar and chill in the refrigerator until required.

3 Whisk the egg yolks and caster sugar using an electric whisk until the mixture holds a figure-of-eight when the whisk is lifted out. The mixture should have more than doubled in volume.

4 Put the butter in a heatproof bowl and place over a saucepan of simmering water on a low heat until melted. Stir the cocoa powder into the melted butter, then fold the melted butter mixture into the egg mixture. Add the melted chocolate and gently fold in. At this stage, the mixture will begin to thicken slightly.

5 Remove the cream from the refrigerator and incorporate it gently into the mixture. Transfer the mixture into the lined loaf tin and allow to set in the refrigerator for up to 12 hours, or preferably overnight.

6 Turn it out of the loaf tin and serve in slices. Decorate with a little mascarpone cream cheese and fresh mint and dust with icing sugar.

Health note
Elderly people, babies, toddlers, pregnant women and people who are already unwell should avoid eating uncooked egg yolks.

Deep-filled Apple and Strawberry Crumble

Crumble may be a traditional dessert but it's one which is always very popular. It can be made well in advance and frozen until required. This one has a sweet pastry base as well as the crumble topping, which makes it even more divine.

Serves 10–12

Sweet Pastry:

300g/11oz/2 cups plain flour, plus extra for dusting
110g/4oz/½ cup caster sugar
150g/5oz/1¼ sticks butter, cut into pieces, plus extra for greasing
1 large egg

Fruit Compote:

4 large cooking apples, peeled and diced
150g/5oz strawberries, hulled
110g/4oz/½ cup caster sugar
1 tbsp water

Crumble Topping:

200g/7oz/1⅓ cups plain flour
110g/4oz/1 cup porridge oats
150g/5oz/1¼ sticks butter
110g/4oz/½ cup brown sugar
pinch of ground cinnamon

1 To make the sweet pastry, sift the flour into a large bowl along with the caster sugar. Rub in the butter using your fingertips until the mixture resembles fine breadcrumbs. Beat the egg, add to the dry ingredients and mix until it all comes together. Mould the mixture into a ball, wrap in clingfilm and put in the refrigerator to rest.

2 To make the fruit compote, put all the ingredients in a large saucepan, set over a medium heat and bring to the boil. Bubble for 3–4 minutes, then remove from the heat and allow to cool.

3 Put all the ingredients for the crumble topping in a large bowl and rub together well.

4 Preheat the oven to 180°C/350°F/Gas Mark 4 and grease a 25cm/10in round, fairly deep tart mould or tin. Roll out the sweet pastry on a lightly floured board and use it to line the mould.

5 Spoon all of the fruit compote into the pastry-lined mould – it should end up about half full, leaving space to sprinkle the crumble mixture on top until the fruit compote is well covered. Bake in the preheated oven for 30–35 minutes until the crumble and edges of the pastry are golden brown. It is best to leave the crumble in the tin to cool down slightly before cutting.

Bread and Butter Pudding

This pudding can be made in so many ways, but I prefer the classic method – a soft set with a wonderful, buttery top. It can also be fabulous made with day-old brioche or croissants instead of the traditional white bread. Custard is the classic accompaniment – if desired, double the quantities for the custard topping and keep half to serve alongside.

Serves 6

75g/3oz/¾ stick butter, at room temperature
12 slices of white medium-sliced bread, crusts removed
50g/2oz/scant ½ cup raisins
pouring cream or extra custard (make double the quantity below), to serve

Custard Topping:

300ml/10fl oz/1¼ cups double cream
300ml/10fl oz/1¼ cups milk
4 eggs
75g/3oz/¾ cup caster sugar
½ tsp ground cinnamon

1 Generously grease a 20cm/8in square ovenproof dish. Spread the remaining butter all over the slices of bread, coating both sides, then cut each slice into quarters on the diagonal.

2 Arrange one-third of the bread triangles in a single, slightly overlapping layer in the bottom of the greased dish. Scatter over half of the raisins, then place the next third of bread triangles in another layer on top, and scatter over the remaining raisins. Press the layers down gently with a fish slice or spatula. Keep the final third of bread triangles for later.

3 To make the custard topping, heat the cream and milk in a saucepan until almost boiling. Remove from the heat and set aside. Meanwhile, whisk together the eggs, sugar and ground cinnamon in a large heatproof bowl set over a pan of gently simmering water, until thick enough that the whisk leaves a trail in the mixture. Remove from the heat, pour in the cream mixture and beat until well combined.

4 Pour two-thirds of the custard over the layered-up bread triangles and leave to stand for about 30 minutes, or until the bread has soaked up all of the custard.

5 Preheat the oven to 180°C/350°F/Gas Mark 4. Pour the remaining custard over the pudding and arrange the rest of the bread triangles on top. Press down firmly with a fish slice or spatula so that the custard comes halfway up the bread triangles. Bake in the oven for 30–35 minutes until the custard is just set and the top is golden brown. Serve with a separate jug of pouring cream or some additional custard.

Barbecued Banana Split

A simple dessert, ideal for cooking on the barbecue if you wish. It might even be good for you – bananas are an excellent source of potassium and dark chocolate helps with the reduction of blood pressure!

Serves 4

4 bananas, peeled and sliced
    lengthways
50g/2oz/¼ cup brown sugar
110g/4oz/²/₃ cup dark
    chocolate drops
50g/2oz/½ stick butter, cut into
    4 pieces
4 scoops of vanilla ice cream

1 Light the barbecue or preheat the oven to 190°C/375°F/Gas Mark 5. Cut out four large squares of foil.

2 Place a banana in the centre of each square of foil and top with some brown sugar, dark chocolate drops and a piece of the butter. Bring the edges of the foil together to close up the parcel and seal well to keep all the juices inside. Put on the barbecue for 5 minutes, or cook for about 10 minutes in the oven.

3 Remove the foil parcels from the barbecue or oven and open at the top using scissors. Pop the open parcels directly into bowls and serve each one with a scoop of ice cream.

Knickerbocker Glory

The knickerbocker glory originated in 1930s America. When devising this particular version I was conscious of the fact that everyone has a very different and unique recipe for it – some people include jelly, nuts, all sorts of different syrups, and more! No method is right or wrong, so just have fun!

Serves 1

50g/2oz/½ cup mixed berries
3 scoops of ice cream (flavour of your choice)
50ml/2fl oz/¼ cup whipping cream, whipped
2 tbsp chocolate sauce
3 tbsp strawberry sauce
25g/1oz/¼ cup flaked almonds (optional)
100ml/3½fl oz/scant ½ cup red (or pink) lemonade
1 tbsp coloured sprinkles

1 Put all the mixed berries in the bottom of a large, tall glass or sundae dish.

2 Add the scoops of ice cream, then top with whipped cream, chocolate sauce, strawberry sauce and flaked almonds, if you like.

3 Pour over the lemonade and sprinkle with the coloured sprinkles.

Rhubarb Crème Brûlée

The secret to a good crème brûlée is to place the individual ramekins or pots in a shallow roasting tin so that the mixture heats up evenly. My wife, Catherine, loves this creamy dessert and of all the recipes I have tried, this is her favourite.

Serves 6

Rhubarb Compote:

4 ripe rhubarb sticks, chopped
  into bite-sized pieces
110g/4oz/½ cup caster sugar
2 tbsp cold water
2 tsp grenadine syrup

Egg Custard:

1 vanilla pod
50ml/2fl oz/¼ cup milk
425ml/15fl oz/generous
  1¾ cups double cream
5 free-range egg yolks
110g/4oz/½ cup caster sugar,
  plus extra for glazing

1 Preheat the oven to 130°C/250°F/Gas Mark ½.

2 To make the compote, put the rhubarb into a small saucepan with the caster sugar and water. Bring to the boil, then reduce the heat to a gentle simmer and cook until the rhubarb has stewed or softened down completely. Stir in the grenadine syrup and allow to cool completely.

3 To make the egg custard, split the vanilla pot lengthways and use a small sharp knife to scrape out the seeds. Put the seeds and the pod into a large saucepan with the milk and cream and bring to the boil, then simmer gently over a low heat.

4 Meanwhile, using a large, spotlessly clean bowl and a whisk, beat the egg yolks and sugar together until light and creamy. This will take about 2 minutes. Pour the boiled milk and cream mixture onto the eggs and mix well. Transfer to a large pouring jug, discarding the vanilla pod.

5 Divide the stewed rhubarb among six 150ml/5fl oz ramekins. Pour the egg custard on top and transfer to a large roasting tin. Pour water into the roasting tray to come halfway up the side of the ramekins and bake for up to 55 minutes, or until set but with a little wobble in the centre. Allow to cool completely.

6 To glaze, dust the top of the cooled crème brûlée with a thin layer of caster sugar. Pop under a preheated grill for 2–3 minutes or use a chef's blow torch to glaze the top of the brûlée and get a thin layer of hardened caramel on top. Serve and enjoy.

Tip:
When pouring egg custard on top of the stewed rhubarb, pour it very slowly to avoid getting the rhubarb mixed in with the custard.

Plum **Pudding**

The pudding is best made 4–6 weeks before Christmas. In our house it is a full family activity and each of the children gets their own special job – weighing out ingredients, stirring and mixing. Nowadays I tend to use melted butter instead of suet.

Serves 6

Dry Ingredients:
110g/4oz/²/₃ cup sultanas
110g/4oz/ scant 1 cup raisins
110g/4oz/generous ²/₃ cup currants
30g/1oz/¹/₈ cup chopped **glacé** cherries
50g/2oz/¹/₃ cup mixed peel
75g/3oz/1¹/₂ cups white breadcrumbs
45g/1¹/₂oz/scant ¹/₃ cup plain flour
110g/4oz/generous ¹/₂ cup (solidly packed) dark brown sugar
50g/2oz/¹/₃ cup nibbed almonds
¹/₂ tsp ground nutmeg
¹/₂–1 tsp mixed spice
pinch of salt

Wet Ingredients:
100ml/3¹/₂ fl oz brandy plus 3 tbsp for sprinkling
100g/4oz/1 stick butter, melted, plus extra for greasing
2 free-range eggs

Brandy Butter:
110g/4oz/1 stick butter, softened but not melted
50g/2oz/¹/₂ cup icing sugar
50ml/2fl oz/¹/₄ cup brandy

1 Place the dried fruits in a small bowl with 100ml/3¹/₂ fl oz of brandy. Cover with clingfilm and leave the fruit to marinate for 2 days.

2 Transfer the marinated fruit to a large bowl. Add the remaining dry ingredients, pour in the wet ingredients and mix well. Tip into a well-greased 850ml/1¹/₂ pint/3¹/₂ cup bowl. Cover with two well-greased pieces of baking parchment, ensuring there is a fold across the middle. Place a double layer of foil or the lid of the pudding bowl on top.

3 Place the pudding bowl into a large saucepan half-filled with water. Bring the water to the boil, then reduce to a very gentle simmer. Steam for 6 hours, making sure that the pan does not boil dry – you may need to top up the pan with more water from time to time.

4 When cooked, lift the pudding bowl from the pan and remove the lid and baking parchment. Sprinkle with 3 tablespoons of brandy. Allow the pudding to cool down completely. When cold, re-cover as before with fresh baking parchment and store in a cool place until needed. On Christmas morning, you will need to steam the pudding for 3 hours. The process is the same as above.

5 To make the brandy butter, mix all the ingredients together until thoroughly combined. Transfer to a serving bowl and chill in the refrigerator until required.

Gooseberry Sponge
with Butterscotch Sauce

Every summer, a very good friend of mine calls by, laden down with a large bag of juicy gooseberries. Of course, the disadvantage is that I'm expected to return the favour (and some of the gooseberries) in the form of a pudding. This is a real feel-good dessert, with the sweetness of the sponge and the tangy berries making a perfect combination.

Serves 8

Gooseberry Compote:

450g/1lb/3 cups gooseberries
150g/5oz/¾ cup caster sugar
2 tbsp cold water

Sponge:

6 large free-range eggs
175g/6oz/generous ¾ cup
   caster sugar
175g/6oz/generous 1 cup
   self-raising flour
50g/2oz/½ stick butter, melted
   and then cooled
icing sugar, for dusting

Butterscotch Sauce:

50g/2oz/½ stick butter
50g/2oz/¼ cup (solidly packed)
   brown sugar
4 tsp golden syrup
250ml/9fl oz/generous 1 cup
   pouring cream

1 Begin by making the gooseberry compote. Top and tail the gooseberries and place them in a large saucepan with the sugar and water. Stew very gently over a low heat for 10–12 minutes, or just until the gooseberries begin to soften. Allow to cool completely.

2 Preheat the oven to 180°C/350°F/Gas Mark 4.

3 To make the sponge mixture, beat the eggs with the sugar in a large bowl until light and aerated and more than doubled in size. The whisk should leave a figure-of-eight on the surface of the mixture when it is lifted out.

4 Using a large metal spoon, carefully fold in the flour. Try not to be too vigorous at this stage, as you could knock the air out of the mixture, which would prevent your sponge rising – be gentle! When the flour is almost fully incorporated, gently fold in the melted butter.

5 Transfer the gooseberry compote to a large baking dish. Pour the sponge mixture on top and bake in the oven for 35–45 minutes depending on the size of your dish, or until light and springy to the touch. Invert the sponge onto a serving plate.

6 To make the butterscotch sauce, melt the butter and brown sugar in a medium saucepan over a gentle heat. Add the golden syrup and pouring cream and whisk continuously until the mixture comes to the boil. Simmer for 2–3 minutes. Remove from the heat and pour into a serving jug.

7 Dust the sponge with icing sugar and serve drizzled with creamy butterscotch sauce.

Tiramisu

This is Italian trifle and contains all of life's pleasures! If you love strong coffee, brandy and wine, this is the perfect dessert for you. We often put this on the menu at the hotel, and two or three portions always make it back over to our house, where it is enjoyed at leisure.

Serves 6–8

110g/4oz/generous ½ cup caster sugar

100ml/3½fl oz/scant ½ cup water

4 free-range egg yolks

225g/8oz/1 cup mascarpone cheese

200ml/7fl oz/generous ¾ cup double cream, lightly whipped

1 double espresso or 1 cup of strong coffee

25ml/1fl oz/2 tbsp brandy

90ml/3fl oz/1½ cups marsala wine or Tia Maria

24–30 sponge finger biscuits

50g/2oz/½ cup cocoa powder

1 Put the caster sugar and water into a small saucepan, bring to the boil and boil until it reaches the softball stage (this is when a teaspoon of the boiling sugar dropped into cold water sticks together in a little ball). Take care because it is extremely hot at this stage.

2 Beat the egg yolks in an electric mixer for 4–5 minutes, or until very pale and creamy. Reduce the speed of the machine to low and slowly pour in the boiling sugar mixture. Beat for 8–10 minutes, or until the mixture has cooled down completely. Add the mascarpone cheese and beat until combined. Gently fold the whipped cream into the cheesy mixture by hand.

3 Mix the coffee, brandy and marsala together. Dip half the biscuits into the coffee mixture one by one and arrange flat on the base of a shallow serving dish or in pretty martini glasses. Spread half the creamy mixture on top of the biscuits, then repeat with another layer of dipped biscuits and another creamy layer.

4 Smooth the top of the cream mixture with a warm palette knife and dust with cocoa powder. Chill in the refrigerator for 2–3 hours before serving.

Black **Cherry** Bakewell **Tart**

This is a variation on the classic Bakewell tart and uses black cherries under a delicate layer of frangipane, an almond flavoured pastry cream. Serve with vanilla ice cream for an after-dinner treat.

Serves 12

1 x 400g/14oz tin of good-quality black cherries, drained

Sweet Pastry:

75g/6oz/1½ sticks butter, softened, plus extra for greasing

75g/6oz/generous 1½ cups icing sugar, sifted

2 free-range egg yolks, beaten

1 tbsp double cream

300g/11oz/2 cups plain flour, sifted

Frangipane:

225g/8oz/2 sticks butter

225g/8oz/scant 1¼ cups caster sugar

¼ tsp almond extract

4 free-range eggs

225g/8oz/generous 2 cups ground almonds

75g/3oz/½ cup plain flour

1 To make the pastry, gently cream the butter and sugar together in a medium bowl until pale and fluffy. Slowly add the egg yolks, mixing well after each addition. Stir in the cream, then tip in the flour and mix to a smooth paste. Cover with clingfilm and leave in the refrigerator to rest for at least 4 hours (overnight is best).

2 Preheat the oven to 180°C/350°F/Gas Mark 4.

3 To make the frangipane, cream the butter and sugar together in a large bowl with the almond extract until light and fluffy. Beat in the eggs, ground almonds and flour. The mixture should resemble a sticky consistency. Gather this together into a ball and refrigerate for a few minutes.

4 Grease a 25cm/10in fluted flan ring and line with the sweet pastry. Scatter the drained cherries around the pastry base. Using a piping bag fitted with a large plain nozzle, pipe the frangipane all around the top of the pastry, then use a palette knife or dessertspoon to spread it carefully over the cherries. Cut long, thin strips from the remainder of the pastry and arrange in a trellis or diamond pattern across the top.

5 Bake for 35–40 minutes, or until a skewer inserted into the middle comes out clean. Allow to cool slightly in the tin before transferring to a serving plate.

Treacle Tart

A traditional English dessert that is very simple to make provided you follow one key rule! Use good-quality golden syrup (like Lyle's Golden Syrup) and not dark black treacle, which can make the tart quite bitter.

Serves 12

Sweetened Shortcrust Pastry:

225g/8oz/1½ cups plain flour
pinch of salt
50g/2oz/⅓ cup caster sugar
110g/4oz/1 stick butter, chilled
2 free-range egg yolks, beaten

Filling:

450g/1lb/1⅓ cups golden syrup
zest and juice of 1 lemon
½ tsp ground ginger
225g/8oz/4 cups fine fresh white breadcrumbs
icing sugar, for dusting

1 To make the pastry, sift the flour and salt into a large mixing bowl. Add the sugar and butter and rub the butter in until the mixture resembles fine breadcrumbs. Mix in the beaten egg yolks, a little at a time, to bind the mixture together. Knead gently, then cover with clingfilm and leave in the refrigerator for at least 4 hours (overnight is best).

2 Preheat the oven to 180°C/350°F/Gas Mark 4. Use the pastry to line a 23cm/9in loose-bottomed flan ring and chill in the refrigerator until required.

3 To make the filling, gently melt the golden syrup with the lemon juice in a medium saucepan until just softened. Stir in the lemon zest, ginger and breadcrumbs. Pour the mixture into the chilled pastry case. If you wish, create a lattice effect across the top of the tart with any remaining pastry. Bake for 30–35 minutes, or until just set and soft to the touch.

4 Dust generously with icing sugar. Serve piping hot with egg custard or ice cream.

Pear William Gâteau

This is my version of the French classic named after the very delicious pears, and it's a lovely dessert for a special occasion. You can make one sponge and cut it in two and then freeze the other half for later use.

Serves 12

butter, for greasing
18 sponge finger biscuits
20ml/¾fl oz/4 tsp juice from
  the tinned pears
1 x 400g/14oz tin of pears, in
  syrup, diced
cocoa powder, for dusting
melted chocolate, to decorate
  (optional)

Sponge Base:

7 large free-range eggs
200g/7oz/1 cup caster sugar
200g/7oz/1⅓ cups self-raising
  flour, sifted

Vanilla Bavarois:

225ml/8fl oz/1 cup milk
1 vanilla pod, split lengthways
3 large free-range egg yolks
50g/2oz/⅓ cup caster sugar
3 leaves of leaf gelatine
225ml/8fl oz/1 cup double
  cream, lightly whipped

1 Preheat the oven to 180°C/350°F/Gas Mark 4. Grease and line a 25cm/10in round springform tin with baking parchment.

2 To make the sponge base, beat the eggs with the sugar in a mixing bowl until light and aerated. The whisk should leave a figure-of-eight on the surface of the mixture when the whisk is lifted out. Gently fold in the sifted flour using a metal spoon, avoiding knocking out any air from the mixture. Pour into the tin. Bake for 35 minutes until well risen and golden brown. Allow to cool, then slice the sponge in half horizontally.

3 Place the ring of the springform tin on a large, round serving platter. Line the sides of the tin with upright sponge finger biscuits. Trim the circular disc of sponge to fit tightly inside the ring of biscuits.

4 Pour the fruit syrup over the sponge base. Spread the pears out evenly on the sponge.

5 To make the vanilla bavarois, heat the milk and vanilla pod in a medium pan over a low heat until it is just about to boil. Cream the egg yolks and sugar together in a bowl until light and creamy. Pour the hot milk over the egg mixture, tip back into the pan and return to the heat but do not boil.

6 Soak the gelatine in cold water for 10 minutes. Strain off the water and whisk into the egg custard. Allow the custard to cool and thicken slightly.

7 When the egg custard is beginning to thicken, gently fold in the whipped cream, then pour the vanilla bavarois over the top of the pears and soaked sponge. Place in the refrigerator to chill and set for 4–6 hours. To serve, dust with a little cocoa powder or drizzle with some melted chocolate and cut into thin slices.

Plum and Almond **Cobbler**

A wonderful all-in-one dessert that is similar to the classic Eve's pudding, but with a crumblier topping! We are lucky enough to receive bags of plums from our friends' gardens in late summer – a perfect base for this dessert. However, you can use other fruits – it's particularly delicious with gooseberries or rhubarb.

Serves 8–10

900g/2lb small ripe plums (taste to make sure they are nice and sweet)
200g/7oz/1 cup caster sugar
½ tsp ground cinnamon

Cobbler Topping:

300g/11oz/2 cups plain flour
1 rounded tsp baking powder
1 level tsp ground cinnamon
110g/4oz/generous 1 cup ground almonds
110g/4oz/generous ½ cup (solidly packed) soft brown sugar
110g/4oz/1 stick butter, cut into pieces
2 large free-range eggs
125ml/4fl oz/½ cup milk

To Glaze:

1 egg, beaten with a little milk
50g/2oz/¼ cup (solidly packed) demerara sugar
75g/3oz/¾ cup flaked almonds

1 Cut each of the plums in half, remove the stone and then cut the flesh into pieces. Put all the chopped plums into a large bowl, sprinkle with the sugar and cinnamon and leave to rest for 20–30 minutes while you are preparing the cobbler topping.

2 Preheat the oven to 180ºC/350ºF/Gas Mark 4.

3 For the cobbler topping, sift the flour, baking powder, cinnamon and ground almonds together into a large bowl. Add the sugar. Gently rub the butter into the flour mixture until it resembles fine breadcrumbs. Stir in the eggs and milk to achieve a sticky consistency.

4 Transfer the plum mixture to a large baking dish. Spoon the cobbler mixture on top. The more haphazard you spoon, the better the finished product will look. Brush with the egg wash, sprinkle with the demerara sugar and flaked almonds and bake for 30–35 minutes. Serve with lingering warmth.

Apple Charlotte

Like all good classic desserts, this is simple in its preparation and execution. The beauty is that it can be made in advance, refrigerated until required, then baked just before serving. You could also try using pears in place of, or in addition to, the apples.

Serves 6

110g/4oz/1 stick butter, melted, plus extra for brushing dishes
1 loaf of bread, cut into slices about 5mm/¼in thick, crusts removed
whipped cream, to serve

Apple Mixture:

75g/3oz/¾ stick butter
150g/5oz/¾ cup (solidly packed) soft brown sugar
8 large dessert apples, peeled and cored and cut into 7–8 wedges
½ tsp ground cinnamon

1 This can be baked in one large ovenproof pudding basin or six individual ramekins (150ml/5fl oz capacity). Brush the base and sides of the dish(es) with melted butter. Also brush the bread slices with the butter.

2 Cut out disc(s) of buttered bread for the top and bottom of the basin or ramekins. Put the disc(s) in the bottom first with the buttered side pointing downwards. Retain the disc(s) for the top of the pudding(s). Cut the remaining bread into strips about 2cm/¾in wide.

3 Use the strips of bread to line the basin(s) all the way around, and overlap a little so that there is no overflow at a later stage. Ensure that the buttered sides face outwards. Chill the basin(s) in the refrigerator until required. Preheat the oven to 170°C/325°F/Gas Mark 3.

4 To make the apple mixture, melt the butter slowly in a large pan over a low heat. Gradually add the sugar and stir until all the sugar has dissolved. Do not try to do this too quickly, as the caramel will have a higher risk of burning. Add the apples and toss around for 3–4 minutes, or until they begin to soften slightly and take on a golden brown colour. Sprinkle in the ground cinnamon, then allow the mixture to cool.

5 When the mixture has cooled a little, take the basin(s) out of the refrigerator and add the apple and cinnamon mixture. Cover with the final disc(s) of bread, with the buttered side facing up. Gently push the top disc down to keep it secure.

6 Transfer the basin(s) to a baking sheet and bake for 25–30 minutes, or until the bread has turned golden brown. Allow the pudding to rest for 5–10 minutes, then invert onto a serving plate. Serve with freshly whipped cream.

Easter Bunny Gâteau

An Easter triumph! You can decorate it as you wish –
I like to use mini chocolate eggs or baby chicks. You can
also adapt this basic recipe with different flavourings
(such as 1 tablespoon of cocoa added with the flour, or
the zest of an orange or lemon added when creaming
the butter). You could also add food colourings.

Serves 10–12

Sponge:

300g/11oz/2¾ sticks butter,
 plus extra for greasing
300g/11oz/1½ cups caster
 sugar
zest of 1 lemon or orange
6 free-range eggs
300g/11oz/2 cups self-raising
 flour

Buttercream:

300g/11oz/2¾ sticks butter,
 softened
600g/1lb 5oz/6 cups icing
 sugar
pink, green and yellow food
 colouring

1 Preheat the oven to 180°C/350°F/Gas Mark 4. Grease and line a
23cm/9in loose-bottomed springform (cheesecake) tin.

2 To make the sponge, cream the butter, sugar and zest together in
a bowl until light and fluffy, then add the eggs and flour and mix
thoroughly. Pour into the cake tin and bake for 35–40 minutes, or until
the mixture comes away from the sides of the tin and a skewer inserted
in the centre comes out clean. Gently remove from the tin onto a wire
rack and allow to cool completely.

3 To make the buttercream, beat the softened butter and icing sugar
in a mixer until light and fluffy. Divide the buttercream equally among
three bowls. Add one or two drops of food colouring to each mixture
and beat well.

4 Slice the cake horizontally in four equal layers with a sharp bread
knife. Make sure they are level, so take your time doing this. Spread
or pipe the top of each layer with one of the coloured buttercreams.
I usually keep the yellow for the top, but that's just a personal thing!
Stack the layers on a serving plate.

5 If you have buttercream left over, pipe birds' nests on the top of the
cake and fill with little mini eggs. The top tier could be decorated with
little fluffy marshmallows, too.

Tips:
Store the cake in an airtight container for 5–7 days (if it lasts that long!)
The sponge part of this cake can also be made in advance and frozen
until required.

Chocolate and Orange Cake with Grand Marnier

If you want something extremely indulgent and incredibly naughty, then look no further. I like to make this for special occasions, and I usually whip one up as a treat for Catherine on St. Valentine's Day.

Makes 12 slices
Sponge:
225g/8oz/2 sticks butter, softened, plus extra for greasing
150g/5oz/1 cup plain flour
50g/2oz/½ cup cocoa powder
150g/5oz/scant 1½ cups ground almonds
150g/5oz/1½ cups icing sugar
zest and juice of 1 orange
7 large free-range eggs, separated
2–3 drops of lemon juice
150g/5oz/¾ cup caster sugar
melted white chocolate, white chocolate curls, or red berries, to decorate

1 Preheat the oven to 190°C/375°F/Gas Mark 5. Grease and line the base of a round 23cm/9in loose-bottomed springform tin with baking parchment.

2 To make the sponge, sift the flour, cocoa powder and ground almonds together. Cream the butter and icing sugar together in a large bowl or in a food mixer until the mixture is light and fluffy. Add in orange zest and juice, then gently mix in the egg yolks.

3 In a separate bowl, whisk the egg whites with the lemon juice until they are quite stiff. Mix in the caster sugar (almost as if you were making a meringue).

4 Gently fold the sifted flour and ground almonds into the creamed butter and sugar. The mixture will be quite dry and stiff at this stage, but don't worry. Beat half of the egg whites into the mixture to soften and loosen it, then gently fold in the remaining egg whites using a metal spoon, making sure you retain as much air and lightness in the sponge as possible.

5 Pour the mixture into the prepared cake tin and bake for 35–40 minutes, or until the cake is well set. A skewer inserted into the centre of the cake should come away spotlessly clean and dry. Allow the cake to cool in the tin, as it will still be quite soft at this stage. When cool, invert the cake onto a plate. The top of the cake is now the base.

6 To make the mousse, melt the dark chocolate in a bowl set over gently simmering water. Whisk the egg whites in a large bowl until they are quite stiff.

Dark Chocolate and Orange Mousse:

400g/14oz good-quality dark chocolate

4 large free-range eggs, separated

450ml/16fl oz/2 cups double cream, very softly whipped

50ml/2fl oz/¼ cup Grand Marnier liqueur

Stock Syrup:

250g/9oz/1¼ cups caster sugar

200ml/7fl oz/generous ¾ cup water

1 orange, cut into wedges

7 Whisk the egg yolks into the melted chocolate. Don't panic, as the mixture will immediately begin to thicken up. Allow the mixture to cool for 4–5 minutes. Mix in half the whipped cream to loosen the mixture a little, then fold in the remainder of the cream with a metal spoon. Next, fold in the beaten egg whites – be very gentle at this stage, as the egg whites give lightness to the mousse. Finally, pour in the Grand Marnier and gently mix it into the chocolate mixture. Cover with clingfilm and refrigerate until required.

8 To make the stock syrup, place the sugar, water and wedges of orange in a saucepan and gently bring to the boil. Allow to boil for 2–3 minutes, then remove from the heat and allow the syrup to cool.

9 To assemble, slice the chocolate sponge horizontally into three equal layers. Place the bottom layer on a thin 23cm/9in cake board. Using a pastry brush, lightly brush the sponge with the stock syrup to moisten it a little. Spread a layer of the chocolate mousse onto this disc – not too much, as there is only so much decadence one can take!

10 Repeat this process with the two remaining cake layers, ensuring that you brush each layer with stock syrup, and press each layer of the cake down with your hand to give an even finish at the end. Cover the top and sides of the cake with an even layer of mousse.

11 Transfer to a large serving platter. If you wish, decorate with a drizzle of melted white chocolate, some white chocolate curls, or some fruit. Serve and enjoy!

Strawberry and Passion Fruit
Pavlova

Crisp on the outside, soft and light on the inside, piled high with sweet strawberries and freshly whipped cream – what could be more delicious than pavlova? We usually make one for family parties, and the children always eat their main course when they know what's for dessert.

Serves 6–8
Pavlova:
6 free-range egg whites
350g/12oz/1¾ cups caster
    sugar
½ tsp vanilla extract
½ tsp cornflour
½ tsp white wine vinegar

To Decorate:
250ml/9fl oz/generous 1 cup
    double cream, very gently
    whipped
16–20 strawberries, cut into
    quarters
2 passion fruits

1 Preheat the oven to 120ºC/240ºF/Gas Mark ½. Line a 33 x 23cm/ 13 x 9in baking tray with baking parchment.

2 Put the egg whites into a spotlessly clean mixer bowl and beat on full speed until quite stiffly beaten. Turn the speed of the mixer down and slowly add the sugar, adding just a little at a time. When all the sugar has been incorporated, add the vanilla extract, cornflour and vinegar and give one final whisk on high speed. The mixture should be glossy and when the bowl is turned upside down, the mixture should remain firmly in the bowl. Either spread all the mixture out on the baking sheet or spoon into a piping bag and pipe out into individual nests.

3 Bake in the oven for 1 hour, or until the meringue mixture is very firm to touch but still soft in the middle. I usually leave mine to cool in the oven with the door ajar.

4 When cold, transfer to a serving plate and decorate with some freshly whipped cream. Pile the strawberries on top of the pavlova and drizzle the seeds of the passion fruit all over the top. Serve immediately.

Dedication

To my beautiful wife Catherine,
who is and always has been
my tower of strength

Acknowledgments

Compiling a cookery book is a long, laborious process
and I have been blessed with wonderful assistance, for
which I am truly grateful.

I would like to thank Edward Hayden for his unyielding
commitment and dedication to this project.

I would also like to thank Helen Donnelly, who assisted in
the testing of the recipes.

Jenny Heller, Ione Walder and Lesley Robb offered
tremendous support and encouragement, and I greatly
appreciate the part they have played in this book.

This paperback edition published by Collins in 2010.
First published in 2009 by Collins, an imprint of
HarperCollins Publishers, 77-85 Fulham Palace Road,
Hammersmith, London W6 8JB

www.harpercollins.co.uk

Collins is a registered trademark of HarperCollins
Publishers Ltd

14   13   12   11   10
5   4   3   2   1

Text©Kevin Dundon
Photography©Noel Murphy

All rights reserved. No part of this publication may
be reproduced, stored in a retrieval system, or
transmitted, in any form or by any means, electronic,
mechanical, photocopying, recording or otherwise
without the prior written permission of the publisher.

A catalogue record for this book is available
from the British Library.

Editorial Director: Jenny Heller
Editors: Ione Walder & Lesley Robb
Design: Heike Schüssler
Layout: Jeremy Tilston
Cover design: Anna Martin and Kate Gaughran
Photographer: Noel Murphy
Senior Production Controller: Chris Gurney

ISBN   978-0-00-736405-3

Colour reproduction by Colourscan
Printed and bound by Printing Express, Hong Kong

Glossary

UK	US
almonds, flaked	almonds, slivered
arborio rice	risotto rice
aubergine	eggplant
bacon rasher	bacon strip or slice
baking parchment	waxed paper
sponge finger biscuits	ladyfingers
button mushroom	white mushroom
chips	fries
clingfilm	plastic wrap
cocoa powder	unsweetened cocoa
coriander (fresh)	cilantro
cornflour	cornstarch
cos lettuce	romaine
cream	
crème fraîche	sour cream — crème fraîche is available only in gourmet stores
double	heavy
single	light
digestive biscuits	graham crackers
flour	
plain	all-purpose
self-raising	self-rising
French beans	green beans

UK	US
golden syrup	corn syrup
icing	frosting
mangetout	sugar snap peas
minced (beef, pork)	ground
mixed peel	candied peel
mixed spice	allspice
monkfish	angler fish
Parma ham	prosciutto
pepper	bell pepper
piping bag	pastry bag
nozzle	tip
prawn	shrimp
rocket	arugula
salad leaves	salad greens
scones	biscuits
spring onion	scallion
sugar:	
caster	superfine
demerara	raw brown
icing	confectioner's
sultanas	seedless white raisins
swiss roll	jelly roll
tiger prawn(s)	jumbo shrimp

Index

WARWICKSHIRE
COUNTY LIBRARY

013492691 0

Askews

641.5   £14.99

2915373

244L

ⓉⓂ ADJUSTABLE LYFJACKET

BOOK PROTECTORS & CO.
PROTECTOR HOUSE, 70 SOUTH GROVE, LONDON E17 7LL

This bestselling cookbook from renowned chef and hands-on dad **Kevin Dundon** shows how easy it is to put great food on the family table every day. Kevin shares more than 120 of his favourite recipes, including well-loved classics and some exciting new twists.

Packed with simple and delicious ingredients, and explained in his warm, straightforward manner, these meals are perfect for the busy, budget-conscious cook, proving that great home-cooked food need never be a chore.

Now includes brand new recipes!

'Home-cooked, uncomplicated food.'
BBC Good Food Magazine

'Delicious family-friendly recipes.'
Bella

LOVE THIS BOOK? WWW.ROOKARMY.COM

UK £14.99 *

ISBN 978-0-00-736405-3

01499 >

*recommended price

9 780007 364053

KT-382-372

RUNNER'S WORLD® THE
RUNNER'S
‹DIET

RUNNER'S WORLD. THE

RUNNER'S
‹DIET

THE ULTIMATE EATING PLAN

THAT WILL MAKE EVERY

RUNNER (AND WALKER)

LEANER, FASTER, AND FITTER

Madelyn H. Fernstrom, PhD, CNS

RODALE

Notice
Mention of specific companies, organizations, or authorities in this book
does not imply endorsement by the publisher, nor does mention of specific
companies, organizations, or authorities imply that they endorse this book.
Internet addresses and telephone numbers given in this book
were accurate at the time it went to press.

© 2005 by Madelyn Fernstrom

All rights reserved. No part of this publication may be reproduced or transmitted
in any form or by any means, electronic or mechanical, including photocopying,
recording, or any other information storage and retrieval system, without the
written permission of the publisher.

Runner's World® is a registered trademark of Rodale Inc.

Printed in the United States of America
Rodale Inc. makes every effort to use acid-free ♾, recycled paper ♻.

Book design by Anthony Serge
Front cover photography © Steve Thornton/CORBIS

Library of Congress Cataloging-in-Publication Data

Fernstrom, Madelyn H.
Runner's world the runner's diet : the ultimate eating plan that will make
every runner (and walker) leaner, faster, and fitter / Madelyn H. Fernstrom.
p.   cm.
Includes index.
ISBN-13 978–1–59486–205–2 paperback
ISBN-10 1–59486–205–2 paperback
ISBN-13 978–1–59486–458–2 hardcover
ISBN-10 1–59486–458–6 hardcover
1. Runners (Sports)—Nutrition.   2. Athletes—Nutrition.   I. Title.
TX361.R86F47   2005
613.2'024'79642—dc22   2005006342

Distributed to the trade by Holtzbrinck Publishers

2   4   6   8   10   9   7   5   3   1   paperback
2   4   6   8   10   9   7   5   3   1   hardcover

We inspire and enable people to improve their lives and the world around them

For more of our products visit **rodalestore.com** or call 800-848-4735

DEDICATION

> To John, Aaron, and Lauren

CONTENTS

Chapter 4: The 50-25-25 Plan for Weight Loss 49

Why this six-step plan works for runners (and walkers)

Chapter 5: Let's Get Physical 74

Identify the problem in your running/walking program—and figure out how to fix it

Chapter 6: Your Drink Tank 101

Analyzing a runner's fluid intake—and how to determine the balance between salt, water, and other components

Chapter 7: Dietary Supplements 121

When it comes to nutritional supplements, less is always more

Chapter 8: Putting It All Together 141

The final push you need to follow the Runner's Diet for life

ACKNOWLEDGMENTS

My most heartfelt thanks to Jeremy Katz at Rodale for his support and his belief that "I have a book in me" the very first time we met. Special thanks to Ted Spiker, whose exceptional journalistic and editorial skills were of great help in making this book most reader friendly. I am indebted to Heidi Rodale, always a willing ear ("Heidi, do you have a minute?"), who provided many good suggestions and overall support.

My husband, John Fernstrom, PhD, was invaluable as a scientific resource. Perhaps more importantly, his quiet persistence and encouragement allowed me to again rediscover the joy of running. I am deeply grateful for his patience, total support, and tireless rereading of chapters with good humor.

My children, Aaron and Lauren, provided not only encouragement and support but many practical and clever suggestions.

A final note of appreciation to all of my patients, who continue to inspire me with their efforts and commitment to a healthy lifestyle.

INTRODUCTION

THE RUNNER'S DIET

> Why recreational runners need a plan to marry their exercise and their eating—and how they can turn that program into a successful one

Jennifer never had a weight problem when she was a high school cross-country runner. While in college, she maintained her running (to the tunc of 4 miles a day, five times a week). More importantly, she maintained her weight, even though she ate whatever she wanted (while her friends struggled with extra pounds).

After college, Jennifer's free time quickly slipped away when she took a job with a major advertising firm. She had to stop running, and now that she wasn't walking to class with a heavy backpack, her activity dropped to desk-potato level. In her first 2 years out of college, Jennifer gained 25 pounds.

"It just crept up, until I couldn't fit into most of my clothes," Jennifer told me. Left with only one pair of black elastic-waist pants and two loose dresses that fit, she decided to do something about it.

She opted against buying larger clothes—and opted for making a change in herself.

When Jennifer came to see me at the Weight Management Center at the University of Pittsburgh Medical Center, I knew she had a wonderful chance of succeeding. Though she called herself a failure—which she wasn't—Jennifer was honest about her weight gain, recognized the problem, agreed that she wanted to change, was willing to work hard, and sought advice about how to get back on track. All of those qualities made her the perfect candidate to succeed on a program that would become the foundation for the Runner's Diet.

Jennifer is like a lot of the hundreds of patients I see every year as founder and director of the Weight Management Center. Used to being fit and not having to worry much about her weight or what she ate, Jennifer may be a lot like you—someone who's gradually watched the numbers on the scale increase while trying to deal with the stresses of a job, of a family, of living life. I see the same—or similar—problems time after time, and while I enjoy helping all the individuals I work with, I decided there was an even better way to reach all those people who had "always been runners" but had watched their weight steadily increase. The idea for the Runner's Diet came to me after many years of meeting people in the clinic who had stopped running. They stopped not only because their extra weight took the fun out of running but also because the weight gain literally caused a steep decline in miles run because of things like joint pain and overall discomfort. As one patient told me, "I got tired of having my thighs applaud when I ran."

All of these people I worked with had similar questions:

What do I do?

How do I eat?

How can I run like I used to?

The answers aren't so simple. If they were, then everyone would be thin. And that's why I think there's a great need for *The Runner's Diet*—a book that not only helps runners and walkers develop a lifelong eating and exercise plan but also helps runners and walkers address common questions and myths about nutritional requirements for runners.

It seems almost impossible that runners could become overweight or obese. All that running, all those calories burned along city streets and down park paths—how is weight gain possible? But the truth is that runners aren't always ultrathin people on the verge of nutritional deficiency, and that's why many runners are honestly perplexed about why they gain weight. Because we see elite runners and read about their habits (carbo-loading, hydrating, and squirting gooey gels in their mouths), we assume that as recreational runners, we should do the same. But the fact is we're not elite runners. We're average people who use running, walking, or a combination of the two to manage our weight, gain energy, and try to lead healthy lives. I know exactly where you've been—and where you want to go.

I'd always been active, but I didn't even consider running as an activity until I was in college. From my dormitory window in Boston, I always saw so many people running along the Charles River that it looked like fun. So I started walking and running a little, but I never thought of myself as a real runner, because I wore baggy shorts and an old T-shirt instead of short-shorts and tank tops. That was more than 20 years—and 20 pounds—ago. Since then, I've gone through periods when I've run a lot, when I've walked a lot, and when I've struggled to find time to run to the store, let along run for a couple miles. I've run with my kids for sports conditioning (baseball for my son, soccer for my daughter), and I've even cut back my running schedule, because I felt too much pressure to maintain my pace. I have many of the same pressures as you—trying to find time to do my job, take care of family responsibilities, and squeeze in exercise and activity. Especially over the past 2 years, I've found it's been a greater struggle for me to maintain my weight, so to manage it, I've had to adjust my eating and training programs. My point is this: There are lot of people just like us—people who like to run and walk, but people who struggle to find the right balance of eating and exercising in order to lose or maintain weight. And that's why I think you'll gain a lot from the Runner's Diet.

The first thing I want to do is define what a runner is. Many of us feel like we're not really runners if we don't follow the routine that some hard-core trainer prescribed, if we don't have all the gadgets, if we don't run 40 miles a week. Baloney. If you strap on your shoes, get out there, and jog (even if it's only for a few seconds to start), you're a runner. You're a runner even if you haven't run a marathon—or don't even aspire to run one. You're no less of a runner if you don't relish the chance to run a 10-K race every Saturday. And you're no less of a runner even if your pace seems slower than a glacier's. With respect, I paraphrase philosopher René Descartes to offer an important guideline for all of us: "I run; therefore I am a runner."

For the 99 percent of us runners who aren't elite or professional, there is often a pattern in those of us who now struggle with slow weight gain. That's the weight creep—the insidiously rising numbers on our bathroom scales. It's not that we've done anything wrong (give or take a dozen doughnuts); it's only that we've abandoned the positive skills we need to stay focused on keeping our weight in check. Fortunately, the right combination of running and eating can overcome weight creep and provide the optimal set of lifestyle skills for long-term, permanent weight loss or maintenance. It's the same set of skills that also helped Jennifer.

Remember, Jennifer had given up running when she started a busy job, but when she came to me to help her lose the 25 pounds she'd gained, she agreed that she always enjoyed running and that one of her first steps would be to bring running back into her life. She didn't remember exactly when she'd stopped, but she knew it had been at least a year. Jennifer was honest about her eating ("I don't pay attention") and activity ("I want to run, but I can't make the time"), so her first step was to figure out how she could (1) allow running time each day; (2) shop for lower-calorie food; and (3) preplan her food intake and match it to her activity level.

Once she put those three factors in place, she could expect to start her weight-loss journey. During her first month, Jennifer chose to make changes that would optimize her success. First, because her long work hours often prevented her from running outside during the week, she joined a 24-hour gym. To minimize the time commitment, Jennifer initially walked/ran 2 miles, 4 days a week for 2 weeks. By the end of this time, she was able to run her 2 miles comfortably in less than 25 minutes. By the end of 2 months, she was back to running 3.5 miles, 4 days a week. The control Jennifer felt when she was running again was empowering. But she agreed that if she wanted to lose weight too and not just maintain her present weight, she also had to focus on her eating for the first time in her life. Her running stopped her "weight creep," but she wanted faster progress. Jennifer jumped to the challenge, and structured her day to include three meals that follow the nutritional principles of the Runner's Diet. On her running days, Jennifer chose a protein bar and a fruit as her on-the-go breakfast, yogurt and a fruit for lunch, and turkey on a whole wheat pita with a small box of orange juice for a late-afternoon snack. This gave her the added energy for her run and allowed her to choose a lower-calorie meal replacement frozen dinner on nights she didn't want to cook. Jennifer lost 2 pounds a week steadily for 8 weeks, and slowed to about a pound a week over the next 12. With a little attention to her eating and a return to running, in 5 months Jennifer shed the 25 pounds she had gained over 2 years—using both discipline and focus.

It's been almost a year since Jennifer lost the weight, and she's confident in her ability to sustain her effort. Although she still struggles on some days, Jennifer is on track and has made her lifestyle one of weight maintenance—always mindful of calories in and calories out. Jennifer's story always reminds me that no matter what your individual circumstances, it's important to keep up the effort, because it does pay off in the long run.

Jennifer's story has been inspirational to me, because it's one of great personal success. But remember that Jennifer's story doesn't have to serve as an example for everyone—each person has different needs and situations. But it should serve as a reminder that with effort the Runner's Diet will work.

To me, much of the problem for the runner who's gained weight stems from the ingrained habits of eating for energy or performance—with little regard for total calories. But if you learn nothing else from this book, learn this:

Calories *do* count, and our underestimation of the amount we eat and the overestimation of the amount we burn is one of the fundamental reasons that recreational runners need a diet especially for them.

Certainly, all three macronutrients—carbohydrates, proteins, and fats—are essential for both running stamina and weight loss. In this book, you'll throw out much of what you've thought about your earlier eating and running patterns. It's time to take a close look to match your real-life eating and activity to enjoy both running and sustained weight loss.

For many runners, the emphasis has always been on eating for performance, focusing on individual nutrients only at times of physical activity. Couple that with the notion that a carbohydrate-dominant diet fuels performance, and you can see why it's an easy path to weight gain. We simply eat too much—hopeful that the foods we choose will send energy quickly to our muscles. And as our desire to eat for performance outpaces our biological need for calories, we store extra calories as unwanted pounds.

Here's another scary fact: It takes only 100 extra calories a day to gain 10 pounds in a year. That's one high-calorie prerun snack that you don't need. Or one sports drink before a 30-minute walk. And that's not even counting the postrun doughnut or prerun chips. In *The Runner's Diet,* I want you to understand not only what foods to eat and in what proportion but also what foods will maximize your performance without sabotaging your diet (nor the fit of the clothes in your closet). You'll soon be equipped to put together your own weight-loss toolbox with an activity and eating pattern that will lead to realistic and enduring weight loss. When you learn to pay attention to your changing energy needs and take an honest look at the calories you consume and expend, you'll be on your way to lifelong weight control. As you look at your eating habits, you'll also be evaluating your running patterns by deciding things like realistic mileage and a weekly schedule. Structure equals success, and regularity is key to long-term weight regulation. (If you're just starting, there's also a plan for you.)

Ultimately, you'll match your eating schedule to your running pattern. You'll learn to eat an appropriate carbohydrate-rich snack prior to running while consuming more lean protein and heart-healthy fats at most other meals. You'll get quick energy when you need it for a productive and healthy run without feeling like you're running out of steam. And when it comes to such things as sports drinks, vitamins, and other supplements, you'll see that more isn't always better.

There's no doubt that we all have sabotages that interfere with our ability to lose weight. The tough part is recognizing them—and then instituting the changes that will address them. It's important to take a look at your habits and patterns honestly, and recognize the things that are holding you back from losing weight and keeping it off.

Whether it's overeating or a lack of motivation to run, I hope that this book will help you determine not only what you're willing to do but also what you're able to do. These are two distinct concepts that you'll learn to separate, address, and then use to fix your barriers to long-term success.

Of course, our culture is one in which everything is viewed as "instant"—from weight loss to oatmeal. We've learned to expect fast results, or else the effort is a failure. When it comes to losing weight, much of this stems from a loss of control over our eating and activity. My patients tell me the same things when I meet them:

"This just seems too hard."

"I have such a long way to go."

"I just want to run. I don't want to think about the food."

No answer is right for everyone. How to achieve weight loss and maintenance is a very individual choice. The key to long-term success is to make the life change that incorporates both correct eating and running.

By thinking like that—that eating and running are as much of a partnership as Ben and Jerry—then you can expect small changes that will yield large results. A deficit of 500 calories a day, for example, will make you lose a pound a week. That's pretty manageable for most people, but it can be slower or faster, if you like. Getting started is the biggest challenge, because you *must* agree to focus on both eating and running. By maximizing both, you'll be able to set the most realistic plan for your long-term success.

Whether you're running a mile or two 3 days a week, or 15 to 20 miles a week, you can benefit from changing your present habits in both eating and running. You may—as many of my most successful patients do—find the most successful change is with a little bit in both areas.

The balance and the choice are up to you.

That's because I believe that the best way is your own way.

CHAPTER 1

ON YOUR MARK, GET SET . . .

> Assessing your eating habits and activity patterns will help get you out of the starting blocks

In one way, most of you are used to change. You change your clothes, you change the oil in your cars, you change your hairstyles, and you change the channels. But when it comes to your body—and especially to behaviors pertaining to your body—changing is just about the hardest thing you've ever had to. It's not that you don't *want* to change; the very fact that you're reading these sentences means that you want to change. You want to lose weight, and you want to find the right balance between two things you really enjoy: running and food.

I believe this balance is at the heart of engaging in a successful lifestyle plan. It's not the plan, the motivation, or even finding the right goal that's so hard. It's the fact that you have to change behaviors relating to food and activity that feels like the biggest barrier. When it comes to the weight-loss race, the starting line is the hardest part. But the finish line—reaching your weight-loss goal—is so rewarding once you cross it.

Of all the things that I want to help you accomplish in the Runner's Diet, the vital first step isn't the one at the start of the run. It's the one in which you need to assess where you and your body stand—and where you want to go. In my practice, I see many different ways that people try to lose weight, many misconceptions people have about food and running, and many drastic measures people take. In a way, we've been programmed to think that weight loss should be like putting a quarter in a gumball machine—you put something in, you better get something out of it. But weight loss, eating, and running are a lot more complex than that, and our bodies don't work in instant-gratification dieting. It not only takes effort and willingness to change; it also takes knowledge. So before you lace up your running shoes, hoof through your neighborhood, and swear yourself to a green-bean-only diet forever, I want you to sit down and assess your current habits. If you figure out the little changes you can make in your habits, you'll see the big changes you can make to your body.

To this end, I think it will help you to know about some of the people I've met through my practice. They're some of the people who more than likely share your common obstacles of being an active person who likes to exercise but who also faces challenges, temptations, and misunderstandings when it comes to eating. In my experience, most dieting runners who don't accomplish their goals fall into the following three categories.

The Drastic Dieter: Amy, 38 and active, had struggled with the same extra 20 pounds for about 10 years. The 20 pounds didn't pose an immediate health threat, but being overweight made her feel "old and out of shape." So what did she do? She went into "diet mode"—as if she could program her body to punch a few buttons and achieve her goal. In a way, that's exactly what she did. She went into an almost robotic transformation. She monitored calories, ran 3 miles four times a week, and adopted a rigid diet: whole wheat toast and peanut butter for breakfast, frozen entrees for lunch, an apple for a snack, and grilled chicken or fish with vegetables for dinner. She'd deprive herself of evening snacks, saying, "I don't care; I want to lose the weight." And you know what? She did. She could eliminate those extra pounds pretty easily and quickly when she followed her automatic-pilot principles of dieting. Sure, that sounds like a perfectly nutritious eating plan, her exercise was admirable, and she lost weight, so on the surface, nothing seems wrong with Amy's approach. But check back in with Amy after 1 or 2 months, and you know exactly what went wrong.

Amy's problem was one of consistency. After a couple months (or sometimes a few weeks), Amy would lose interest in dieting the way kids lose interest in old toys. She would become busier at work and she couldn't make time to shop for her frozen entrees and fresh fruit; so she wound up sharing pizzas at lunch and running to the vending machines for a late-afternoon snack. Losing her focus made it easier for her to skip breakfast, as well as make less nutritious choices at dinner. "I just ate whatever I wanted, and that made me feel even worse," she said. When she started to gain weight again, she felt sluggish and slow—and that made her lose interest in running, which made her pack on the pounds even faster and caused her weight to creep up again in about 3 months.

Amy's problem wasn't that she did the wrong things; in fact, many of the things she did were exactly right. Her problem was that she made too many changes at once. You don't have to be named Emeril to know that's a recipe for disaster. That's because it's extremely difficult to make—and then stick to—so many behavioral changes at once.

Amy's solution? After she recognized that she was overdoing it, she simplified her plan to accept slower and more consistent weight loss. She agreed to decrease her mileage (making it more compatible with her schedule than her original goal, which overwhelmed her). She designed her Sunday schedule so she could shop for and prepare healthy meals for the week, and we also designed some part of every day where she could have a snack of her choice (which was of no more than 150 calories) so that she no longer felt deprived at night. She simplified her changes so she could get started. Amy lost her 20 extra pounds in 4 months—a lot slower than she expected and originally wanted, but it proved to be the right pace to make a long-term commitment. She's maintained her weight loss for nearly a year and is confident that she can do so with her present balance of eating and running.

The Panicked Dieter: At 40, Gary was happy in his work as an accountant. He had a very structured (and sedentary) life. After gaining 15 pounds over the past 5 years, it hit him. "I've noticed it, but now it really shows and my clothes don't fit," he said. When he realized he had to change, he panicked. He had that initial feeling of being out of control and that he had to lose weight immediately. So he picked up the same exercise plan he did when he played football in college—running 6 days a week. "Runners are skinny," Gary figured, "and I don't want to change much about my eating." But 20 years and 15 pounds later, running that often proved to be too much. "I tried to get my act together to run," he said, "but I couldn't stick with it for more than a week."

The first step in Gary's readjustment was for him to learn that he didn't fail; it's just that he failed to choose the right running plan. Gary is typical of so many men and women who want to make some progress but always start with unrealistic goals and changes. So we created a plan that fit his schedule—and his mind-set. Gary would run on Saturdays (still keeping Sundays free) and on his choice of 2 days during the week to get started. After a month of sticking to that schedule, we added one more day.

In terms of eating, Gary only needed to make minor adjustments and calorie cutting, since he had a healthy lifestyle. Gary agreed to limit dessert to two evenings a week (two low-calorie, sugar-free ice pops replaced his high-calorie items on the other 5 days). He also agreed to limit his alcohol intake to four beers a week; this worked better for Gary in terms of choice (two beers twice a week, or one beer four times a week). Gary lost 2 pounds a week in the first 2 weeks, and then a pound a week over the next 12 weeks. He has maintained this for 6 months. Gary feels secure that he can manage this plan, since he set the guidelines, and he readily accepted the fact that his loss was expected to be greater some weeks than others. To him, the most important thing is that the scale keeps going down, not up. To get started, we all must do something, which is always better than doing nothing—and certainly better than trying to do *everything*.

The Impatient Dieter: Ten years ago, Emily ran 4 miles 4 days a week. But that was one husband and three children ago. Though she's maintained a stable weight, Emily felt that she could stand to lose 5 pounds. Emily was actually surprised—and maybe somewhat offended—when I suggested she walk 2 miles a day 3 days a week. Emily, 36, loved running, and she loved being outside. Now that her children were all in school and she had a part-time job, she finally had the time to pick up her running career. She viewed my recommendation as "not enough," since she was able to do so much more than that a decade ago. Emily—like many of us—had an issue of patience. And that's actually one of the biggest barriers to getting started on a running plan—trying to compare how we ran months, or years, ago with how we run today. But if you want to achieve long-term success, comparing yourself today with yourself yesterday is like going down on an up escalator—it won't get you anywhere.

Emily had to agree that in order to get started and sustain the effort, she could not jump back into running. She had a walk/run routine after 2 weeks, and in a month, she was running 2 miles a day three times a week. As she progresses, she'll add days and mileage to her program while still trying to balance work and family responsibilities.

And that's what we're really talking about here. Getting started means making some small changes. For most of us, we want to jump into a diet like the way we jump into a swimming pool on a hot day. But jumping in too quickly sets you up for one thing—disappointment. The message that we really hide from ourselves is that with a big effort, we never really expect to stick with it over many months or years. And that's a difficult concept to accept. We come from a society where major efforts translate into major rewards—at work, on playing fields, everywhere. But when it comes to weight loss, the only way to get major rewards is through one minor effort at a time.

So you've read about Amy, Gary, and Emily, and chances are you fit one of the dieting patterns—or maybe a little bit of all three. Before you begin your journey of minor changes, I think it's important to really think about what kind of dieter and runner you are. Knowing where you stand on the weight-loss spectrum gives you an idea of where you need to go. So I've created some rating scales to help raise your own awareness about the kind of changes you'll need to make to achieve long-term weight-loss success. For some, the major change will come with eating; for others, it will be in physical activity. Most often, though, you'll have to address both areas.

To achieve success, you need to build on your strengths and overcome your weaknesses. So use your score on the Eating Awareness Rating Scale to help you identify your eating style and degree of control. Your score for the Physical Activity Rating Scale will not only focus on your walking/running activities but also address your views on physical activity in general. Answer these questions honestly, total your score, and you'll have a good idea of where you need to begin.

EATING AWARENESS RATING SCALE

Answer each question and keep track of your total points.

[1] Do you think before you eat?
    a. Never. I eat everything in sight. I'd eat the napkin if I could. (+1)
    b. Occasionally. (+2)
    c. Almost always. Nothing goes in my mouth without my thinking about it. (+3)

[2] Are you able to easily stop eating?
    a. Forget it. I eat until my plate looks like it's gone through the car wash. (+1)
    b. Sometimes, but usually I'm pretty full. (+2)
    c. I always know stop before I'm completely full. (+3)

[3] Do you count calories in an effort to maintain or lose weight?
    a. Hardly ever. It's such a hassle. (+1)
    b. Sometimes, but I always try to look at labels. (+2)
    c. I have an Excel spreadsheet from the past year. (+3)

[4] Do you eat breakfast?

    a. Does coffee count? (+1)

    b. Sometimes, when I remember or squeeze something in. (+2)

    c. Almost always. I make a point of it. (+3)

[5] Do you snack between meals?

    a. All the time. My middle name is Dorito. (+1)

    b. Sometimes, if food is around. (+2)

    c. Almost never. I'm usually never hungry between meals. (+3)

[6] Do you tend to eat most of your calories in the evening?

    a. Yes, I'm too busy during the day to eat. (+1)

    b. Not really, though it does happen. (+2)

    c. I usually spread my calories out through the day. (+3)

[7] Do you pay attention to the texture and mouthfeel of different foods?

    a. Huh? What's mouthfeel? (+1)

    b. Occasionally, if I like the food. (+2)

    c. Always. I have a degree in food appreciation. (+3)

[8] Do you eat when you're stressed out?

    a. How do I spell relief? I-C-E C-R-E-A-M. (+1)

    b. Sometimes. I occasionally have bad days. (+2)

    c. Rarely. I use other ways to deal with it. (+3)

[9] Do you eat when you're bored?

    a. All the time. (+1)

    b. Occasionally, but I try to stop myself. (+2)

    c. No, only when I'm hungry. (+3)

[10] Do you do a lot of eating when you're alone?

 a. Most of my eating is by myself. (+1)

 b. Sometimes, but not every day. (+2)

 c. Not at all. I usually eat with others. (+3)

YOUR EATING AWARENESS SCORE_____

Your Score: Eating and Weight Loss

24–30: You have pretty good control over your eating environment. You may eat too much at times, but you know you're doing it. You have reasonable control and don't do much "mindless eating." You may need to work on consistency to stay on track for weight loss. Your major changes will be in activity.

16–23: You are uneven in your approach to food. Although there is some "mindless eating" to minimize, you lack control in many areas. One area will be in consistency. If you're a regular exerciser, the eating program will be your area of focus.

15 or less: Your eating is out of control, meaning that you're doing a lot of "mindless eating." Whether or not your exercise is on track, you still need to make significant changes in your eating to lose weight. You may need to beef up both your eating skills and your activity skills.

PHYSICAL ACTIVITY RATING SCALE

Answer each question and keep track of your total points.

[1] When you feel the urge to get up and move, do you ignore it?

 a. All the time, unless I have to go to the bathroom. (+1)

 b. Sometimes. I ignore it when I want to. (+2)

 c. Rarely. I always get up and do something. (+3)

[2] Do you try walk at least 30 minutes a day?

    a. Hardly ever, unless you consider 6,000 trips from the couch to the fridge. (+1)

    b. About 3 or 4 days a week. (+2)

    c. Almost always. It's rare when I don't. (+3)

[3] Do you save running, walking, or other physical activity for the weekend?

    a. Yes, I'm too busy during the week. (+1)

    b. Mostly weekends, but I try for some weekdays. (+2)

    c. I'm active most days. (+3)

[4] Do you have time to run or walk briskly three or four times a week?

    a. Forget it. I'm lucky if I can do it once a week. (+1)

    b. Always on the weekend, and I can manage another day or two. (+2)

    c. No problem. I do that most every day. (+3)

[5] Do you run or walk for distance or for time?

    a. Time. I'm lucky I get anything in. (+1)

    b. I try to think about mileage, but it's mostly about time. (+2)

    c. Most often distance; rarely is time an issue. (+3)

[6] Do you need a companion to get your walking or running done?

    a. Absolutely. I can't get motivated by myself. (+1)

    b. Sometimes. It's much easier with someone else. (+2)

    c. No, I do this on my own, but company is also fine. (+3)

[7] Do you find it hard to stay focused, and do you stop your running or walking before you've reached your goal for the day?

a. I typically stop before I planned to. (+1)

b. I mostly complete what I start. (+2)

c. I always finish my goal, no matter how I feel or what the weather's like. (+3)

[8] Do you feel overwhelmed by the idea of running or walking more than twice a week?

a. Twice? How about once? (+1)

b. I could do more but usually don't. (+2)

c. Not at all. I could do more most weeks. (+3)

[9] How do you feel after completing a run or a brisk walk?

a. Sweaty and exhausted, like I've just moved a piano—by myself. (+1)

b. Pretty good, but happy it's over. (+2)

c. A strong sense of well-being—I look forward to the way I feel afterward. (+3)

[10] Do you want to pick up the pace to burn more calories?

a. No, I'd rather eat less. (+1)

b. I think I'm able to walk/run to burn enough. (+2)

c. I want to be or stay a runner and gain consistency in my running to make this work for weight loss. It takes the pressure off the eating for me. (+3)

YOUR PHYSICAL ACTIVITY AWARENESS SCORE: _____

Your Score: Activity and Weight Loss

24–30: You're doing great. You enjoy the benefits of exercise and likely consume too many calories despite your activity. You tend to overestimate the calories used by exercise and underestimate your food intake. You need to keep up the consistency in your walking/running and make some changes in your eating patterns.

16–23: You probably lack consistency in your activity. Focus on regular, modest activity and packing more exercise into limited time. You'll have to work on your food intake, to balance the amount of exercise you're willing and able to do to lose weight.

15 or less: You may think about activity, but you're not doing enough. Whether from time or interest, you need to pick up the pace to lose weight, even with changes in your food consumption. The burden of weight loss cannot be on caloric intake alone. If you are not willing to be more physically active, this may not be the right time for you to lose weight. Even if you can lose weight without activity in your life, it's going to be especially hard to keep your weight off for the long term.

Activity and Awareness Scores

Total your scores from the two tests and add them together.

Eating Activity Rating Scale Score: _____ (out of 30)

Physical Activity Rating Scale Score: _____ (out of 30)

Total Score: _____

Ultimately, it's not one score or the other that is going to determine your success; it's the interaction of these scores that will help you get started—and help produce short- and long-term success. Nobody (including me) has a perfect score of 60. Perfection may be nice to think about for bowlers and plastic surgeons, but perfection is rare and unrealistic when it comes to maintaining long-term results.

I'd like you to make sure that you're no less than a total score of 40 and then strive for 45. Your goal should be to hit 50. While you may hit the high fifties on some days, the important thing to do is stay consistent with your approaches to eating and running. The best way to improve your number is by looking at your responses—and then selecting one behavior to change at a time. You can—and will—build on your success if you tackle them one concept at a time. Even if you're on the low end of the score sheet, it doesn't mean that you can't lose weight; it just means that your starting point will be different. Once you know where your problem areas are, we can figure out how to fix them.

What I hope to do in the book is help you address some of the areas that can adjust your attitudes (and behaviors) so that you can lose weight. When you know the critical areas that cause many of us to stumble along the path, you can better adjust to oncoming obstacles. These are the guidelines I'd use when just starting out.

Don't give up. So many former runners have given up due to lack of time, interest, bad joints, and many other reasons. No matter whether you run 1 or 6 miles a day, you're a runner—and have joined the ranks of greater activity. If you had been a runner and are plagued by bad joints or other health issues, then walking is the best substitute. The calories used for walking and running are equivalent based on distance; it just takes longer to walk 3 miles than it does to run it.

Don't underestimate. We're all guilty of underestimating our caloric intake and overestimating calories used for running or walking. Be realistic. The best way to take the pressure off of the necessary food restriction needed to lose weight is to burn more calories by running or walking. It takes the pressure off all of the eating changes alone. It is this combination that is so powerful.

Retake the test. Use your scores as a starting point to determine where you can make some changes. Be honest with yourself, and you will make progress. Revisit these rating scales every 2 weeks until you're in a comfort range of around 50. That's the surest way to long-term success.

THE RUNNER'S DIET CHECKLISTS: GO!

To know where you're going, it's always best to know where you've been. That's why I want you to fill out these few checklists. They'll not only improve your chances of success, but they'll also give you baseline numbers to use for comparison as you progress from month to month.

GETTING-STARTED CHECKLIST

Whether you're new to running or were the Division I cross-country champ in college, answer the following questions. Your best success will occur when you can answer yes to all of them.

I have medical clearance from my primary care doctor (see "Medical Clearance" on page 17).
Yes_____   No_____

I have a pair of well-fitting running shoes.
Yes _____   No_____

I am willing to make time to run (or walk/run) at least 2 or 3 days a week.
Yes_____   No_____

I want to increase my mileage.

Yes_____   No_____

I am willing to eat fewer calories than I do now.

Yes_____   No_____

I am willing to make consistent changes in my eating and activity.

Yes_____   No_____

THE BODY CHECKLIST: CALCULATE YOUR BODY MASS INDEX (BMI)

While most of us know—or can feel—when we need to lose weight, we don't always know by how much. The best way to estimate your healthy body weight is by calculating your body mass index, or BMI. BMI calculations are the weight charts of the new millennium (you remember those charts—your height in 2-inch heels with a small, medium, or large frame). Knowing your BMI eliminates a lot of guesswork about your bone structure and gives you a guideline for how much weight you need to lose—based on large-scale studies, which estimate the ideal weights in relationship to height. Here's how it works: The higher your BMI, the greater your risk of health problems. The lower your BMI, the lower your risk of health problems. To calculate your BMI:

Take your weight in pounds and multiply it by 703.

Divide that number by your height in inches.

Take that number and divide it again by your height in inches.

That's your BMI—and you can see how you stack up in the chart below. Surprised? Everyone is. We all have a mental disconnect of how we look and what our health risk is for any given weight.

TABLE 1.1 BODY MASS INDEX (BMI) AND WEIGHT CLASSIFICATION

BMI	Classification
Below 18.5	Underweight
18.5 – 24.9	Healthy
25.0 – 29.9	Overweight
30.0 – 34.9	Moderate obesity – class I
35.0 – 39.9	Moderate obesity – class II
40 or above	Severe obesity

Your Height_____ Your Weight _____

Your BMI _____

BODY MASS INDEX (BMI) CHART

HEIGHT	WEIGHT (IN POUNDS)								
4'10"	91	96	100	105	110	115	119	124	129
4'11"	94	99	104	109	114	119	124	128	133
5'0"	97	102	107	112	118	123	128	133	138
5'1"	100	106	111	116	122	127	132	137	143
5'2"	104	109	115	120	126	131	136	142	147
5'3"	107	113	118	124	130	135	141	146	152
5'4"	110	116	122	128	134	140	145	151	157
5'5"	114	120	126	132	138	144	150	156	162
5'6"	118	124	130	136	142	148	155	161	167
5'7"	121	127	134	140	146	153	159	166	172
5'8"	125	131	138	144	151	158	164	171	177
5'9"	128	135	142	149	155	162	169	176	182
5'10"	132	139	146	153	160	167	174	181	188
5'11"	136	143	150	157	165	172	179	186	193
6'0"	140	147	154	162	169	177	184	191	199
6'1"	144	151	159	166	174	182	189	197	204
6'2"	148	155	163	171	179	186	194	202	210
6'3"	152	160	168	176	184	192	200	208	216
6'4"	156	164	172	180	189	197	205	213	221
	19	**20**	**21**	**22**	**23**	**24**	**25**	**26**	**27**

Note: I just want to mention one thing about the variability of muscle mass and differences in bone structure. I am often asked if BMI is correct, because "I am a large-boned person" or "I work out so my weight is muscle and not fat." Both are valid questions. Although not a perfect index (nothing is), the BMI is a *guideline,* independent of the "small-medium-large" frames. Because the BMI chart is a range of pounds for particular height, the normal variation in frame size is already accounted for. But what about muscle? It is possible to be "overweight" without being "overfat" according to the BMI charts. For the vast majority of people, short of some competitive weight lifters and professional athletes, a higher

WEIGHT (IN POUNDS)

134	138	143	148	153	158	162	167	172	177	181
138	143	148	153	158	163	168	173	178	183	188
143	148	153	158	163	168	174	179	184	189	194
148	153	158	164	169	174	180	185	190	195	201
153	158	164	169	175	180	186	191	196	202	207
158	163	169	175	180	186	191	197	203	208	214
163	169	174	180	186	192	197	204	209	215	221
168	174	180	186	192	198	204	210	216	222	228
173	179	186	192	198	204	210	216	223	229	235
178	185	191	198	204	211	217	223	230	236	242
184	190	197	203	210	216	223	230	236	243	249
189	196	203	209	216	223	230	236	248	250	257
195	202	209	216	222	229	236	243	250	257	264
200	208	215	222	229	236	243	250	257	265	272
206	213	221	228	235	242	250	258	265	272	279
212	219	227	235	242	250	257	265	272	280	288
218	225	233	241	249	256	264	272	280	287	295
224	232	240	248	256	264	272	279	287	295	303
230	238	246	254	263	271	279	287	295	304	312
28	**29**	**30**	**31**	**32**	**33**	**34**	**35**	**36**	**37**	**38**

BMI is associated with increased fat mass (stored fat) and not increased muscle mass. However, it is for this reason that other factors need to be included for your total health index. An estimate of body-fat percentage (and lean body mass) is readily available at most exercise facilities. If you can locate a facility using underwater weighing or with a whole-body scanner, those methods have

---

MEDICAL CLEARANCE

When Michael came to see me, he said, "I haven't been to my doctor in years." When he visited his doctor, he was cleared to start a running plan, but Michael's doctor noticed that his blood pressure was borderline for high blood pressure. This was Michael's wake-up call—and a great motivator. Michael kept up with his running (3 miles three times a week) and began monitoring his food intake. With modest changes in eating and his sustained running schedule, Michael lost 18 pounds in 3 months. Upon a return visit to his doctor, Michael's blood pressure had dropped to a healthy range. In this case, Michael responded to his wake-up call.

Whether you want to change your eating patterns or your exercise regimen, you'll want to check with your primary care doctor. This is most important if you're presently inactive and want to begin a regular activity schedule. Only your doctor can give you medical clearance to begin or increase your exercise—even if you think you are in great health. Joint pain, heart problems, breathing problems (including asthma), and others need special attention, and although you may know your body, your doctor needs to help you avoid injury and prevent you from damaging your health. Oftentimes, this is the time to start fresh and reconnect with your primary care doctor. Get in the habit of a yearly checkup if you have no specific health reason to see your doctor more often. Your doctor will welcome this new partnership, where you are taking control and making a positive change for life.

more precision than a body-fat scale or trainers measuring areas of fat with calipers.

THE HEALTH CHECKLIST

While it seems that you have one goal (lose weight), your overall health picture is a little more complicated than that. Yes, you want to lower your BMI—or even maintain it, which can be a challenge itself. But if you're in the obese BMI categories, you should also be concerned with decreasing other substances in your body—that is, the substances than can put you at risk for such things as heart disease, diabetes, and other conditions. No matter where you're headed, it's important to know that sometimes even a small change in weight can produce a big change in blood fats, blood sugar, and blood pressure. So, you should see a doctor for a blood test so that you can record your starting position for the following numbers. Use them as a baseline for your total health picture—gathering information for the future.

☐ Blood pressure _____

☐ Total cholesterol_____

☐ (Good) HDL _____

☐ (Bad) LDL _____

☐ Triglycerides _____
   (fasting)

☐ Blood sugar _____
   (fasting)

☐ Insulin _____
   (fasting)

THE GEAR CHECKLIST: THE BASICS

Every walking and running program needs the most basic piece of equipment: shoes. Finding the right shoe can help you stick with a program, rather than providing another excuse (blisters, numbness, injury) to stop.

SHOE FITTING

Shop for shoes later in the day when your feet are at their largest. Get proper fit by going to a respected athletic store where a skilled sales-person can "size up your feet" and help you select your shoes.

Measure both feet for length and width. Often one foot is longer than the other. Fit your shoes to the longer foot.

Allow at least ½ inch of room at the toe. Wiggle your toes to make sure there is sufficient room.

Look for cushioning to absorb shock and help stability. You want both side-to-side stability and heel-toe shock protection.

Remeasure your feet every time you replace your shoes; feet change with time.

Wear socks that you will use during your walk/run for optimal fit.

Try on at least three different brands of shoes, particularly if you are buying your first pair.

Make sure your heels don't slip when you walk.

New shoes should be comfortable at purchase and not require a major break-in period.

Ask for models that are specifically made for wide or narrow feet, rather than adjusting by going up or down a size.

Avoid walking or running in nonrunning shoes, to minimize discomfort and injury during exercise.

Check your shoes at least monthly for wear and tear (shoes usually last about 300 to 500 miles). Excessively worn shoes can contribute to leg and foot pain and other injuries.

GEAR FOR WARM WEATHER

Wear lightweight, light-colored, loose-fitting clothes.

Cotton is absorbent and will stay wet as you sweat. For greater comfort, try nylon, spandex, cotton/polyester blends, and CoolMax clothes.

Avoid wearing "rubberized" clothing to increase sweating.

Wear sunscreen and lip balm to avoid burning.

GEAR FOR COOL WEATHER

Hats, gloves, and scarves minimize loss of body heat.

A light, breathable base is the best underlayer; minimize 100 percent cotton and use synthetics to help maintain body heat; top with a protective outer shell (water resistant and windproof).

Use sunglasses and lip balm to avoid sun glare and wind chapping.

Wear sunscreen to avoid burning.

CHAPTER 2

MENTAL MOTIVATION

> You can make your success a reality by making your goals realistic

Are you ready to change? The very question evokes all kinds of emotions and feelings. But to me, when I ask you the question—*Are you ready to change?*—I want you to know how you really feel. The question isn't a challenge, but more like a reality check. You only need to be ready to make some change, not ready to make every change in your long-term goal.

Of course, being ready pops up in unusual ways for all of us: when a button pops off your pants, when it takes your breath away to walk a flight of stairs, when you see yourself in pictures. Typically, people know when they're ready. It usually comes through in the form of statements like "I really need to do something" or "I have to get going again." These statements are the best signs for a runner—or soon-to-be-runner—to get started. While scientific models point to the official stages that people go through to prepare for change, a simpler model that I use is the same model that kids use when they play hide-and-seek: You're either ready or you're not.

Patients tell me all the time they'll do anything to lose weight. I admire their passion, but I don't totally believe them. Unfortunately, no matter how much weight you have to lose—or how badly you want to lose it—the fact is that you may have been, up to now, unwilling to do anything to lose weight. Your lifestyle, schedule, physical ability, mental endurance, and so many other factors make it impossible to do that. Losing weight (and keeping it off) requires you to be prepared to change *something*, not *everything*. So the key factor in determining whether you're really ready to lose weight is not just what you're *willing* to do but what you're *able* to do.

If you learn the difference between the two, you'll be set for success. Use the following chart to determine which goals are more realistic—and will keep you on the road to meeting your goals.

Unrealistic Goals (Good Intentions): *I'm willing to . . .*	Realistic Goals (Success): *I'm able to . . .*
Go to the gym every day	Go to the gym 3 days a week
Run 3 miles 6 days a week	Run 3 miles 3 to 4 days a week
Walk 3 miles in 45 minutes daily	Walk 2 to 3 miles 4 or 5 days a week
Run and lift weights 5 days/week	Run 3 days and lift 2 days a week
Skip a late-afternoon snack	Plan for a low-calorie snack
Never eat after 7 p.m.	Allow one mini-meal at night
Avoid all fast foods	Choose a "kid's meal"
Pack a lunch every day for work	Eat a protein bar and a fruit
Cook a low-calorie dinner every night	Keep frozen entrees on hand
Never eat dessert	Share a dessert

The reason you want to make the distinction between the two types of goals is that you put too much pressure on yourself to attain weight loss quickly—and you view lifestyle activities as a temporary fix. Richard, whose weight had crept up as he entered his forties, went from a comfortable 160 pounds to an uncomfortable 185 pounds in 5 years. "I can do anything for a month," he said. So he adjusted his long-term goals. At first, he wanted to reach his high school weight of 150, which he agreed would take more effort than he was willing to commit (a perfect example of the battle between "willing" and "able"). He was ready to choose a few permanent changes to get himself away from his record of failing because he attempted to "change everything." Richard's original goal had been to run 3 miles 6 days a week. That goal had gone by the wayside, so he wasn't running at all. He adjusted his schedule to 3 miles 3 days a week (with an optional fourth day). He agreed to eat at least five servings of vegetables and fruits a day and to limit his between-meal snacking. For Richard, this was a realistic and effective combination.

You also must learn to set up a realistic plan. This is hard to do and is the single biggest sabotage that runners face when trying to lose weight. Failure is only the lack of finding the right set of goals; it is not a lack of readiness, willpower, or ability. That's why it's important for you to determine how ready you really are to start on your path to weight-loss success.

ARE YOU READY? THE QUIZ

All or nothing may work in poker, but it doesn't work in weight loss. You have to decide that some change is possible—and that some change is what will help you achieve your goal. It would be easier to make excuses (you have no time to cook, you're too embarrassed to exercise, your grocery doesn't carry healthy food). But excuses only stand in the way when you try to change too much at once. Whether you've slipped out of a regular walking or running routine or want to start one, all you need is a small amount of discipline to make a new habit. Making small changes allows you to determine reality-based readiness—the level of preparedness you have that will make changes. Fernstrom's Readiness Quiz will allow you to stay connected to your own action plan. It allows for the variability in motivation that occurs with daily life (yes, it's real life that sometimes you *are* too busy to run 4 miles).

Simply put, this quiz is pretty lenient, and allows anyone to pick and choose goals for a particular day or week. Here's how it works: If you can honestly answer yes to four or more of the eight questions, you are ready to make (and sustain) some type of change in your lifestyle. In the beginning, the act of initiating the change is more important than the intensity of the change. Revisit these questions at least once a month to size up your attitudes. You'll find you'll be saying yes to different questions at different times, but as long as you pick four, you're okay. It doesn't mean you'll lose weight any faster, but it does help with the acceptance that you are on track and can maintain your focus for long-term commitment.

Note to those who score less than four: Doing something is always better than doing nothing, and any sustained effort will help you maintain a sense of control. If you score less than four, you may not be able to make any significant changes right now. Whether you are overcommitted with family or work, this may be a time to tread water and stay even. Revisit this quiz in a couple of weeks after you've had a chance to digest the concepts. I'm sure you'll see that four is not a magic number—just a starting point to help set you up for realistic change.

FERNSTROM'S READINESS QUIZ

1. *Do you accept partial responsibility for your weight gain? Yes/No*
Because so many factors contribute to weight gain, we don't want
to find a single reason and we don't want to point fingers or direct
you to a mirror. You gain weight for lots of reasons, including biological ones (genetics, brain chemistry, metabolism) and behavioral ones (environment, psychological). I like to think of these
elements as different pieces for your own individual weight-gain
puzzle. No two people are the same, but you must accept the fact
that there are things you can do to contribute to the overall effort.
Genetic and other biological factors may make you more vulnerable to weight gain, but they cannot take full blame for your failing
to lose it.

2. *Do you acknowledge that you eat too many calories for your
body's needs? Yes/No*
If you put too much water in a bucket, it's going to spill over. And if
you put too many calories in your system, they will find a place to go,
which is why fat overflows on your stomach, thighs, and other parts
of your body. Simply, weight gain results from too many calories in,
not enough out. It's a simple concept, but a tough one to accept. Even
if you have biological factors that contribute to the way your body
processes food, you need to agree that you must ingest fewer calories
than you do now if you want to lose weight.

3. *Are you willing to work on regaining control? Yes/No*
The common theme I always hear is of a feeling of being "out of control." The reason? Most often, it's lack of daily structure. Though it's
not always easy, you're on your way to workable solutions if you're
willing to consider ways to incorporate structure of both eating and

activity into your daily living. You may have to try different strategies to find the right combination of tools to give you control, but if you're committed to the effort, you will gain (or regain) a better sense of control to sustain your positive changes.

4. *Are you willing to commit to at least one health-promoting activity each day? Yes/No*
I have yet to see someone serious about losing weight *not* be able to answer this question positively. One activity a day—you get to choose. It can be as simple as eating five fruits and vegetables a day or as challenging as walking or running your way to 10,000 steps a day. The commitment is one of consistency; you must do it every day.

5. *Are willing to confront your eating sabotages? Yes/No*
The first step in breaking barriers that prevent us from making changes is identifying them. That's not so easy for many of us; it's easier to pretend they don't exist. Of course, we want to always focus on the positive things we do, but a chain is only as strong as its weakest link. So list the things that sabotage your efforts (stress, all-you-can-eat buffets, or workplace munchies). Agree to change them—one at a time. Confronting these issues is the only requirement to getting started on the path to meet your goals.

6. *Are you willing to consider a realistic (not dream) goal weight? Yes/No*
Always dream with your feet firmly planted on the ground. Think big, but think realistically. Choose a short-term weight-loss goal to set yourself up for success. Don't worry about your ultimate goal. Concentrating on losing 5 pounds at a time gets you to your goal faster than trying to chip off 25 pounds all at once.

7. Are you willing to partner with someone/some group to meet your goals? Yes/No

If it were easy, everyone would be thin. But losing weight is hard work, and everyone needs support. Whether it's a family member, friend, or group of co-workers, you need that support to help you through the times when your motivation plummets. And knowing that others are counting on you is a motivator, too. To optimize success, choose someone or some group with similar goals and at the same fitness level. Although face-to-face is always best, online support can help some people, too. Choose the system that works best for you.

8. Are you willing to consistently increase both your everyday activity of daily living and your running/walking duration and/or intensity? Yes/No

The most important key word here is *increase,* but that doesn't have to mean a big increase. Small changes add up. The second important key word is *consistently.* Your willingness to make changes in both activity of daily living and in structured walking or running is essential to supporting a successful weight-loss effort. You can't reach your goal by focusing on only one or the other.

THE THREE QUALITIES OF READINESS

As you can see, there's a lot more to being ready than buying a pair of running shoes and pressing the button on your stopwatch. Being ready is about being mentally prepared for the long effort—not necessarily physically prepared to make a long run. To prepare for the long-distance journey of weight loss, it's important to practice, develop, or acquire the three qualities necessary for success.

QUALITY 1: SUPPORT

Most of us need support in everything we do—whether it's at work or at home. So why should you set out on this journey alone? Many people feel it's a sign of weakness to seek the help of others in losing weight, especially when it comes to running. Take Julie, who never initially believed that she needed company to keep up her motivation to meet her running goal. She was a hard-driving, independent individual who always plowed into any effort with a single-mindedness and a belief that she could do anything all on her own. "The power of one is most important," she often stated. "I should be able to do this on my own." But she wasn't able to, and decided that a little support could keep her on track on the days she was less motivated. On the weekends, Julie ran alone, but she walked 2 days a week at lunchtime—with a co-worker at the same fitness level. They could power-walk 3 miles in 30 minutes, with no more effort than putting on running shoes. This gave her the structure she needed to keep up her pace when she was tempted to use busyness as an excuse to beg off. Needing an exercise buddy does not mean you are less motivated.

One of the main problems is choosing the right support system. First, you need to determine the kind of support you need to stay on your lifestyle track (for both making and maintaining changes in your eating and physical activity). To do that, answer the following questions.

Do you need total lifestyle support?

Do you need someone to be available "just in case"?

Do you need help avoiding stress eating?

Do you need someone to walk or run with?

Do you need a sympathetic ear when your motivation is dropping?

Once you know when you most need support, it's easier to identify whom to ask for help when you need it. The ideal supporter will have the same focus on running—for both intensity and time devoted, and a similar plan to pick up the pace and increase weekly mileage. This person will be at about the same fitness (or unfitness!) level as you. This is important, because someone far below your level will not allow you to maximize your workouts; a person way above your level makes you set unrealistic goal and sets you up for failure. (*Note:* The latter setup can work if your buddy agrees to match your pace and goals.) A support system won't work unless your support buddy has the same long-term goals as you.

While many people want a spouse or sibling to be a lifestyle buddy, you have to be careful. Laura, for instance, wanted her husband to be her running buddy, because he ran four times a week, logging 3 to 5 miles in 30 to 40 minutes. Laura's rekindled interest in running made him a natural support, she thought. But they got off to a rocky start. At first, she was frustrated, complaining, and not at all enjoying a run. She ambitiously wanted to run 4 miles up and down the hills in her neighborhood, thinking this would jump-start her efforts to get back into running. Laura took a step back to evaluate the problem. Once she saw that she was sabotaging her efforts by trying to do too much too soon, Laura decided to run on her own for a couple of months. Running 1 or 2 miles at first and working up to 3 or 4, Laura got into shape enough to rejoin her husband. The change in plan made a big difference in her program. Laura enjoyed the experience and companionship—and that kept her on track. Running became a positive experience only when she felt good about her own performance.

Similarly, if you need a support person for your eating habits, both your eating patterns need to be somewhat compatible. Someone who does a lot of restaurant eating is not a good match for you if you prefer to eat at home. Buddies with incompatible eating styles wonder why they seem to sabotage each other. Meat eaters do not do well with vegetarians. Even those who prefer fish often can't connect with the carnivores. But the most problematic are those who are grazers (they eat six to eight mini-meals per day) trying to buddy with the three-meal-a-day, no-snack eater.

Because you might not live with someone who shares your eating goals, you must seek those with eating styles similar to your own. Dee, for example, had a big problem with eating in the evening after dinner. No matter what she did, she couldn't make it through the evening without grazing every hour or so. Dee's husband wasn't an evening eater, and he couldn't understand the problem. "Just stop," he would tell her. This, of course, made Dee eat even more. The solution came through a casual acquaintance that Dee met at a community meeting. Dee and Diane found they had the same struggle, and agreed to call each other nightly, and not just talk, but have a warm beverage and snack "together." This plan is working well for both of them, and they are managing their own personal sabotage with mutual support.

While we all need different levels of support, most of us need someone when we're feeling vulnerable. Maybe we don't need support when we're in cruising mode—training for a 10-K race or eating a grilled chicken salad for lunch with the dressing on the side. But there are times when we're not in control, not focused, and not self-motivated. These are the times when enthusiasm drops, and we need someone to help us stay focused and motivated.

WHEN TO LOOK FOR SUPPORT . . .

When you're stressed at work or at home

When you're bored

When you feel overwhelmed

When you don't feel like paying attention to your eating

When you feel "lazy" and don't want to run or even walk

When you go to a buffet

Any holiday season

When you just need a little encouragement (and we all do!)

Make no mistake about it. You need support to initiate and sustain change. It takes a little work, but once you find the right person (both mentally and physically), you'll have the strength to know that you have a mental safety net to overcome short-term temptation and achieve long-term success.

QUALITY 2: PATIENCE

One look at a store full of unruly toddlers (and their parents) makes you aware that some people have an inborn sense of patience and others do not. But if this doesn't come naturally to you, you need to work on developing patience for successful long-term weight loss and maintenance. The first step: Accepting you are in this plan for life allows you to put together a daily routine that you are both willing and able to follow. Focusing on small changes forces you to make a realistic set of changes over time. Goal setting is important, but setting the path is the challenge. Runners often want to return to their previous mileage schedules immediately, forgetting the time and energy it took to increase both the duration and intensity of running to their top performance.

Because we live in a culture expecting a quick fix for everything, there's an enormous amount of frustration when we try to lose

THE GREAT MOTIVATOR: SEEING SUCCESS

Carolyn, 28, mother of two young boys and a home-based business owner, had never been particularly active or particularly obese, but she could always stand to lose a few pounds. "I remember when I thought about losing 25 pounds, but I still felt good and looked good." After two pregnancies, unlimited eating, and no exercise, Carolyn found herself faced with a walloping 80 pounds to lose. When she came to see me, she had no major health problems, but she knew these issues were on the way, saying, "If I don't do something, I will keep gaining."

But Carolyn had all three qualities for reaching her goals: support, patience, and positive thinking. Carolyn would always bring her husband, Roger, to her appointments. He was supportive and willing to help Carolyn any way he could. Carolyn agreed to keep food records for 2 weeks, and focus on the Runner's Diet eating plan, with her major source of carbohydrates coming from vegetables and fruits. She had never thought about running, but agreed that she would start walking 1 mile every day. Needing a way to exercise at home, she purchased a treadmill, recognizing it was the only way she could realistically keep up with her plan. She argued that it didn't sound like much at first, but I assured her that it was a great start and would help take the "pressure" off the changes in eating. Well, Carolyn was bitten by the running bug and wanted to do more. After clearance from her primary care doctor, she picked up the pace. By the end of 2 months, she was slowly jogging 3 miles every day, and feeling great. Coupled with a calorie intake limited to 1,600 calories, which she logged daily, Carolyn lost her 80 pounds in a little more than a year—and has kept it off for 2 years. The steady effort paid off for her. In fact, the biggest barrier for Carolyn was making the time for her daily run. Having the treadmill at home was the biggest help, and Roger's support to stick with the plan, even on days when she was not "in the mood," was key. Although Carolyn has since moved to another city, we have stayed in touch. Her greatest weight-loss problem now? "My treadmill is worn-out and I need to buy another."

weight. It's just never quick enough. It takes time and effort to detach yourself from this mentality and decide that slow and steady weight loss (derived from slow and steady changes in your lifestyle) will be permanent. You can set the best path for weight loss when you are honest about realistic expectations. For instance, you can lose 10 pounds in a year simply by cutting out 150 calories a day (a pound a month), or 10 pounds in 6 weeks (a pound a week) by cutting out 1,000 calories a day. The choice is yours. Any plan is realistic only if it works for you.

QUALITY 3: POSITIVE THINKING

It's so easy to beat yourself up when you feel you aren't making progress—or the progress isn't as much as it should be. It's especially hard on runners who have reduced or even stopped their running altogether. But you can sabotage your plan with these three words: "I used to."

Susan, 32, used to run 3 miles 3 days a week, lifted light weights twice a week, and was a part-time yoga instructor. But a car accident left her with a back injury that made it difficult for her to return to the level of activity she expected of herself. After her accident, Susan was unable to exercise for 6 months and gained 30 pounds. Frustrated that she wasn't physically able to jump into her old routine, she had to wait another 6 months before returning to her yoga classes. Her back pain prevented her from running, and at first Susan didn't want to consider walking as an alternative. But she agreed to try to use some extra calories. "I have never been this inactive," she said. She began walking 3 miles in an hour 3 days a week, and found that this was a reasonable substitute for her running. Once she agreed that comparing her past activity with the present wasn't productive, she began to enjoy her walks more than she originally thought she would. She later made the time to add a 4th day of walking. Rather than focus on what she could not do, Susan chose to move ahead and think about what she could do. She is allowing herself 9 months to lose the 30 extra pounds—a realistic and sustainable goal. It just took an attitude change to get Susan to the next step.

CHAPTER 3

THE RACE TO LOSE

The biological basis of weight loss—and why traditional nutritional principles don't always work for runners

Perception versus reality. That's the classic conflict that magicians capitalize on but that drives you crazy because it's one of the reasons some runners have trouble losing weight. How so? If you look at winners of marathons and all the runners that get the most media attention, you get the perception that they're all thin. Really thin. So the myth that all runners are thin is perpetuated. Because you run, you need special dosages and proportions of nutrients. Because you run, you will lose weight. Because you run, you can eat whatever you want. Because you run, you will be thinner than a garden hose.

But the reality is far from the perception. There are many reasons elite distance runners are so lean. They may have inherited thin genes. They probably have training schedules that look like your work schedule—which means essentially that their "jobs" are to burn calories all day. Looking at these super-thin runners has given you—everyday runners—many misconceptions about how you need to fuel yourselves.

For example, I see recreational runners who make many dietary mistakes, including:

They eat doughnuts, cookies, or candy bars because they think it's the best source of prerun energy.

They drink high-calorie energy drinks during short runs, because they think the drinks will keep energy high and prevent muscle fatigue.

They bulk up on chips, because they think chips provide a quick source of salt and carbohydrates for a run.

They avoid fiber, because they think it makes them bloated before a run.

They eat like a herd of hogs after a run, because they think it's necessary to avoid nutrient depletion.

My reaction when I hear any of these habits? Mistake, mistake, mistake, mistake, and—oh, yeah—mistake. Some of these habits may work for the runner who logs more miles than a truck driver, but for the average person who runs to stay healthy, lose weight, or maintain weight, those dietary tactics will derail your plan and consequently deflate your motivation. That's because there are some weight-loss basics that don't change, and it all starts with the most important relationship: *calories out versus calories in.*

Many runners have spent more time thinking about heel counters and interval splits than they have thought about this basic nutritional premise. That's because for many runners food seems to center around performance, and not necessarily around weight loss: What food will help me run faster? What foods will give me more energy? What foods will make me recover quicker? How can I power my engine to make it through my next run? Anybody have a pack of GU? Sure, many of us make healthy choices the rest of the day, but we tend to consume far too many calories in the name of performance. But to lose weight, you have to stop counting carbohydrate grams, stop thinking that your run needs to be jet-powered by chocolate, and stop believing food marketers who insist that all exercise needs to be supplemented with "power" this or "energy" that. You need to focus on your 24-hour eating/exercise cycle. Calories out versus calories in.

To lose a pound, you need to burn 3,500 calories; you can do that in a number of ways. You can burn it through exercise, you can reduce your calorie intake through your food choices while maintaining the same activity level, or you can combine both methods. So, to lose a pound every week (which is a reasonable and safe goal), all you need to do is trim 500 calories from your daily intake. You can do that pretty efficiently by increasing your running (or walking) and by reducing your intake. Running or walking 2 miles will expend 200 calories (walking will just take longer). Couple increased activity with removing 300 calories from your current eating plan, and you can lose weight at a steady and motivating pace. There are endless combinations to this method, and the way you choose to lose weight is based on what will work best for you and what you can continue over the long haul. So I'm not going to tell you that there's only one way to burn calories. What I want to show you is how to understand your body in terms of how it works—both when you're running and when you're not—so that you can be more knowledgeable and your body can be more efficient in the calorie-burning process.

One of the most important things to realize about the process is how your body views food. Your body needs it, craves it, and can't function without it. If you try to lose weight by depriving yourself of food through skipping meals, your body shifts into starvation mode. Not only does that set you up for an eating disaster, but it always leads to weight-loss failure. Why? With prolonged food restriction, your body panics (oh, no! famine approaching!), so it stimulates your appetite to overeat at your next meal to compensate for the perceived lack of food. In effect, you've made your body think it needs to prepare for a period of starvation. So when the opportunity comes to eat the next meal, you become overhungry (which is an actual biochemical signal) and eat like you've just finished 39 days on *Survivor*. In runners, the effect is even more pronounced when they skip a meal, go for a run, and then feel ravenous when looking for a postmeal snack. Max, who routinely skipped lunch and ran after work, overate during his postrun snack before dinner. "I didn't realize I was so hungry," he said. So he ended up having a snack, further stimulating his appetite rather than satisfying it, and he kept eating, from dinner all the way through bedtime. Sound familiar?

You can erase this pattern by creating a mental shift in the way you eat. Don't have a daily caloric goal or try to track every single piece of food. The strategy I like to employ is to "think backward." Instead of trying to calculate how many calories you need to eat, the first step is to think before you eat—and find ways to cut out extra calories in each meal or snack. This is what I call staying connected. In that way, you learn to understand how to create a daily caloric deficit for sustained weight loss, because you're constantly thinking of the changes you can make and the new habits that will contribute to your weight loss. By understanding the contributions diet and exercise have on metabolism, you can design your own weight-loss plan that is essentially a partnership between your eating and running.

CALORIES OUT: DAILY ENERGY EXPENDITURE

While it'd be nice if our bodies worked under the "what goes in must come out" theory, they don't. What goes in can stay in, and it can form a basketball-size pouch on our guts. Luckily, though, our bodies do have ways to burn the nachos and burger that you had for dinner. It's called energy expenditure, or daily caloric usage. Our bodies have three ways of burning calories, and two of them work automatically. They are:

• Resting metabolic rate (RMR): This is the rate that your body burns calories by doing nothing—just to maintain the livelihood of your organs—and it accounts for between 60 and 70 percent of your total calorie burn.

• Thermic effect of food (TEF): This is the rate at which your body burns and digests food. Accounting for 10 to 15 percent of your daily calorie usage, this is also preprogrammed genetically. Since our bodies are not 100 percent efficient in processing ingested calories, we waste some calories during digestion—literally. Some of us, of course, waste more than others; the average person eliminates about 200 calories in a daily intake of 2,000 calories. These calories are blown off as heat by the body, but we don't feel it happening. The more efficient a body is in processing calories, the easier it is to gain weight. The winners of the genetic lottery are those few who are very inefficient with caloric use and storage. That allows for many wasted calories—meaning that they'll have no weight gain with little effort.

So that means that 70 to 85 percent of our daily energy expenditure is biologically set. It's a genetic predisposition, and it accounts for the variability in what we call a "healthy" body weight on the body mass index charts. But that 70 to 85 percent leaves 15 to 30 percent of calorie burn that you can control. And that's through the caloric wild card: physical activity. The more you exercise, the more calories you can burn. And most runners—because of the efficiency of running—can put those burning levels at about 30 percent of all calories burned.

The effect is not only that you burn calories during exercise but that you can also increase your resting metabolism as well through exercise. Although we cannot permanently increase the resting metabolism, running sustains an increase in RMR for several hours afterward. Translated into calories, this means the more you run, the more calories you will burn both during and after the run.

Now, one of the tricky parts about metabolism is that it's not always constant; your RMR naturally decreases about 5 percent every decade (biologically, we're not sure why this happens). And that's important, especially when you look back on what running used to do for your body 10 or 15 years ago—and what you expect it to do now. For example, a runner consuming 2,400 calories a day at age 30 needs to consume 120 calories fewer each day *to remain the same weight* if he or she is running the same amount. This fact alone helps explain weight gain among many runners.

Just consider the number of runners struggling with being overweight or obese. An estimated 21 percent of runners under 30 are medically classified as overweight (that's a BMI of 25 to 29.9), and the number increases to 30 percent for runners ages 45 to 49. Translated into mileage, runners need to run an additional 1.4 miles a week to remain the same weight between the ages of 20 and 50, or cut out 150 extra calories in food. And that's just because of the aging process alone—not even accounting for any changes you've made in how much you eat or how much you run.

So it shouldn't come as a surprise that as you age, weight gain creeps up for both men and women. It's simply not metabolically possible to maintain body weight over time if your running and eating patterns stay the same. The key for the successful weight loss is to maintain, at the very least, a running (or run/walk) schedule of about 4 miles a day of total activity (that's 10,000 steps or 400 calories a day). Whether it's relaxed running, intensive time and mileage, or a combination of the two, it is distance, not time, that is the important consideration.

I've heard from so many patients who say they've been out for "more than an hour a day," but they count the time, not the distance, for their caloric usage. A 3-mile walk in an hour burns the same calories as a 3-mile run in 35 minutes. Take your pick.

CALORIES IN: THE ROLES OF CARBOHYDRATES, PROTEINS, AND FATS

Just as we struggle with overestimating the calories burned from running, we do the opposite with eating. It's simply human nature to underestimate how many calories may come in a slice of meat loaf or a piece of pie. Part of the confusion, I think, stems from the mixed messages we hear about the big three nutrients: carbohydrates, proteins, and fats. (These are macronutrients; micronutrients are vitamins and minerals.) Particularly among runners, there's more discussion on the pros and cons of each nutrient than on virtually any other topic (aside from maybe heel pain or chafed thighs). And I'm always amazed at the passion with which people discuss how they work. I've heard it all. Carbohydrates make you fat, keep you thin, cause diabetes, prevent diabetes, stimulate appetite, reduce appetite, put you to sleep. Protein keeps you full, makes you hungry, kills your liver and kidneys, makes you constipated, builds muscle, makes you faster, makes you slower. And fat clogs your arteries, clears your arteries, keeps you full, makes you fat, causes heart disease, prevents heart disease. Well, as with political and sports talk, everyone's a little bit right.

When you think about macronutrient use, I want you think in terms of the way we used to eat—as animals whose job it was to forage for food and run away from predators. While we don't run from woolly mammoths or hunt for food in terrain no more unknown than the local market, our bodies still respond like we do. Here's how they work biologically.

Carbohydrates: They are the preferred energy source of your body. How? Your body's cells are fueled by a digested carbohydrate (it's called pyruvate) that triggers a chain reaction: The chain reaction (called the Krebs cycle) is what uses calories for energy. Our bodies do not store carbohydrates readily; we use them and have only small stores for "emergency" use (like to run away from a predator).

Proteins: Our bodies use proteins to produce muscle, brain chemicals, and enzymes that drive various biological reactions. Although these are the preferential uses for proteins, they are available to also produce pyruvate, that carbohydrate breakdown product needed to drive cell activity.

Fats: Fats support cell structure, cushion organs, help produce hormones, and can also serve as an energy source for the body. That occurs when fatty acids (a result of fat metabolism) convert to acetyl-co-A for energy production via the Krebs cycle.

From a practical standpoint, the key is that we consume these macronutrients for different reasons than the body does. When we eat, we eat for taste, smell, and a host of other reasons. But your body doesn't give a flip about how creamy the pudding is or how sizzling the steak; it sees the nutrients through digestive eyes only—in terms of what the body needs from those nutrients.

The specifics of digestion vary depending on what you eat, and thus reflect our ability to perform and fuel our body systems. But the fact is that even though you aren't running from mammoths, you are running—and that makes us a bit different from other parts of the population in terms of what your body needs and how you may have perceived what your body needs.

There's no doubt that you've had enough prerace spaghetti-dinner invitations to believe that a diet composed mostly of carbohydrates is the one that will give you maximum performance. But that's only partly true. Your carbohydrate intake depends not on the fact that you run but on things like the total number of calories you consume each day, as well as the duration and intensity of your run. Metabolically, it's pretty hard to deplete carbohydrate stores with a run, even a high-intensity workout, of under 3 hours. But still, runners think carbohydrates are like gas for your car—you need to keep your tank constantly filled so you don't run out of fuel. In reality, though, one of the major ways that runners sabotage their diets is by eating too many carbohydrates as a percentage of total calories.

Now, that's not to send carbohydrates to eternal damnation, like some diets do. Carbohydrates are extremely important for runners, but so are all calories in terms of the way your body uses them for fuel. There's no doubt that carbohydrates are the only source of carbohydrate storage in the muscles and liver necessary to avoid fatigue during robust activity (and avoiding muscle fatigue is a major concern for of all runners). Muscles do prefer to use carbohydrate as the first line of energy (glycogen is stored carbohydrate) but can utilize protein (amino acids) or fat (fatty acids) as well. It is most fuel efficient to take some of these stored carbohydrates and break them down into usable carbohydrates (although amino acids and fatty acids can be converted into the same sources with a little more work). Since our bodies are hardwired to store only small amounts of carbohydrates, it will seek to use this source first. So, your goal with carbohydrates is to avoid depletion by providing amino acids as an alternative source or replenishing them with carbohydrate foods. But that's not to say you should overload on carbohydrates. Your needs will be defined as a function of your intensity and duration of effort. Remember, *there is no biological requirement for carbohydrates.* Carbohydrates can be converted from either protein or fat, although it takes a little more time to do this.

CALORIES OUT AND CALORIES IN: REBUILDING THE FOOD PYRAMID

When it comes to carbohydrates, or any nutrient for that matter, one of the great dietary mistakes you can make is counting and tracking grams of any macronutrient, rather than monitoring total calories. Total calories are the only way to determine your energy expenditure versus intake. Instead, when you consider the three macronutrients, you need to think more in terms of guidelines for total consumption. The federal guidelines provide a fairly large range of ideal consumption percentages, with 45 to 65 percent of calories coming from carbohydrates of all types (fruits, vegetables, bread, rice, pasta, potatoes), 20 to 30 percent of calories from fat, and at least 15 percent coming from protein.

At first glance, it would appear that eating from the food pyramid is the runner's best strategy, since the base of the pyramid is carbohydrates. But when it comes to losing weight, if you eat from the food pyramid, you'll look like the food pyramid.

The biggest problem with eating from the food pyramid is the disconnect between portion size and number of servings. The food pyramid encourages variety, but without any connection to what is a "standard" serving. Nowadays, everything we order is the supersized version, rather than the standard-size version—it's kind of like getting an alligator helping when all you need is the lizard.

So when we look at the recommended six to 11 servings of carbohydrates per day, it reinforces the idea that healthy guidelines say we needs lots of carbohydrates. And that's exactly where we all get into trouble. We love all the starchy carbohydrates (bread, rice, pasta, and potatoes), and feel we need this anchor to improve performance. With bagels weighing in at 5 ounces—that's five servings of a carbohydrate—at close to 500 calories (without any toppings), you see where the problem starts. It's easy to think that this is one serving, because it's one item. But it's five servings—almost a day's carbohydrate guideline in one food item. Even a 100 percent whole wheat bagel has the same calories—more fiber, but the same calories. So, if your goal is to lose weight, you have to pay attention to portion and serving sizes, as well as how to distribute your calories throughout the day.

What runners need to do is to flip the food pyramid and make fruits and vegetables the base. This provides fiber-rich carbohydrates, with quick energy but with far fewer calories than many of the starchy items. The extra water and fiber in fruits and vegetables help keep us satiated. It doesn't mean avoiding all starchy carbohydrates; it means making better choices. For both weight loss and performance, you want a diet that is broken up like this—in a 50-25-25 ratio—for the best combination for sustained weight loss, keeping your appetite satisfied, and avoiding postrunning fatigue.

Fifty percent carbohydrates: I've reduced the percentage of carbohydrates from federal guidelines, because 50 percent will allow you sufficient fuel for a workout to offset glycogen depletion and maintain the small carbohydrate stores that regularly need to be replenished. The best carbohydrates are ones that are high-fiber, complex carbohydrates that come in the form of fruits, vegetables, and whole grains. The high fiber and water content and low fat content naturally occurring in fruits and vegetables promotes lower calorie intake with greater fullness, calorie for calorie. Whole grain starchy carbohydrates that are fiber rich also help reduce the amount you eat (fiber is a great stomach filler and slows the rate of stomach emptying for even fueling after eating). You want to avoid processed carbohydrates that provide a lot of hidden calories in fat and sugar, which are major contributors to the extra calories. I'm not suggesting that you can't have an occasional doughnut or finger swipe of icing, but you should always focus on the healthy carbohydrates, which maximize energy utilization with minimal extra calories. They're best eaten before running.

Twenty-five percent protein: I've increased the protein because of its power in controlling appetite—and its role in building muscles you'll need for running. Though proteins and carbohydrates both have 4 calories per gram, protein is biologically more satisfying than an equivalent amount of carbohydrate. The effect: You're more content with fewer calories. Protein should be high in quality and low in fat, like chicken, fish, egg whites, and veal.

Twenty-five percent fat: Fat is also important, because it provides necessary fatty acids for performance and also slows the rate of stomach emptying. That gives us the sense of fullness, but you can't eat too much (the average American has 35 percent of calories from fat). But you need to eat heart-healthy kinds of fat—unsaturated fat in vegetable oils, and foods like nuts, olives, and fatty fish. Saturated fats like whole-fat dairy and meat are more easily stored as fat on your body. As you'll see in later chapters, your fat intake will be distributed mostly during periods of the day when you will not be running. Because the rate of stomach emptying is slowed by fat ingestion, the goal is to minimize fat before a run but include it prudently in other meals—to enhance contentment after eating.

Typically, after I show runners the 50-25-25 eating program, the first question they ask is "Is this enough carbohydrates?" Yes, *sí, oui, ja,* yes, yes, yes—I can't think of enough ways to tell you. It's the best way to save calories and maximize fullness, especially because the main source of carbohydrates comes from fruits and vegetables. This balance provides the right combination of nutrients to energize, satisfy, and avoid the boredom of what I call "phobic" eating—deleting whole groups of foods perceived as "bad." (For those of you new to running, you might think that 50 percent sounds like an awful lot of carbohydrates as a percentage of daily calories. It's not. But if your comparison is coming from a restricted, no-carbohydrate diet, then you need to rethink your eating strategy. This balance fulfills your physiological requirements, even if your psychological ones need adjustment.)

As runners, we like to think we need more carbohydrate calories than we do. And often, we'd like to give ourselves permission to overindulge not only on fiber-rich whole grains but also on sugar- and fat-loaded processed carbohydrates—neither of which is advantageous for performance or weight loss. I do believe that learning what foods to eat and when is the easy part; portion control is a lot tougher. And for the runner, timing meals and snacks becomes an important issue, too—when you eat plays as much of a role as what you eat. Those are some of the issues I'll address throughout the book, but know this: This plan allows you the ability to choose the foods to give you quick energy and satisfy cravings without giving you extra calories. This eating plan is not only about good health but also about working on the mutual long-term goals of weight loss and energy for fitness.

CHAPTER 4

THE 50-25-25 PLAN
FOR WEIGHT LOSS

> Why this six-step plan works for runners (and walkers)

The 50-25-25 plan says that 50 percent of your daily calories should come from carbohydrates, 25 percent from protein, and 25 percent from fat. And it helps you keep that ratio without being obsessed with every bite you eat. Counting every calorie you consume and every calorie you burn is like saying you're going to wash your new car every day. It sounds wonderful in theory, but it's nearly impossible to manage in practice. That's because it's difficult to account for every single calorie in and calorie out. So what happens? We all tend to overestimate how much we burn during exercise (the machines are rarely accurate) and underestimate how many calories we actually eat. In a way, we don't know what to count—or how to count it, so we end up in information overload of calories, grams, or points and wind up with diets that instruct us with words like "don't" and "avoid" and "fill 'er up with blue cheese dressing."

Instead, the 50-25-25 plan provides a balanced, manageable strategy. It allows you to think of your caloric requirements in daily groups. It also does four important things:

It allows you to incorporate a moderate amount of carbohydrates in your daily diet.

It gives you sources and options for foods that give you quick energy for physical activity.

It provides the right balance of protein and fat to give you continued energy.

It allows you to remain content and satisfied throughout the day while still losing weight and having enough energy.

While the 50-25-25 plan works on a daily ratio of total calories (50 percent from carbohydrates, 25 percent from protein, and 25 percent from fat), every food doesn't need to be in that perfect ratio. Keeping that ratio throughout your daily food intake will, however, satisfy your energy needs by providing you with quick energy when you need it, and a slower, sustained energy level when you're more sedentary. The dual goals mean that you have plenty of choices of what to eat—without having to deprive yourself. To start the 50-25-25 eating plan, you'll follow this simple, six-step process.

STEP 1: PICKING YOUR DAILY CALORIE GOAL

To lose a pound a week, you must have a caloric saving of 500 calories a day. That comes through eating, exercise, or both. You must either eat 500 calories less, burn an extra 500 calories through added activity, or both eat less and exercise more. Is reducing your intake by 500 calories difficult? The answer depends on how much you're eating right now. There's a big difference between saving 500 calories if you're currently eating 1,500 a day (33 percent reduction) and saving 500 calories if you're eating 3,000 (17 percent reduction). And as a runner or walker, you'll have calories burned during your running or walking to factor in. (Remember, the calories used to walk or run a mile are the same; what differs is the time it takes you to finish.) Whether you walk or run, use this equation:

1 mile = 100 calories = 2,500 steps

So your rate of loss can be as speedy as a pound a week if you cut out those 500 calories a day, or as slow as a pound a month if you cut 150 calories a day. Now, what happens when you start running a lot? There may be times when you can consistently eliminate 1,000 calories a day and increase your loss to 2 pounds a week—if you can commit significant time to exercise.

So, start by figuring out your daily caloric intake. If you have no idea how many calories you ingest, start with 2,000 calories a day, and work down if you need to. One way to estimate your daily calories for maintaining your current weight (not losing weight) is to take your present weight and multiply by 15. That total number covers your metabolic needs for the day and factors in a little bit of light activity. Subtract 500 calories from that number, and that's your starting point for daily calories for weight loss.

One of my patients, Lisa, weighed 150 pounds, and her goal was to lose 20 pounds. To maintain her current weight, she'd need 2,250 calories a day (150 multiplied by 15). But to lose a pound a week, a number Lisa felt was manageable, her estimated intake should be around 1,450 calories. Lisa added a 2-mile walk/run every day and kept her food intake between 1,500 and 1,600 calories. After 6 weeks, Lisa had lost 7 pounds and, as she said, "It's never been easier. I don't feel the pressure of food all the time." For Lisa, that release of pressure came from having a little buffer where exercise could compensate for additional eating on certain days—and a bigger savings when she limited her intake to 1,500 calories. But the best part about Lisa's story is what she said at the 6-week mark: "I can keep this up." Her confidence convinced me that she would.

STEP 2: DISTRIBUTING YOUR CALORIES

Though some people clearly follow the three food groups of hamburgers, milk shakes, and french fries, there's really only one way to divide your food intake when monitoring calories for weight loss: carbohydrates, proteins, and fats. Although we don't use the metric system much in our country, the standard understanding of calories is based on grams of foods. As an index, there are 30 grams to 1 ounce of food. All carbohydrates and proteins contain 4 calories per gram of food, and all fats contain 9 calories per gram of food. (For the record, alcohol falls in between, with 7 calories per gram, but more on that in Chapter 6). This difference is explained as "caloric density." There are twice as many calories packed into each gram of fat as in a gram of either carbohydrate or protein.

So why are carbohydrates so different from proteins? Our bodies see different foods differently. We have dozens of pathways to convert one nutrient to another. While carbohydrates are the body's preferred source of energy, there is no biological requirement for carbohydrates, because all necessary carbohydrates can be converted from either protein or fat. But while conversion to carbohydrates is always happening, the process is too slow to provide quick energy for intense physical activity. So we need carbohydrates in order to store them so that our bodies can call upon them for running and other athletic activity. With a readily available source of carbohydrates both before and after exercise, we have a quicker response to our energy needs—and thus greater energy that contributes to our performance. The reverse is also true: When we limit carbohydrates, particularly before and after activity, we feel sluggish and fatigued. And that's exactly the opposite of what we expect from exercise—whether it's a leisurely walk or a high-intensity run.

Ian came to the clinic, reporting major fatigue about 15 minutes (1 mile) into his 3-mile jog. Trying to lose 15 pounds, Ian had been skipping lunch and going for his run after work. Although he did eat a modest breakfast, he was out of fuel by the time he was ready to exercise. He drank 16 ounces of water before the run and took a 16-ounce bottle of water with him, so he didn't think that dehydration was the source of his sluggishness. Ian's fatigue, in fact, came from insufficient quick energy available for his run. Although his body could convert stored fat to carbohydrate, it could not keep up with the quantity needed for his energy output. This is a very fixable problem. Ian agreed to have a midafternoon meal, a 220-calorie protein bar plus a tennis ball–size apple (totaling 300 calories), and to wait 90 minutes after the meal to run. He also maintained his water intake before and during the run.

Hesitant at first, Ian thought those extra calories would ruin his weight-loss effort. Once he recognized that he needed the fuel for his run, his commitment to exercise strengthened, because he felt much more energized after the run. Ian began to look forward to his runs, rather than dreading them as "something I have to do to lose weight." He even added an extra running day. For Ian, recognizing that food was an important tool for his running success was the simple change he needed in his behavior to make a major change to his life—and weight.

As I'll discuss in the next few sections, *when* you eat is as important as *what* you eat, so you'll want to keep in mind the ebb and flow of your daily activities by selecting foods based on how you structure your day. The guideline goes: Choose a greater proportion of carbohydrates—either whole grain starches (rich in fiber) or fruits and vegetables (rich in fiber and water)—before and after your walk/runs (keep the protein and fats limited). Focus on protein and some heart-healthy fat throughout the rest of the day, with added vegetables and salads to round out your selections.

50-25-25 CALORIE DISTRIBUTION			
Daily Calories	Carbohydrate Calories	Protein Calories	Fat Calories
1,200	600	300	300
1,400	700	350	350
1,600	800	400	400
1,800	900	450	450
2,000	1,000	500	500
2,200	1,100	550	550
2,400	1,200	600	600
2,600	1,300	650	650

STEP 3: SELECTING CARBOHYDRATES

In this country, we've had more carbohydrate debates than presidential ones. One reason the pendulum of viewpoints swings so wide is that there's no dietary requirement for this nutrient class. Think about it—there are no guidelines explaining the recommended daily intake that will help prevent a carbohydrate deficiency. That's because there are no essential carbohydrates as there are essential proteins and essential fats. Carbohydrates can be produced in lots of different ways in our bodies. That's where the problem lies. Without knowing the minimum, how can we know how much we really need—or what kinds? Are there are truly good carbs or bad carbs, or is there any difference? The answer depends not only on the food itself but also on your goals and what you're asking the food to do.

For weight control, for example, it's a matter more of portion control and having the energy when you need it in order to complete your goal activity than whether a carb source is good or bad. As a runner, you need to have a regular source of quickly available carbohydrates to maintain stamina. Without it, you're setting yourself up for long-term failure—in both performance and weight control.

People who focus on a high-protein and very low-carbohydrate diet all report the same thing: They run out of energy halfway through their runs. Karen, for instance, thought she was doing everything right to lose weight. She monitored her calories, and as she proudly told me, "I avoid all carbohydrates," as if this were the purple heart of dieting courage.

Karen combined a walk/jog regimen of 2 miles four times a week. But she reported that she felt drained just 1 mile into her activity, even though she carried water and was drinking liberally throughout her jog. Karen, as is the case with many dieters who severely restrict carbohydrates, lacked the quickly mobilized energy that only carbohydrates can provide. Sure, fat can be converted to energy, but not at the rapid rate that she needed to feel energized during and after her exercise. So what happens? If you don't feel energized, you don't run. If you don't run, you don't burn calories as quickly. If you don't see results, it's a deterrent to doing anything at all.

Feeling fatigued during and after your exercise is actually one of the greatest threats to establishing a long-term walking or running program. To change, you have to listen to your body and carefully choose a pre-exercise meal or snack. And you need to time and select the food based on two factors: (1) the time that you exercise and (2) the duration and intensity of your exercise.

Even runners can be subjected to bad examples. At some 5-K races volunteers serve fresh whole fruits, cut-up melons, doughnuts, and chocolate-chip cookies. The problem is in our perception. If race organizers are providing these carbohydrate-rich foods, then they must be good for you. But really, the organizers aren't offering a food because it's the optimal thing to eat before or after your run; they're offering it because many participants demand it or because that's what has been donated. So we excuse our indulgences and rationalize our feasting by saying that these sugar/fat combination foods serve the purpose of providing a source of quick energy.

But if you want to lose weight, you need to accept a few basic concepts.

1. Calories count, even when you'll be exercising and using some.

2. Carbohydrates give you quick energy, but you will need to avoid sugar/fat combinations or other refined-carbohydrate sources.

3. The best carbohydrates are fiber rich and/or have a high water content.

The reason for following these concepts is so that you think of carbohydrates the way your body sees them—not the way your eyes and taste buds see them. By eating fiber-rich or high-water-content carbohydrates, you'll slow down the rate your stomach empties, which will help you feel more contented on less food. So the healthiest carbohydrates to have before a race are fruits, vegetables, and whole grains.

The danger of eating other kinds of carbohydrates is that you can ruin your diet with the mind-set that you'll offset the calories of some sugar- or fat-rich pastry just because you run. That assumption is based on wishful thinking—not calories. Take the case of Ellen, who monitored calories and allowed herself a prewalk meal. "I'm maintaining, but I can't seem to lose," she lamented. When asked what her prewalk meal was, she said: a large cherry Danish from a local coffee shop. Ellen finally calculated the calories and was amazed to learn that her Danish contained a whopping 600 calories, while her walk burned only 300 calories. This left her with 300 extra calories to compensate for—just to maintain her present weight. Indeed, Ellen was saving 300 daily calories during her meals, which she thought would lead her down the road to weight loss. Instead, this was just the balance she needed not to gain weight. So we adjusted Ellen's prewalk meal to keep the taste of what she wanted—"sweet cherries" and the soft, creamy texture of a pastry dough. Ellen now has a slice of 100 percent whole wheat bread, topped with a teaspoon of creamy peanut butter and a tablespoon of no-added-sugar cherry preserves. Totaling 100 calories, this snack provided the sensory stimulation Ellen wanted and the quick energy she needed. That adjustment meant that she saved 500 calories a day—without a sacrifice in taste or satisfaction. Now Ellen was on her way with a slow, steady weight loss of 1 pound a week.

As you have seen, you need to focus on calories, not anything like net carbs or usable carbs. But you also need to be aware of refined carbohydrates—ones not found naturally in the food supply. Sucrose (table sugar) is a refined carbohydrate, while fructose (the naturally occurring sweetness of fruit) is not. Now, to confuse the issue, some other refined carbohydrates use fructose as a sweetener, as if that were a more "natural" food. Well, there's no such thing as a doughnut tree or a brownie bush, so you need to be careful of cookies and other products that are labeled "naturally sweetened with fructose." They're still considered refined carbohydrates containing high sugar, added fat, and way too many calories for their size, known as "high caloric density" foods. Fruits and vegetables should remain your main carbohydrate sources, because of the fiber and the fact that the calories by weight are lower due to the large amounts of water in them; these are called "low calorie density" foods. Your second choices will be whole grain breads and cereals in premeasured amounts; the high fiber content feeds your energy, and measured amounts make calorie counting easier and more accurate. Does this mean you'll never touch a piece of cake or a cookie again? Of course not. But don't be fooled into thinking you can substitute a treat item for a healthy carbohydrate source for quick energy needed for activity. You can have that special treat occasionally, but include it in your diet not as a "carbohydrate" but as a sugary fat treat that you'll eat sparingly without guilt or justification.

As runners and walkers, we need carbohydrates for quick energy. So use the snack list on page 71 to find the good combinations of carbohydrate-containing foods to sustain your energy before, during, and after your run or walk. It is important to pace the timing of your eating with what I call the "1-hour rule." You want to eat no sooner than 1 hour before your run, and no later than 1 hour after your run. A postrun snack or meal can prevent your getting "overhungry" later on, which leads to overeating and a loss of control.

BEST-CHOICE CARBOHYDRATES

(Serving sizes are listed as a caloric guideline: You can always adjust up or down.)

CHOOSE OFTEN:

Fruits (about 60 calories per serving)

Apple, orange, pear, nectarine: 1 small (tennis-ball size)

Banana: 1 small (5-inch)

Peach, plum: 1 medium (fist size)

Kiwi: 1 whole

Grapefruit: ½ whole fruit

Green or red grapes: 1 cup (about 20)

Melon: 1 cup, cut up

Berries: 1 cup

Mango, papaya: ½ small

Apricots: 4 small

Prunes: 3 small

Cherries: ½ cup

Tangerines: 2 small

Fresh pineapple: ¾ cup, cut up

Canned fruit: ½ cup (in its own juice)

Orange juice—Tropicana Low Sugar: 8 ounces

Low-starch vegetables (about 25 calories per serving)

Raw vegetables: 1 cup

Cooked vegetables: ½ cup (including carrots, celery, cabbage, brussel sprouts, broccoli, cauliflower, eggplant, leeks, onions, green beans)

Green pepper: 1 whole

Asparagus: 7 spears cooked/14 spears raw

Lettuce/raw greens: 1 cup

100% tomato or vegetable juice: ⅓ cup

CHOOSE WITH CAUTION (WATCH THOSE PORTIONS!):

High-starch vegetables (about 80 calories per serving)

Beans (lima, navy, pinto): ⅓ cup

Corn: ½ cup

Corn on the cob: 1 medium ear

Peas/lentils: ½ cup

Baked white or sweet potato with skin: 1 small (tennis-ball size)

**Pasta/rice, cooked (about 80 calories per serving—
you can choose less)**

Couscous: ⅓ cup

Brown or white rice: ⅓ cup

Noodles/pasta (whole wheat or white): ½ cup

Bulgur (cracked wheat): ½ cup

Kasha (buckwheat groats): ½ cup

**Breads/cereal/crackers
(about 80 calories per serving)**

Tortilla (white or or whole wheat): 1

Mini pita bread (5-inch): 1

100% whole wheat bread: 1 slice

Light 100% whole wheat bread (Country Hearth): 2 slices

Light bread with added fiber: 2 slices

Light hot dog or hamburger bun: 1

100% whole wheat matzo: 1 sheet

Mini bagel: 1

English muffin: ½

Eggo Special K waffle: 1

Pretzels: ¾ ounce or 8 sourdough nuggets

Popcorn (air popped): 3 cups (Orville Redenbacher Smart Pop mini bags and Pop Secret popcorn sugar-free kettle corn mini bags contain 110 calories each)

Saltine crackers: 6

Triscuit Thin Crisps: 8

Rice cakes—all varieties (large): 2

Rice cakes—all varieties (mini): 6

High-fiber cereal (Kashi Good Friends, Kashi Go Lean, All-Bran): ¾ cup

Low-sugar cereal (anything from Special K to reduced-sugar frosted flakes): ½ cup

Puffed Kashi: 1 cup

Oatmeal: ⅔ cup cooked or 1 instant packet

STEP 4: SELECTING PROTEINS

Protein is the Swiss army knife of your body, because it serves a lot of purposes and does a lot of things well. To let protein do its job, however, you need to be sure you're getting the right kinds of protein. Amino acids are the building blocks of protein. These amino acids come in two forms. First are essential amino acids, which you need to get from food, because your body doesn't produce them. Second are nonessential amino acids, which are present in food, but your body also can make them. Some foods are called complete protein sources, because all of the amino acids are present in that food source. That's the case for all animal sources of proteins, but not usually true for vegetable-derived proteins. For vegetable proteins, two sources must usually be mixed to provide the complete profile of essential and nonessential amino acids. Simply put, if you don't want to worry about meeting your complete protein needs without a lot of effort, stick with at least some animal-based protein. Otherwise, it takes a lot more effort to maintain adequate complete protein intake.

While protein serves the primary role of maintaining muscle integrity (muscle is a protein, and you need essential amino acids to build it), it also has a significant role in food intake. Ounce for ounce, protein makes you feel fuller than an equivalent amount of carbohydrate. This fact alone is what helps those embracing a high-protein intake to stay on their eating programs—for a while, at least. Eating too few carbohydrates, however, sets people up for a dietary *Titanic*, because they can't stick with the diet over the long term. Joan, a devotee of a severe protein regimen, said she'd kill for a piece of bread. Melinda said she got so sick of protein that she couldn't deal with it anymore. And Cheryl said, "If I eat any more chicken wings, I'll grow wings and fly away." These three women are victims of the all-or-nothing approach, where so much protein and the elimination of other macronutrients promote an aversion to protein—essentially a protein burnout. And that's not a good thing when you're trying to lose weight. If you mix protein with fats and carbohydrates, you dilute the taste and avoid burning out on the sensory stimulation of having too much concentrated protein day after day.

What most people don't know is that different amino acids have different tastes. As individual molecules, some are sweet, some quite bitter, some bland. That combination in different acids contributes to different tastes in different protein sources. When people complain of "protein aversion," it's usually to a specific type of protein. When you overconsume protein—and avoid other macronutrients—everything you eat starts to taste the same. When it comes to protein, you want to pay attention to your taste buds: What you like is what you should eat. In our country, it is virtually impossible to be protein deficient unless you're unable (because of disease or because of an eating disorder) to eat.

When you choose proteins, lean is always best (see the list on page 64). But fat adds flavor. A good rule of thumb is the fattier the protein is, the smaller the serving should be. Ed swore off meat, because it was "too fatty," so he didn't feel it could be part of a heart-healthy or weight-loss plan. That was a huge sacrifice, because he really loved the taste of beef. But his view of beef was a 12-ounce porterhouse steak. With some preplanning and marinating, Ed could incorporate red meat into a healthy and weight-reducing program. He cut his portions to 6 ounces of the much leaner flank steak. Because he no longer felt deprived, he enjoyed his double servings of green vegetables even more. Avoiding starch at dinner allowed him to include a protein and still remain within his daily 1,600-calorie limit.

How much protein? Most Americans consume two to three times as much protein as they require. For a sedentary person, protein intake should be 0.80 gram per kilogram of body weight. For someone who participates in moderate exercise, protein intake should be 1.0

gram per kilogram of body weight. The biggest concern for most of us is limiting the calories consumed by eating proteins.

Mike, an administrator with 20 pounds to lose, increased his protein and was walking/running 4 miles 3 days a week. But he struggled terribly. He couldn't lose weight, and he even had trouble maintaining his weight. Frustrated and defeated, he said, "I'm doing everything right." It sounded that way, until we looked at his food records. He consumed lean protein (at least 12 ounces), and he added protein powder to his skim milk twice a day. All that led to 300 to 500 extra calories a day. He reduced his portions to 8 ounces of lean protein at a meal and cut out the protein powder. With only these changes, Mike began to lose weight slowly and steadily. At the end of the first month, he had lost 4 pounds, and after 2 months, an additional 3 pounds. Now close to the end of his third month on this program, he's down another 3 pounds. For Mike, a 10-pound loss in 3 months was worth waiting for. Because Mike had considered himself a "good eater," it was ironic that too much of a good thing—protein—had been sabotaging his weight-loss plan.

BEST-CHOICE PROTEINS

(3 ounces of any protein is about the size of a computer mouse or deck of cards)

Very lean (about 35 calories per serving)

Chicken or turkey breast, white meat, skinless: 1 ounce

Fish fillet (all whitefish): 1 ounce

Canned water-packed tuna: 1 ounce

Shellfish: 1 ounce

Egg whites: 2 large

Egg substitute: ¼ cup

Lean protein (about 55 calories per serving)

Chicken or turkey breast, dark meat, skinless: 1 ounce

Salmon, swordfish, herring, trout, bluefish: 1 ounce

Lean beef (flank steak, top round, ground sirloin): 1 ounce

Veal or lamb (roast or lean chop): 1 ounce

Pork (tenderloin): 1 ounce

Canadian bacon: 1 ounce

Low-fat hot dog: 1

Low-fat luncheon meat: 1 ounce

**Dairy products (about 90 calories per serving—
select smaller serving if desired)**

Fat-free or 1% fat cottage cheese, calcium fortified: 1 cup

Low fat, sugar-free yogurt: 3/4 cup

Fat-free, sugar-free yogurt: 1 cup

Fat-free , sugar-free yogurt minis (6-pack): 2 mini cups

Low-fat cheese (all types): 2 ounces

Light mozzarella sticks: 2 sticks

Laughing Cow Light: 3 wedges

Mini-Bon Bel Light: 2 individual pieces

STEP 5: SELECTING FATS

Fat is a lot like a rebellious teenager—it sounds really bad, but it's often so misunderstood that you can easily overlook the good parts.

One thing's for sure: It's one of the hardest nutrients to keep under control when it comes to losing weight and preparing for physical activity. Fat is an extremely satisfying caloric source because of its caloric density (remember, it has twice the caloric content of an equivalent amount of carbohydrate or protein). And that makes it all the harder to monitor, because of all the "hidden" sources of fat in our food supply. Of course, fat provides a smooth and creamy mouthfeel, and it also a lot of taste and flavor. Only when it's missing do you notice that food tastes "thin" or "dry."

The body does require some fats—*essential fatty acids*—but we don't have to worry about meeting the requirements. There's been no known fatty acid deficiency in our country. So what does that mean? Choosing a diet lower in total fat is a learned behavior. So, when we decide to lose weight and to lose calories with the least effort, what do we do? We cut fat out of our diets like we cut a money-hungry relative out of a will—quickly and immediately. The problem is that we don't just cut pastries, cookies, ice cream, and other junk food sources of fat that are laden with white sugar and loads of calories. We also cut fatty foods that are quite healthy, including nuts, nut oils and nut butters, and olives and their oils. (Heart-healthy unsaturated fat and artery-clogging saturated fat contain 100 calories per tablespoon.)

To reap the benefits of fat while avoiding a caloric overload, choose foods that contain *some* fat. Foods with some fat slow the rate at which the stomach empties (a major role of fat in digestion) and provide a sense of fullness. Whether you're trying to lose weight or maintain your weight, that sense of fullness helps you avoid overeating. This was the case with Sarah, who struggled with the same 10 pounds for 5 years. Sarah was active and walked 2 miles four or five times a week, but she couldn't lose those pounds. Perplexed by her failure to lose, Sarah was confused. "I avoid fat, and don't get more than 10 percent of my calories from fat. I don't know what I'm doing wrong," she lamented. "But I feel like I'm hungry all the time." Sarah's problem was that she viewed fat like Superman views kryptonite—something to stay away from. And she was also unaware that low fat does not always mean low calorie. While she was avoiding dietary fat, she thought that she was cutting down her calories. She did cut down her fat intake, but she focused only on carbohydrates and proteins. Lack of adequate fat meant that her meals emptied very quickly from her stomach. So Sarah felt hungry shortly after eating—and couldn't figure out why. Once Sarah acknowledged that she was ready to add some fat back into her diet at times when she needed more contentment, but not before her 2-mile walks, she had far better control of her food intake. Midmorning and midafternoon were her "vulnerable" times, so when Sarah incorporated a low-fat yogurt, a cheese stick, or a dozen nuts at these times, she had a good combination of protein and fat (with a small amount of carbohydrate) to keep her satisfied and content. To prepare for her walks, which were in the morning before breakfast, she ate a cup of melon and a half dozen melba toast rounds, giving her about 100 calories to sustain her during exercise. By incorporating some fat into her meals, Sarah could sustain contentment after eating, and achieve better control when she needed it.

Now, in choosing a source of fat (see the Best-Choice Fats list on the following page), it's optimal to select heart-healthy vegetable and nut sources. However, your main goal is to eat both the right amount and the right kinds of fats. We sometimes like to fool ourselves into thinking that because unsaturated fat is "healthier," it somehow doesn't have the same caloric impact on our bodies as saturated fat. While this is wrong, if you choose your fats wisely, you can manage both greater contentment on less food and a sustained sense of control. By providing yourself with 25 percent of your daily calories from fat, you will be liberated from the chains of fat restriction—and make fat work for you, not against you.

BEST-CHOICE FATS

Full-calorie fats (about 50 calories per serving)

All oils (canola, olive, other vegetable): 1 teaspoon

Avocado: ⅛ (medium)

Nuts

    Almonds, cashews, filberts: 6

    Peanuts: 10

    Pistachios: 12

Olives, green or black: 8 medium

Peanut butter (creamy or chunky): 1 teaspoon

Reduced-calorie fats (about 25 calories per serving)

Light tub margarine: 1 teaspoon

Light mayonnaise/salad dressing: 1 teaspoon

Light cream cheese: 1 teaspoon

Fat-free salad dressing: 1 tablespoon

"Free" fats (1 serving = 0 calories)

I Can't Believe It's Not Butter spray: 1 spray

Pam spray (original, butter, olive oil): 1 spray

STEP 6: MATCHING EATING PATTERN TO EXERCISE STYLE

The reason the 50-25-25 plan works is that you are not denied any foods or food groups. You understand that a 50 percent carbohydrate plan doesn't give you license to gorge. You can enjoy any foods on occasion, of course. But the wild card in the 50-25-25 eating plan is incorporating eating into your running/walking schedule. Choosing foods that will give you energy to run/walk will inspire you to keep exercising. That will play a role in reducing your daily caloric intake and in using more of the calories you burn (and have stored in your body). This efficiency will reduce your poundage. To optimize everything you eat, you should select combinations of carbohydrate-rich foods with less protein and fat at times you will be more active, because the carbs give you quicker energy. Eating your proteins and fats at times that your body has more time to process them into energy gives you sustained energy. Planning *when* and *what* to eat requires you to have some structure throughout your day—to establish a dietary and exercise ebb and flow. But it also means that you need to listen to your body—and identify the key features of your eating personality and what you perceive to be your walk/run style.

Though there are some nutritional fundamentals you need to follow, a successful diet acknowledges not only what you're willing to do but also what you're able to do. Similarly, your exercise pattern—whether it's all walking, only running, or a mix—must be realistic for you, and not for anyone else. Developing your eating/exercise plan starts by looking at your current habits and picking which habits are easier to change now and which ones you won't realistically change until later. First, start with your activity. When do you feel most willing to make time to walk/run? When are you willing to do this—not now and then, but regularly?

Juanita wanted to lose 20 pounds. She set a goal to get up at 5:30 a.m., walk with her neighbor 2 miles in an hour 3 days a week, and then get ready for work. At the same time, Juanita complained she had no time to do this. Her life and schedule were so busy that this was the only time she could manage. "I have to do it this way," she said. At her 2-week follow-up visit, Juanita said she had walked only twice in 2 weeks. "It was just too hard. See, I told you I had no time!" Juanita struggled with the self-fulfilling prophecy; she anticipated that she'd fail and she did. But had she known it all along? She had chosen times incompatible with her life. It sounded right, because so many people she knew got up early to walk and she enjoyed socializing. But Juanita didn't listen to herself and chose a pattern she couldn't sustain. Admitting the flaws in her plan, Juanita strategized to come up with a workable plan. First she agreed that she enjoyed walking, and 3 days a week was reasonable. She also liked the company of her neighbor. Our solution was for her to walk with her friend on one weekend day when she had more time. She also agreed to walk at lunchtime for 30 minutes 3 days a week to meet her other 3-mile goal. On some days, she doubled up, and walked 45 minutes on 2 days to meet her 3-mile goal. What counted was her weekly mileage. I also raised the issue of running, or to walk/run to shorten the time to cover her miles. But Juanita now knew herself well. "No," she said, "I don't like getting sweaty at work, and I enjoy chatting with my friend, so I don't think that will work for me." Juanita is keeping up her schedule and has already lost 8 pounds in 4 months. Slow and steady for Juanita, but a plan she can realistically manage.

So pick the time to exercise that works for you. Early morning, lunchtime, after work, after the kids go to bed—it's up to you. In Chapter 5, you'll learn the specifics of setting up your own walk or walk/run pattern. Even if you've been a runner in the past, it's a good idea to start with a walk/run until you're back in the running groove. If you get trapped in the idea of "what you used to do," you run the risk of jumping back into a regimen that's too taxing on your body.

So where does eating fit in? A lot depends on the intensity, duration, and time you exercise. This is the "matching" part of eating to your activity. For those walking and/or running 3 or fewer miles at a time, the only physical requirement for you will be fluid, preferably water (see Chapter 6). But you can still have a snack before you run. A basic concept of weight loss is to not go too many hours without eating. Why? Because you can become overhungry, with your brain's signaling starvation mode and stimulating your appetite even further. So, these are the five basic guidelines for matching your running and eating:

1. Have a morning, an afternoon, and an evening meal.

2. It's okay to have a snack midmorning and/or in the afternoon and/or after dinner, as long as you stay within your caloric range for the day.

3. Eat at regular intervals and match the larger caloric intake to times that are not just before exercise.

4. If you don't feel hungry before an early-morning run, drink 8 to 10 ounces of water. You'll have enough stored carbohydrates to meet your energy needs, assuming you will cover no more than 3 miles without stopping. If you like to eat something before the exercise, eat fruit or half an English muffin with jelly (and keep tabs on the calories).

5. No matter when you run, it's important to eat sometime soon after your exercise—to refuel—if you didn't eat beforehand.

BEST-CHOICE SNACKS (AROUND 100 CALORIES)

Some pre- or post-run/walk snacks:

1 mini pita bread + 2 tablespoons hummus

1 5-inch tortilla + 1 teaspoon peanut butter

½ English muffin + 1 teaspoon peanut butter + 1 teaspoon low-sugar jelly

1 Slice Country Hearth Light 100% whole wheat bread + 1 Laughing Cow light spreadable cheese wedge

8 Triscuit Thin Crisps + 1 mini Bon Bel light cheese wedge

1 mini bag single-serve light popcorn

1 mini bag single-serve light kettle corn

½ cup Kashi Good Friends + ½ cup fat-free milk

1 board 100% whole wheat matzo coated with I Can't Believe It's
Not Butter spray and 1 teaspoon jelly

10 sourdough pretzel nuggets

1 medium fruit (tennis-ball size) + 1 light cheese stick

1 Pria protein bar (regular, not low carb)

**Some fun snacks (treats—not for exercise preparation or recovery;
limit to 150 calories per day or less):**

1 ounce baked chips or light chips + salsa (120 calories)

1 Tootsie Roll Pop (60 calories)

Jell-O Sugar Free pudding (60 calories)

Nabisco 100 Calorie Packs—all varieties (Chips Ahoy!, Oreo,
Wheat Thins, Cheese Nips) (100 calories)

1 fun-size candy bar (90 calories)

Sugar-free Creamsicle (25 calories) or Fudgsicle (40 calories)

½ cup sugar-free, low-fat ice cream (100 calories)

Nestle fat-free hot chocolate mix (25 calories)

Some "Free" snacks (select anytime you need a little something . . .)

Sugar-free gelatin

Sugar-free ice pop

Diet soda (no calories)

Diet iced tea

Coffee (think decaf)

Tea (think herbal)

No-calorie sweeteners: Splenda, Equal, Sweet'n Low, acesulfame K

"Diet" juice drinks: 10–20 calories per 8 ounces

Dill pickles

All low-starch vegetables (see the list on page 59)

Sugar-free mints

Sugar-free gum

IMPORTANT NOTE: Any of the foods listed in the carbohydrate, protein, and fat tables can be used for snacks. Select your portions carefully and monitor the calories per serving. These samples are provided only to get you started. Let your imagination be your guide. This is all about choice and avoiding deprivation.

Brian said he was quite fatigued after his daily 2-mile jog. He went directly from work at 5:30, after having had lunch around 1:00. "I thought it wasn't good to eat before exercising, and besides, I thought I could save some calories for dinner," he said. Brian was right in some ways. You don't want a steak the size of Texas before exercising, but we added to his diet a can of a high-protein meal replacement, containing roughly 240 calories. Brian drank this about 4 p.m., which allowed sufficient digestion time. Brian told me he felt great after his run and was surprised to find that he was less hungry for dinner after he began to add his late-afternoon snack.

The lesson here is to listen to your body. It is okay to use calories and not "save" them for another time. This is a great mistake we all make. You want to plan your eating and activity so they work together and complement a total lifestyle.

CHAPTER 5

LET'S GET PHYSICAL

> Identify the problem in your running/walking program—
> and figure out how to fix it

No matter how active (or inactive) you are, your body burns calo-ries. It burns calories to digest food and to keep your organs work-ing properly, but it also burns them anytime you move. Walk to the bathroom? That's a calorie burn. Carry groceries into the house? Calorie burn. Chase your kids between racks of clothes? Calorie burn. Those, of course, are the activities of daily living that you do with-out even thinking—the calories you burn simply because you get up and move. The other way you burn calories through physical activity—exercise—takes a lot more thinking, planning, and effort. But it's im-portant to understand that for successful long-term weight loss and maintenance, you have to think of physical activity not just in terms of exercise but also in terms of everyday activities. When you think about staying active throughout the day—and not just for the 20 or 30 minutes you set aside to specifically run or walk—you're increas-ing the number of calories you're burning exponentially.

Whether your brisk ½-mile walk is on a track or treadmill or from your parking lot to your workplace, you're using the same number of calories for the task—and improving your fitness level at the same time. Taking stairs instead of elevators, parking further from the supermarket entrance, and playing ball instead of video games with your kids all raise the number of calories used. These changes take focus and commitment—but not that much effort—in order to make them habits. When something becomes a habit, you've automatically intensified your daily calorie burning. (See the table on page 91 for other ways you can get extra activity in your day.)

Why is habit changing so important? As recreational runners and walkers, you have this mind-set: "I've already exercised. I don't need to do anything more." But treating physical activity as some kind of quota that you stop doing once you fulfill it for the day only limits the strides you can make (both literally and figuratively). Take Kathy. A working mother of three teenage boys, Kathy would diligently run/walk on the treadmill 4 miles 3 days a week (using about 400 calories per run). She monitored her eating but still struggled with 10 extra pounds that stuck around like annoying party guests—she never could get rid of them. Discouraged, Kathy figured her treadmill work was no longer worth the effort. When we spoke, Kathy acknowledged that she relied on her treadmill time as her sole activity. "I'm always pressed for time, so I save as much time as I can, and this means parking close wherever I go." She also admitted that she never took the stairs in her office building, although she had to go only four flights.

Kathy agreed she had no time to increase her mileage or frequency on the treadmill, but she did want to otherwise increase her physical activity. We added regular activity of daily living to include an extended walk (5 minutes) from her parking spot into the main office entrance twice each day; walking up the steps three times a day at work (10 minutes); and being less efficient in her house—adding 15 minutes of extra walking while doing daily chores at home. This 30 minutes gave Kathy about an extra 100 calories in exercise. It took a year, but Kathy lost her 10 pounds with a very modest change in exercise. Sometimes, the smallest changes yield the biggest results.

It's this very kind of mindful daily activity that can enhance your regular walk/run program and promote successful weight loss. Kathy already had half the battle won—she was a devoted treadmill user—and just needed to do a little more, but not in a structured exercise mode.

More common, however, are the former runners or distance walkers who simply do nothing now—and they're frustrated by their inability to "just start up again" with the same mileage where they left off. They feel like novices—and they hate the fact that their starting point is so far behind where they last ended. The best way to get restarted isn't by trying to plan out a detailed running/walking plan; for many people, getting started means being generally more active every day. That's the most practical way to jump-start a renewed interest in a recreational running program.

Ron, an ex-runner in his early thirties, told me he hadn't run regularly for about 10 years, although he still considered himself a runner. "I just can't get moving," he said, citing his stressful job. "I never worried about having a piece of apple pie for dessert, because I knew I would run it off, and I guess it really caught up with me."

That piece of pie led to another and another—in the form of a 6-pound weight gain over the past 2 years. It was nothing drastic, but Ron feared he was losing control. At 5 feet 11 inches and 176 pounds, with a body mass index (BMI) of 24, Ron was still within the healthy-weight guidelines, but he felt that he would continue to gain if he didn't change something. Smart guy.

Ron expressed his concern to his doctor, who encouraged him to run again and cleared him medically to do so (10 years of inactivity is a long time, and medical clearance is a must at any age). Ron focused on exercise as a calorie saver with only a modest adjustment in food intake, because he controlled his eating fairly well. Because of his job demands, Ron agreed he could manage to run 3 miles 3 days a week. Three miles (roughly 300 calories) took less than 45 minutes, which was a comfortable pace and time frame for Ron, especially because he didn't want to push too hard. That, coupled with a daily reduction of 150 calories (his choice of where to cut), allowed Ron to lose about 2 pounds a month with ease, losing his 6 extra pounds in 12 weeks—and with an attitude that he would maintain this modest effort for the long-term.

Making changes in physical activity can be tough. No one *has* to exercise, and now that we've gained remote controls and lost the woolly mammoths, no one has to do a whole lot of moving in order to survive. But you do have to eat, and that's why many weight-loss programs focus so much on the eating component—the calories in. Exercise becomes an afterthought—something you'll do only if you have time. Because we spend so much time on not eating, we often lose focus or energy for physical activity. What a mistake. In reality, if you agree to regularly use 200 to 300 calories a day through activity, you'll lose weight a lot easier and faster than if you stayed at your current activity and eating level. Just think of it in terms of calories (which I always do). When you're using more calories in activities, it boosts the effort you're making to reduce your calories—your net deficit (that is, how many calories you're saving from both eating and exercise). Every single patient I see knows that activity is as crucial to weight loss and maintenance as controlling eating habits. You'll also get the "value added" of a short-term boost in metabolic rate after each activity bout.

Kelly, thin and active in college, had gained 25 pounds during the 2 years after graduation. She had taken an office job, and the weight had just crept up at pace of 1 pound a month. One morning, Kelly woke up and decided she needed to lose the weight. She just didn't feel like herself, and she wanted to return to regular activity. Having always enjoyed running (she had done so recreationally in college), Kelly still never considered herself a runner. So, at first, Kelly began walking 3 miles in an hour 4 days a week, until she could form the habit of daily exercise, which took about 3 weeks. Next, she began a walk/run pattern, completing her 3 miles in 40 to 45 minutes and adding a fifth day. It's a comfortable schedule for her, and it's one she's maintained for the past 6 months. Kelly also agreed to add some extra steps in her daily activity, even on her walk/run days, and we trimmed 200 daily calories from her food intake. It has taken 7 months for Kelly to lose 25 pounds. The pressure of food restriction is gone, because her caloric use from running is calculated into her daily allotment. Kelly is confident and in control—and now has a structure to maintain her weight.

Another common problem comes in the form of the active recreational runner who can't figure out why weight is creeping up despite what seem to be high levels of activity. Donna, who began running in her thirties as a social activity with friends, has continued a daily 2-mile jog 6 days a week for the past 5 years. She enjoys the occasional 5-K race and has run/walked a 10-K with friends, but she couldn't figure out why she had gained 30 pounds over those 5 years. "I'm out of control, and I don't know what the problem is. I exercise every day and I'm gaining weight. I'm almost hysterical," Donna said. She's the kind of exerciser who's doing everything right, but she's ignoring the eating issues. "I always thought I could eat whatever I wanted because I'm so active," Donna opined. Unfortunately, "whatever she wanted" isn't a category of food endorsed by any nutritional organization, especially when she included one or two doughnuts before a run, and a daily dessert of cake or pie.

Donna did have a lot of variety in her eating but enjoyed treating herself ("Why not? I run," she told me). When she understood that her running didn't completely use the calories in her treats, she agreed to maintain her present running schedule but increase to 2½ miles at least 3 days a week, with the goal of increasing over 3 months to 6 days a week. She adjusted her food intake to allow one doughnut only on weekend days (with some fresh fruit added) and replaced her high-calorie desserts with a small bag of graham cracker sticks (limited amounts of refined carbohydrates are okay). Over 4 months, Donna lost about 15 pounds with very little change in her routine. She's patient, knowing that her long-term goal will be met over the next 4 or 5 months with slow, steady progress. Donna became successful when she finally recognized that like all of us, she greatly overestimated the calories used in exercise and underestimated those that she ate.

Chances are, you're like one of the people I described above—in your approach to eating or running, or maybe even to what kind of effect they have on each other. So before you decide what kind of plan you need to follow, you should assess what kind of runner or walker you are.

YOUR PERSONAL RUNNING PROFILE

By identifying your running profile, you'll be better able to choose the program that will keep you on track over the long haul. Remember, any change in your exercise pattern needs to be cleared with your doctor or health professional. You need to have the confidence that you are physically prepared—to match your mental preparation and focus. For the following choices, choose the one profile closest to your present lifestyle—not your anticipated lifestyle. (Don't worry; you'll likely switch to another profile within a few months.) This selection will help you balance the eating and exercise changes you need to both lose weight and successfully sustain the loss.

PROFILE 1: ACTIVE RUNNER AND FIT

I consider myself a runner.

I run at least 3 days a week.

I take my running seriously and want to improve my performance.

I want to maintain my present weight.

I will always make time to run/walk. This is a high priority for me.

Your action plan:

Maintain your present walk/run pattern and eating pattern.

If your weight fluctuates more than 3 pounds, pay attention.

Produce a 100-calorie deficit each day from your present lifestyle. Reduce your food intake by 100 calories *or* add 1 mile to your walk/run.

Weigh yourself once a week.

PROFILE 2: ACTIVE, BUT INCONSISTENT

I am active and can run/walk about 2 miles but do not do so consistently.

I do not really consider myself a runner.

I want to lose weight.

I would like to make my exercise time more efficient.

I have limited time but am willing to make the effort.

Your action plan:

View yourself as a runner; you are one. Distance doesn't make the runner; interest does.

Select a base distance of at least 2 miles 3 days a week.

Focus on increasing intensity for these 2 miles, using the rate of perceived exertion (RPE) scale (see page 94).

Cut out 300 to 500 calories a day in eating.

Weigh yourself once a week.

PROFILE 3: WILLING WALKER AND RUNNER

I am not a runner right now but would like to be one.

I don't know if I can run, but I can walk.

I am willing to devote 30 to 60 minutes at least 3 days a week.

I am always struggling with my weight.

I've never been willing or able to focus on regular exercise.

I want to lose weight.

Your action plan:

Using the RPE scale, determine how far (mileage) you can walk in 60 minutes.

Agree to exercise no fewer than 3 days a week.

Add some short bouts of jogging, as comfortable (use the RPE scale).

Cut out 300 to 500 calories a day in eating.

Weigh yourself once a week.

PROFILE 4: FORMER RUNNER

I used to run but have not for at least a year.

I enjoy running but have limited time.

My weight was never a problem until now.

I had a much easier time keeping weight off when I ran/walked regularly.

I want to get back into my running in a realistic way.

Your action plan:

Forget the distance you used to cover and recall the pleasures of running.

Start out with a modest walk/run of no less than 30 minutes, three times weekly.

Pay attention to your food intake, and cut out 300 to 500 calories a day with more than 5 pounds to lose, and 100 to 200 calories a day with less than 5 pounds to lose.

Adapt your eating habits to match your new activity; avoid comparisons with how you "used to when running."

Accept that a consistent walk/run will make the effort easier.

THE RUNNING HOW-TO LIST: THE TOOLS YOU NEED FOR EXERCISE

When it comes to choosing gear for running and walking, it is pretty simple. All you need is some good shoes. But the locker you keep in your mind needs a few more items in it—the tools you'll use to track your progress and overcome obstacles. Below are the important measurements and issues you'll be dealing with as you incorporate more activity into your weight-loss program.

HOW TO TELL THE DIFFERENCE BETWEEN MENTAL FATIGUE AND PHYSICAL FATIGUE

If exercising were easy, we'd be a country of people who looked more like carrots and less like apples. Unfortunately, real life intervenes, and everything from deadlines and schedules to family and illness gets us off track. One of the most common reasons I hear for not getting into a walking or running routine (or having a routine get derailed) is "I'm too tired to exercise."

The first step in facing this challenge is to distinguish between mental and physical fatigue. As I'll describe below, a regularly worn pedometer is the best tool to measure whether your fatigue is physiological (you really are active) or psychological (mental stress is tiring!). Some of the biggest surprises can come from wearing a pedometer for a day and comparing your sense of fatigue and the number of steps you take. Consider Alison, who felt she had an enormous amount of exercise in her daily activity as a representative of a prescription drug company. Alison enjoyed recreational running, but she always felt exhausted at the end of the day of visiting multiple doctors' offices and presenting her products. She complained of being too tired to do more. When Alison wore a pedometer, she was surprised to see she was walking between 5,000 and 6,500 steps per day. When we evaluated her activity, she acknowledged that she parked as close as she could and did very little walking other than to and from her car (lugging her products in a rolling cart). Her tiredness, she agreed, came from the mental exhaustion of selling with her sales tied to her income. When Alison saw the evidence that she was not particularly active, she agreed to boost her activity to 8,000 to 10,000 steps a day in the first 2 weeks of change, and to stay at more than 10,000 steps in the 2 weeks after that.

Within 1 month, Alison almost doubled her steps through a combination of daily activity and weekend running—which turned out to be a great stress reliever. During her workweek, Alison increased her steps to about 7,500 steps a day (an additional mile). She also ran on the treadmill to reach 10,000 steps, adding another mile and an additional 15 minutes of exercise to her day. By including running or walking as a stress reliever, Alison took a positive step toward a sense of well-being and fitness. The bonus was that Alison also found it much easier to maintain her current weight. "I always felt under so much pressure to monitor my eating," she said. "Now it's a lot easier." For Alison, the recognition that her tiredness was mostly a symptom of mental fatigue—rather than physical tiredness—helped her decide to build in extra daily activity and structured running to fight her fatigue.

For all runners, whether you're beginners or elite, you're certain to experience mental fatigue. To fight it, step back and consider your goal for the day. First, consider your overall fitness level and the day-to-day variability in how you feel, based on your level of stress, fatigue, or physical illness. Do not confuse your level of enthusiasm with your level of fitness or physical health. It's great to push yourself to more challenging goals, but you need to identify whether you need to adjust the goal on a particular day. If you can eliminate physical fatigue from the equation, then the best resolution of mental fatigue is to just complete your task. It simply means resetting your goal just a little—move the finish line or change how you want to reach your original goal. This is your reality check that will help you finish up strong and continue to be positive about your efforts. Your sense of mental fatigue really builds when you feel you simply cannot reach any of your goals. You must fight that feeling, because you always can do *something,* which, when it comes to activity, is always better than *nothing.*

IS THIS YOU?	
Problem	**Solution**
You're out for a 4-mile, 45-minute run, and run out of steam in 30 minutes.	Revise your goals and complete the task. Either complete 4 miles in a longer time or complete 45 minutes of activity with less mileage. You will offset the sense of mental fatigue when you have an achievable goal in mind for that particular day. Tell yourself you'll try again, another day, and eventually you will meet the goal.
You plan to run/walk 3 miles in 40 minutes after work. You get home, sit on the couch, and can't face 40 minutes of activity.	Get up and change into your running clothes. Agree to walk/run 1 mile in 10 minutes. With that goal met, you can decide if you want to pursue the second goal of a longer time and more mileage.

Important note to all runners: If you feel unusually fatigued without explanation and are unable to keep up with a regular walking or running schedule, it is important to revisit your doctor. Remember, before even starting or changing an exercise program of *any* type, see your doctor. There might be hormonal, dietary, or other reasons involved. Do not "push through it" if, instead of having the activity re-energize you, you feel de-energized.

HOW TO CALCULATE YOUR RATE OF PERCEIVED EXERTION (RPE)

Any kind of running—whether it's 1 mile, 3 miles, or down the street—is an aerobic, calorie-burning activity. Consistency in a program is always the hardest part; so many of us have started and stopped a routine many times (the first cousin of yo-yo dieting) without understanding why we don't continue. One reason is that it's difficult to monitor how you feel and how hard you exert yourself, so you struggle with a frame of reference. What is your body supposed to feel like when you start a run, in the middle, and at the end? Of course, to increase your efforts, you have to avoid injury and make the exercise enjoyable. To do that, you have to know the line between hard effort that's good and hard effort that's risky. For many years, measuring your heart rate was the gold standard of exercise intensity, also taking into account your age. Besides entailing a lot of math, this method has other disadvantages. Most importantly, it doesn't take into account how you feel—whether you're fatigued or not. For example, you could be exercising well below a recommended heart rate but still feel overly strained, tired, short of breath, or even ready to pass out. Besides being a possible health risk, it's a major deterrent to continuing an exercise program because the activity will feel as energizing as a dead battery.

Another way to measure your effort level is based on the rate of perceived exertion (RPE) scale; it's one of the preferred ways to determine your exercise intensity, because it's based on your overall fatigue and takes into account psychological, musculoskeletal, and environmental factors that change with aerobic activity. Because the RPE scale is a reflection of your personal feelings, rather than the specifics of a heart-rate measurement, one of the tricks is staying focused on your general feeling of physical fatigue and breathlessness—and not the discomfort of starting a new activity. You'll also integrate other factors—like pain related to specific injuries, motivational problems, climate—and end up looking at the whole picture of your activity. The goal is to feel like you're "working" but still feeling comfortable.

This scale works on a 6- to 20-point scale, and you assign numbers to how you feel at a particular moment during your exercise (see the table on page 94). Think of 7 as a walk to the mailbox—very low exertion, while *19* would be a jog up a steep hill. There is no right or absolute answer to your RPE—it's dependent upon your daily state of mind and physical readiness. Some days you may be able to run faster, or choose a hillier course, or shift your run/walk ratio from other days; you must listen to your body and adjust intensity and distance accordingly. This approach provides the best kind of personal control for gradually increasing your intensity and/or duration of effort while still promoting a safe, enjoyable experience. (It also requires clearance from your doctor, to ensure that your own perception of effort is compatible with your body's abilities.) Here are your goals throughout the course of a workout.

Point of Activity	Rate of Perceived Exertion (RPE)	Explanation
Warmup	7 to 9	Allows heart and muscles to prepare for activity
Bulk of workout	11 to 13	Should feel like you are putting out significant effort but are able to hold a conversation without being breathless
Periodic intensity increases within workout	15 to 17	Can do periodically during your run, but not necessarily for weight loss or fitness; based on your personal preference and temperament
Cooldown	7 to 9	Allows heart and other muscles to recover from activity

HOW TO MONITOR YOUR DAILY ACTIVITY

In our daily lives, we track all kinds of stuff—from stock prices to game scores to politicians' hairstyles. So it shouldn't be a surprise that tracking your activity is also important, because it helps you get a better handle on the calories you're using for running and walking. There are lots of ways to do it (neither sweat production nor estimation is a good indication of calories burned), but these are my favorite gadgets for a realistic check.

Low-Tech Options: Using a Pedometer

A pedometer is a great tool for those who get a lot of their activity from "running around during the day" and who don't devote significant time or frequency to recreational running. Some activity is always better than none. For weight loss or maintenance, and improved cardiovascular activity, the best rule to follow is to increase your daily steps. You should record at least 10,000 steps a day. A mile is roughly 2,500 steps for a walker using a 2-foot stride, and about 2,000 steps for a runner with a 2½-foot stride.

If you consider that most of us take about 5,000 steps in normal daily activities, that would translate into needing about 5,000 additional steps, or about 2 miles running or 2½ miles walking, or about 30 to 40 minutes of daily activity. Choose running or walking, but aim for 10,000 steps a day total. Of course, you can divide these 30 to 40 minutes into shorter bouts. Ten minutes three times a day is a great start, with a future goal of up to 60 to 90 minutes if time and health allow. I always qualify this time factor with patients; although some recommendations favor 60 to 90 minutes as the "optimal" exercise time, most people feel this is just too much. It's better to stick with 10,000 steps and 30 minutes every day, thinking of it as a bonus if you go beyond.

High-Tech Options: Measuring Speed and Distance

Garmin International and Timex have teamed up to develop a watch to transmit speed, distance, and pace, with a built-in lap counter. The Timex Ironman Speed & Distance System consists of two pieces—a receiver and a watch/monitor that are connected wirelessly via a radio signal. Satellite positioning signals, complete with atomic clock readings, are sent to the watch to record speed, distance, and pace information in real time. The receiver is small enough to be strapped onto your waistband or arm, and the watch is standard for performance-style watches. Polar Electro, a world leader in heart monitoring, has also introduced a product for all level of runners. Called the Polar S625X, this unit monitors speed, distance, pace, altitude, and heart rate. It's one of the first models including heart monitoring to provide a wireless connection. You can download your running data from the unit via an infrared signal to a compatible cell phone. Optional accessories and software allow you to get an even more detailed look at your run.

But one word of caution: Don't feel you need to purchase an expensive tracking device to truly be a runner. You don't. If it's a motivator for you and you enjoy an upscale gadget, consider a purchase. But remember, all the expensive gadgets in the world will not get you to lace up your running shoes and get going. Only *you* can make running/walking a priority.

HOW TO PICK UP THE PACE: INCREASING ACTIVITY OF DAILY LIVING

Because you must burn 3,500 calories to lose a pound, you can help chip away at those calories by changing your view of nonexercise activity. It's very easy for you to feel exempt from those day-to-day activities when you have structured running and walking in your day. But the best boost for weight loss is to maximize those extra activities, which add steps and calorie usage to our day. This is not an either/or way of thinking; it's a combination that can mean the difference between maintenance and weight loss.

If you have 10 minutes (surely we all have 10 minutes at some point during the day), you can boost your calorie burn in daily activities that you often discount because they don't seem or feel like exercise. Optimally, if you can choose activities that burn 30 calories for every 10 minutes, you can pack in some extra-effective calorie burning to your day. For 30 minutes, you get a 100-calorie savings in addition to your run. It all helps.

GOT 10 MINUTES?
HERE'S WHAT YOU CAN DO

Activity	Calories Burned
Watching television	12
Sleeping	12
Standing	14
Dusting	27
Grocery shopping	35
Painting	35
Light gardening	38
Light housework	38
Cooking	39
Dancing	44
Washing floors	45
Weeding	65
Playing tag	75
Shoveling snow	85

HOW TO CHOOSE BETWEEN RUNNING AND WALKING

I'm often asked lots of questions about whether it's better to run than walk when trying to lose weight (after all, this is the Runner's Diet, right?), and they all come in a variety of ways.

Will I lose weight more quickly if I run?

Will running speed up my metabolism better than walking?

Don't I use more calories while running than walking?

If I run, can I eat more and still lose weight?

How can I change my calories to maximize my running performance and still lose weight?

To go from walking to running, won't I have to add calories to prevent fatigue?

Doesn't running mean I need a lot of carbo-loading?

The answer to all of these questions is uncomplicated, and actually quite simple in concept. When you accept the explanation, you'll easily master the caloric balance needed for weight loss or maintenance, whether you are a new, a renewed, or an established runner. When it comes to losing weight, the greater distance you cover, the more calories you use. Part of figuring out whether you are a walker, a walker/runner, or a runner, is based on the time you have to spend doing the activity. The most important concept to remember is this: One mile traveled burns about 100 calories. For whatever reason, the toughest concept for people to grasp is that whether you run, walk, skip, or hop-scotch a mile, you still burn 100 calories. The only difference is the time it takes you to complete your activity. So, if you can run 5 miles in an hour but walk only 2½, you will have burned more calories while running—but only because you covered more ground, not because you moved faster. This is the fundamental concept to embrace when contemplating distance covered, and whether you run or walk.

WALKING VERSUS RUNNING—A CALORIE-BURNING GUIDE

Distance	Time	Activity	Calories Used (Approx)
1 mi	15 min	Walk	100
1 mi	10 min	Walk/run	100
1 mi	8 min	Run	100
2 mi	30 min	Walk	200
2 mi	25 min	Walk/run	200
2 mi	20 min	Run	200
3 mi	45 min	Walk	300
3 mi	40 min	Walk/run	300
3 mi	35 min	Run	300
4 mi	60 min	Walk	400
4 mi	50 min	Walk/run	400
4 mi	40 min	Run	400

No matter what plan you choose or how fast or far you go, you're a runner. If you combine walking with running, you're a runner. If you run twice a week, you're a runner. If you view yourself as a runner, you will become a better one. If you've never run and want to become one, you can be a runner. All it takes is interest (and a good pair of running shoes). That interest will always be a most important contribution to your weight-loss effort. A consistent run/walk pattern will allow you the freedom to focus on your food intake to optimize your weight-loss effort. Your goal will not and cannot be met by exercise alone, but exercise will enable long-term success.

You need to include moderate-intensity exercise to gain your best return of fitness and weight loss. This exercise may include running and brisk walking (in that 11- to 13-RPE range). More intense exer-

THE RPE SCALE

WHAT THE NUMBERS MEAN

Although the RPE scale is a more intuitive and "easier" intensity gauge than heart-rate measurement, it can be difficult for those just beginning an exercise program. Some reference points may help.

7 = walking to the mailbox. The activity is not strenuous at all.

19 = walking up a steep hill or running from a mean dog. The activity is too intense. You feel that you are going to pass out or cannot continue on.

The most important thing to remember about the RPE scale is that there are no "right" answers. Some days you may be able to run faster or set an exercise machine to a higher intensity level. What's important is that you listen to your body signals and adjust the exercise intensity accordingly. **And always stop exercising if you feel light-headed or dizzy. Get a drink of water and rest for a while.**

THE RPE SCALE

6	No exertion at all
7	Extremely light
8	
9	Very light
10	
11	Light
12	
13	Somewhat hard
14	
15	Hard (heavy)
16	
17	Very hard
18	Extremely hard
19	
20	Maximal exertion

The numeric range for the RPE scale.

cise provides only modest additional benefits to your health. Translated into calories, we're talking at least 1,000 calories a week, or 150 to 200 calories a day for most days. Here's where the goals for weight loss and weight maintenance split. For those at a stable weight who are exercising 30 minutes a week at least three or four times a week (and burning 1,000 calories or more), no changes are required, unless you sense your weight creeping up. Those who are exercising 30 minutes a day and monitoring food intake but failing to lose weight need to reduce food intake further and/or increase their run/walk duration or pace. For most people, a combination of these two applications works best. Increasing activity to 45 to 60 minutes is optimal, but if time is an issue, you can step up caloric use by increasing intensity. Always remember: You have to compromise between what you're willing to do and what you're able to do to create a program you can stick to.

HOW TO CHOOSE BETWEEN DISTANCE AND INTENSITY

Whether you're starting a running program for the first time or the 51st time, your best first step isn't the one you take out the front door. It's taking a mental first step in choosing a distance you *want* to cover and also are *physically able* to cover, given your present state of fitness. It's always hardest for former runners to "start small" and be realistic.

Distance: Start with 1 mile, even if 1 mile seems wimpy to you. It's much better to complete a mile and want to do more than to struggle with a longer distance and be turned off of exercise. Determine the time it takes to cover this mile and increase from there. See the table on page 93 for a guideline of distance, time, and calories for both walking and running. Don't worry if you can't complete a 15-minute mile to start (4 miles an hour on a treadmill). Your goal is to complete the distance.

Course: Whether you're using a treadmill or running outdoors, keep it flat to start. Avoid inclines and hills until you're comfortable with a set distance.

Time: As you progress, you should be aiming to devote a minimum of 30 minutes a day at least 3 days a week. Aim for at least 1½ miles in 30 minutes (3 miles an hour), which is a leisurely walk for most people. Some people can manage 2 miles in 30 minutes (4 miles an hour) without much pushing. To lose weight, I recommend you devote 45 to 60 minutes, even if you need to accumulate it over a few episodes during the day.

Intensity: Once you have set your distance, you want to master a feeling of comfort during your running. Refer to the RPE chart (on page 94) as your guideline. Aim for working "somewhat hard" (about 11 to 13) most of the time, with some attempts at "very hard" (16 to 18), but only if you want to challenge yourself further on particular days. Try it once or twice. You may find you like the personal challenge of a major push.

Once you're settled in this routine, ask yourself if your effort is comfortable. You may decide the distance and time are sufficient to support your weight-loss/maintenance effort. If so, that's great—and there's no need to change anything right now. But if you want to pick up the pace—either for a better rate of weight loss or for a better level of fitness—there are two ways to move ahead. One way is to increase distance without increasing intensity; that is, your present effort stays the same, but you do it for a longer period of time. The second way is to maintain the same time frame but increase the effort you put in, the intensity, to burn extra calories. Both solutions burn more calories. Whether you increase your mileage at the same speed (increase duration) or maintain the same mileage at a faster pace (increase intensity), caloric use will increase. Usually you'll use a combination of intensity and distance. Let your body be your guide.

HOW TO BUILD STAMINA

Whether you increase your exercise by increasing duration or intensity (or a little of both), you need to assess your stamina. While stamina is usually determined by your present physical condition and your type of activity, I like to think of stamina as the end point of both muscle and mental fatigue. When you've reached the limits of your stamina, your muscles are fatigued, and that's caused by the depletion of that muscle's glycogen (the storage form of carbohydrate for the body) used for energy. This fatigue is usually accompanied by mental fatigue with an onset slightly before or slightly after the physiological event. The art and science of conditioning is the gradual increasing of stamina over greater physical challenge, so it's not surprising that this is really a combination of both physiological and psychological factors.

One of the biggest problems many runners face when contemplating weight loss is the mistaken idea that glycogen depletion (and fatigue) can be overcome simply by eating more carbohydrates that can be stored ahead of time—the notion of carbohydrate loading (carb-loading). This tactic is necessary only for long-distance runners; there is very little problem maintaining sufficient muscle glycogen for the recreational runner covering 5 or fewer miles a day. Often recreational runners add hundreds of calories "for stamina"—whether they're hungry or not. Building stamina is not about carb-loading; it's about adding the right fuel before your run. But more so, it's about gradually increasing the time and distance of your run/walks to build up a base that allows you to go longer and stronger.

HOW TO BALANCE EATING, CALORIES, AND EXERCISE PERFORMANCE

It's important to include the fundamental concepts of eating and exercise performance of running and walking in the context of weight

(continued on page 100)

SHOULD RUNNERS LIFT WEIGHTS?

I field as many questions about weight lifting as Alex Rodriguez fields ground balls during practice. Should runners lift weights? Will it help you lose weight? Are there other benefits? Should you just stick with running? For sure, weight lifting has a lot of benefits. It can build muscle mass, increase bone density, and increase flexibility—all important for both running performance and weight loss. But comparing aerobic activities and weight lifting is like comparing sweet and sour. They go well together, but individually they're very different. Lifting weights is one sure way to increase your muscle mass. Particularly for runners, who typically develop increased muscle mass in the lower body (legs), weight lifting can increase upper-body muscle mass.

New muscle tissue can enhance weight loss because metabolically, muscle is more active—meaning that it uses more calories per hour than fat does. There are more energy-producing cell particles (called mitochondria) per gram of muscle than for fat, making muscle more efficient for burning calories. Many people don't realize that muscle development has nothing to do with existing fat mass. Just as inactive muscles do not "turn to fat" with less use, increased muscle mass is not a result of fat's "becoming muscle." Muscles decrease in size when they're not used (it's called muscle atrophy), and muscles build up with continued stimulation. When muscles are pushed to perform, as they are when you lift weights, some small biological damage occurs, causing the muscle to rebuild, thus increasing the muscle mass. This is a good thing, and can help burn more calories per hour, boosting your metabolism during your workouts.

But you should perform any weight lifting using a moderate effort and with comfort. A good rule is to use lighter weights with increasing repetitions, which provides muscle toning. (Avoid starting with heavy weights and few repetitions, which can lead to injury.) For runners, the toning aspects of weight lifting can help you both look and feel better. The optimal way to start, particularly if you are inexperienced, is to arrange a consultation with an exercise physiologist or a certified trainer. You first need to determine your physical limitations and develop a plan for toning your body evenly and proportionally. Any good plan will address arms, back, chest, and abdomen in an integrated, alternating manner. Buildup of your legs, of course, can be supplemented by wearing weights, but your running may satisfy all your needs. Most professional trainers will evaluate your abilities and start you with weights you might think are too light. Start with two sets of 8 to 12 repetitions for a given set of weights, but ultimately, let your exertion level be your guide. The first set of repetitions, or reps, should be comfortable and without strain. The middle sets should be tougher—with the last few reps being a particular challenge.

When doing two sets of 8 to 10 repetitions becomes too easy, it's time to add a third set of 8 reps (toning) or a modest increase in the weight (anywhere from $2\frac{1}{2}$ to 10 pounds), depending upon the body part challenged. Initial weight recommendations are variable, and the best guideline is to underestimate your ability. It's much easier to increase to the next weight than to nurse a sore body. Ask for advice to avoid injury.

If you choose to do both running and weight lifting, do them on alternating days, because both activities use those fast-twitch muscle fibers. Doing both on the same day can excessively fatigue those fibers and make your recovery time much longer. Linda, for example, who enjoys running and lifting weights, had opted to cut out her running due to fatigue. "I work out three times a week at the gym," she told me, "using weights for 30 minutes and doing a 3-mile run. I just can't run any more. My legs feel like jelly." Linda's solution was easy, when she accepted that the physical demands on her body were too much to combine running and weight lifting on the same day. She wanted to lift weights for bone health but found she was gaining weight (5 pounds), even after only 2 months without running. Linda compromised by lifting weights twice a week and devoting one gym day to running, where she was comfortable with a relaxed 6-mile run/walk. Adding a 3-mile run on a weekend day allowed Linda to maintain her weekly mileage. On the weekend, she used a flexible plan that allowed her to cover 3 miles in either one running session or two.

loss. First, for all aerobic activity (running and fast walking), glycogen is the preferred energy source. The liver and muscles store small amounts of glycogen and provide quickly mobilized energy for aerobic activity. When we talk about sources to supply energy to muscles, we're talking about two kinds of muscle fibers—fast twitch and slow twitch. Fast-twitch fibers use glycogen most, to provide quick energy for brief activities like running or fast walking as well as activities like weight lifting. Think of this as the "burst of energy" for muscles needing a quick oxygen supply (for muscle respiration and replenishment). In contrast, slow-twitch fibers have a less intense demand for fuel, using energy more slowly and oxygen more efficiently. They're associated with endurance activities like swimming and rowing. Not surprisingly, fast-twitch fibers tire more quickly than slow-twitch fibers. In order to properly fuel, you can follow the 50-25-25 plan to give yourself the right amounts of carbohydrates at the right time. This correct balance will ensure that you get the maximum performance from your muscle. See Chapter 4 for a list of prerun and postrun snacks. Check out the calorie contents, and do not be surprised that these servings total fewer than 150 calories for both prerun and postrun eating.

CHAPTER 6

YOUR DRINK TANK

> Analyzing a runner's fluid intake—and how to determine
> the balance between salt, water, and other components

No matter where you go, walkers and runners are always carrying
something to drink. Short of martinis, you'll find them carrying just
about anything—designer vitamin waters, bottled water, and sports
drinks. That's because we've been bombarded with the message that
as runners, we need to stay more hydrated than a rose garden. That
message is important, but I think we all have heard it, know it, understand it, and realize that especially in hot weather, we need to take
as much water in as we let out. But the bigger problem—at least when
it comes to weight loss—is finding a balance between calories and performance.

Robert, a professional who takes time from his busy office day as
a hospital administrator to briskly walk 3 miles in 45 minutes, wanted
to lose 15 pounds. Despite his hard work (walking nearly every day
and monitoring his calories), he remained the same weight. The flaw
in his program was a 275-calorie energy drink he slurped down right

before his walk. "I used it to hydrate and give myself the energy to walk up hills," he said. But he did this even though he ate a lunch of yogurt and fruit at 11:30 each day—and he wasn't particularly hungry before his walk. The problem was that Robert was adding what he felt were healthy—but were really wasted—calories. So, not surprisingly, he maintained his weight rather than lost any, because the 300 calories he used in the walk were mostly offset by his sports drink. It was like he had canceled out all his work with a couple of gulps.

Without changing anything else, Robert switched to bottled water and began losing 2 pounds a month. He has lost 4 pounds and is satisfied to continue this pace for the next 3 or 4 months to reach his target. Most importantly, it's a change Robert can manage, and it's made him more aware of the calories in other fluids. So now he chooses water exclusively as his "sports drink" of choice.

Although water is the base of all of the commercially available fluids, these drinks have a wide variety of calories, nutrients, and electrolytes. They all give a variety of explanations about their benefits— how they prevent dehydration, enhance performance, or stave off exhaustion. But the confusion occurs when runners or walkers are trying to lose weight and when they concern themselves more with sustaining energy with these high-calorie drinks than simply trying to stay hydrated with no-calorie water. Because many products promoted for hydration have more calories than a slice of cheesecake, regularly adding them to your eating and exercise regimen puts the "die" in "diet"—because they're surely the death of success.

The main problem I see in the marketing of these products is that while they're promoted as helping with hydration, they're not necessary for the recreational athlete—even if they have "good" nutrients. The scientific claims of these products are supported, but the studies are typically done with conditioned, competitive athletes rather than more modest recreational athletes. Conditioned, competitive athletes like marathoners and professional and Olympic athletes often walk on the metabolic edge of physical performance. They're constantly training—and under many more (and longer) physical demands than the weekday and weekend warrior. So what works for them might not be necessary for us. It just seems that the media, marketers, and even some physicians and nutritionists seem to unnecessarily extend these findings to nonelite athletes.

Biologically, the problem is that our bodies don't sense the calories in liquid in the same way that they sense the calories in food. Studies in everyday people (not elite athletes) clearly demonstrate that calories consumed in liquids are not compensated for by reduced food consumption later on. For the runner trying to lose weight, this means that many hidden calories in calorie-containing sports beverages can add many calories to your daily total without your feeling like you've consumed any extra calories at all. And these calories typically are not justified by any increase in your physical ability to run or walk comfortably, and they really don't contribute to your postrun recovery.

The real benefit to consuming these sports/energy drinks is more of a psychological one. If you think your performance is increased by consuming a power drink, then you may actually feel like it's helped. That can be a good reason to consume a beverage—*if* it doesn't add to your total calories. This is why label reading and understanding the roles of various kinds of drinks will be essential to your program—especially in the way you choose to balance salt and water before and during exercise.

THE ROLE OF HYDRATION

There's no question that your ability to sustain a run/walk—and particularly to increase your effort when you are ready—will be impaired with progressive dehydration. All runners lose heat during exercise, in part by the evaporation of water. Particularly in a dry environment, evaporation of sweat can account for more than 80 percent of heat loss from the body. Of course, as anyone who's been stuck in a crowd in July knows, sweat rates vary from person to person. But everyone loses the same things when they sweat: Besides water, you also lose considerable amounts of sodium (salt) and much smaller amounts of potassium and magnesium (which we'll talk about later). The important thing is to know your body and pay attention to early signs of dehydration, which include headache, fatigue, impaired concentration, and constipation—all of which can influence your ability to perform your workout. (More advanced signs of dehydration can include muscle cramping, nausea and vomiting, dizziness and confusion, and irritable behavior, and dehydration often requires medical attention.) Remember that these effects accumulate over time, so you won't go quickly from fully hydrated to being depleted of fluid, extremely dehydrated, and physically sick. As long as you monitor your fluid intake before, during, and after your run, you can easily avoid dehydration—while adding minimal or no calories. A general rule: Don't wait until you feel thirsty to drink when you're running, and that includes both before and after the activity. If you do, you have gone too long without drinking and put yourself at risk for dehydration. (These guidelines are different from the resting state, where thirst is the best indicator of fluid need.)

Of course, the rate of hydration (or dehydration) is directly related to weather changes, outside temperature, humidity, your selection of clothing, and your percentage of body fat. Don't ignore your body signals, and use the guidelines below to optimize your fluid intake and save calories.

WATER

Making up two-thirds of our bodies, water plays a crucial role in helping our bodies function. You can live for several weeks or longer without food, but only for a week or less without water. Water plays a role in almost every body function, including digestion, excretion, and cardiovascular activity, as well as acting as a carrier for water-soluble vitamins. Water carries nutrients to all body cells and is key to normal cellular function by aiding the normal flow of nutrients in the body, and waste products out of the body, for every cell in the body. It's also a source of hydration for the biggest organ we have—our skin. With this in mind, it's not surprising that dehydration can include both metabolic and behavioral changes, and the onset of a widespread set of reactions.

Following guidelines for water intake can be difficult, because the recommendations must be based on both external factors (temperature and humidity) and internal factors (activity level). On average, we lose about 500 milliliters (about 16 ounces) of liquid every day through daily activities like breathing and sweating in a nonexercising state. Our estimated daily water need, without activity, is at least 1,500 milliliters (50 ounces or six 8-ounce glasses). When it comes to losing weight, I recommend you cut out all the extra calories in sports drinks and stick with water. Water alone is the most appropriate fluid for any run/walk sessions of less than an hour. Surprised? Don't be. The body's mechanisms for fluid regulation are finely tuned, and there is no scientific evidence that a sports drink of water, salt, and added calories for energy will improve hydration for performance—or help you complete the activity and recover from it when you're done.

To ensure hydration, drink 8 to 10 ounces of water 2 to 3 hours before your run/walk. Then, drink another 6 to 12 ounces immediately before you start. Because many of us are slightly dehydrated in the resting state, we often forget to consume liquids of any type regularly. This pre-exercise water consumption will offset any possible fluid depletion you may have and not be aware of. (Important note: This is also an amount of water that will not produce "water intoxication"—meaning you have diluted your body's salt balance by adding too much water and not adjusting your salt intake. This condition of hyponatremia—low sodium levels—is not an issue for the everyday runner and is an issue only in the context of the elite runner.)

Your water intake during your run will vary depending upon your intensity, but you can use the following chart as a guideline to keeping yourself properly hydrated.

GENERAL GUIDELINES FOR WATER INTAKE FOR RUNNERS	
(NOTE: CHOOSE ANY CALORIE-FREE NONCARBONATED BEVERAGE.)	
2 to 3 hours before:	8 to 10 oz
Immediately before:	6 to 8 oz
During:	3 to 4 oz per 20 min or 1 mi (whatever comes first)
Immediately after:	8 to 10 oz

If water isn't your calorie-free beverage of choice, you can substitute any other calorie-free or ultra-low-calorie beverage. Use a guideline of 10 or fewer calories per 8-ounce serving. You also can take a low-calorie product with a higher calorie range—say, 40 to 50 calories per 8-ounce serving—and dilute it by half or more with water. This is more of a mental crutch for those who feel they need a flavored drink before activity. Your goal is to maximize the calories used for your run/walk to contribute to weight loss and to not offset your effort by hidden calories in beverages. Caffeine doesn't add calories, so you can add it if you prefer. If you are not a caffeine user, do not add it to help sustain your effort. (See the section on caffeine on page 116.)

SALTS

Body salts, or electrolytes, help maintain fluid balance in your organ systems. This balance is a highly regulated pathway to maintain the integrity and function of your body.

What drives those physiological functions is the concentration of electrolytes per unit of body fluid. It is not only the amount and type of electrolytes or fluid present in your body but their mix that will determine health benefits or risks. Your normal body function is driven by several major electrolytes, including sodium, potassium, and magnesium.

Because running produces salt loss as well as water loss, your body has natural, automatic mechanisms that kick in to balance salt and water concentrations when your body is challenged. A high body-salt content encourages fluid retention to reestablish the normal balance and dilute the salt content, while too much fluid stimulates salt appetite and/or increased fluid elimination in order to concentrate the blood volume. Like guidelines for water intake, the recommendations for electrolyte replacement after walking or running can vary tremendously with both the climate and your activity.

These electrolytes are also important in a variety of metabolic pathways, including nerve cell function in the brain, protein synthesis, carbohydrate synthesis and metabolism, and acid-base balance in the body. And these actions occur all over the body—at a single-cell level. The "sodium-potassium pump" creates impulses for normal cell activity; what's essential is the balance of these two electrolytes passing across each cell membrane. Because this balance is needed by every cell in the body, deficiencies in these salts can potentially produce effects ranging from muscle cramping to nervous system abnormalities to cardiac problems. For the moderate walker/runner exercising for less than 4 hours in a single session, the body can handle the small degree of electrolyte change without supplementation with products that contain electrolytes.

Of course, we're bombarded with sports drinks that claim to revitalize your energy and enhance your performance. While makers of these drinks don't tout the calories they contain, the makers focus on the electrolyte (salts) "balance" that you can benefit from during or after a walk or run. In truth, there's no need to replace any electrolytes in a single exercise session that's less than 3 or 4 hours—and that's especially true if you've recently had sodium in a meal. Salt balance is another area where the weight-loss runner has struggles. Seeking a high-salt (and usually high-fat) snack before running is like wearing both suspenders and a belt—it's redundant. You can pack in almost 400 calories from a bag of chips that is supposed to contain 2½ servings (even the little bags contain 150 calories). If you're craving a low-calorie source of salt before your run, try a pickle or two. Even for conditioned athletes, the sodium lost in sweat can be replaced simply with a meal or snack. Check out these comparisons, calorie-for-calorie:

One mini whole dill pickle: 290 milligrams of sodium, 5 calories

Two large celery stalks: 100 milligrams of sodium, 20 calories

17-ounce bottle Propel*: 150 milligrams of sodium, 21 calories

20-ounce bottle of Gatorade*: 275 milligrams of sodium, 150 calories

* For other brand names, read labels.

Magnesium and potassium—minerals lost in sweat—are both important for fluid balance and to avoid muscle cramping. But because the loss of these minerals by sweating is considered to be minimal even among conditioned athletes, you don't need to specifically replace them.

Although you may feel like you're oozing nutrients during your walk/run, the fact is that you're not. And maybe the reason you want to replenish your calories is that you want to find a health reason to do so—that if you feel like you're nourishing your body before or after a run or walk, you feel more justified in your caloric choices.

Mark, a recent college graduate, never had any trouble maintaining his weight—even during his first job after college. A runner, he logged 3 miles three times a week and admitted he really didn't worry about his eating. But he decreased his activity as he became more and more tethered to his sedentary job, working for many hours a day on the computer. He was comfortable with his running routine and lifted weights twice a week, but he found he was gaining weight slowly— about a pound a month—and he was about 6 pounds heavier than when he'd started his job 5 months earlier.

This creeping weight gain disturbed him. Rather than pretend it wasn't happening, he decided to attack it head-on. His activity level was stable, robust, and—most importantly—he did not want to add more running. So we focused on his eating and where he could eliminate some calories. Surprisingly, Mark made good choices but noticed he rewarded himself with high-calorie, salty treats before a run, convincing himself that he needed both the carbohydrate energy and the salt to maintain energy balance. He thought he was careful in his choice, selecting a single-serve snack bag containing 150 calories. We solved his problem by substituting two large dill pickles. They satisfied the crunch and salt Mark was looking for, but with far fewer calories—a 120-calorie daily savings. The change resulted in a pound-a-month loss, with no further changes in his food intake.

The bottom line? Nutritionally, sodium is the most important electrolyte for recovery after exercise, but there's no convincing evidence to support that you need to replace any other salt, including potassium and magnesium, with respect to exercise. So, if you are choosing a salty snack—whether it is chips, pretzels, or nuts—to help maintain your energy during your run, save those calories. They don't support endurance or recovery, and they're unnecessary for the recreational runner with a single walk/run session of less than 3 or 4 hours. The best rule is to examine the color of your urine as an indicator of fluid balance. Pale yellow (the color of lemonade) or lighter indicates adequate hydration. A medium-to-dark yellow indicates fluid loss, particularly if the volume of output is low. This is a sign that your body is conserving body fluid and not "wasting" it through elimination. This signals a need for water soon—before biological signs of dehydration set in.

SPORTS DRINKS

You've probably seen enough "ade" commercials to know how effective the marketing is for sports drinks. And I think a lot of our perceived dependence on sports drinks before exercise is based on that marketing and our psychological needs. Somehow, we all feel that those green, blue, red, and purple drinks will give us the energy we need to improve our performance. Water just seems weak by comparison. But really, the only thing sports drinks will absolutely give us is unwanted calories.

When it comes to losing weight, these calories, which are supposedly designed to give you energy, are only a mental crutch, and—in order to meet your weight-loss goal—you need to eliminate them from your program. If you are monitoring your eating and are walking/running multiple times a week but cannot lose any weight, examine your fluid consumption before exercise. Almost every non-loser consumes 20 ounces or more of sports beverage before activity, not realizing this can be a significant source of calories.

Because there's no evidence that you need anything but water for hydration and there's no reason to replace electrolytes for exercise under 1 hour, there's no reason to make a mistake that will ruin your workouts. Consuming those calories before and/or after a run wipes out all the positive effect of doing that run in the first place. The net caloric effect is just the same as sitting on the couch and not doing anything. In Chapter 4 is a list of pre- and postactivity snacks—real food to prepare and replenish your energy and real nutritional needs. Most products promoted to runners are really for those people doing extreme endurance events and sustained running/walking. Liquid carbohydrate sources (like Gu) have 100 calories in just a 1-ounce squeeze, and more popular sports drinks are a mix of carbohydrates, electrolytes, vitamins, and minerals. We'll examine more of the vitamins and supplements in the next chapter, but take a look at the summary on page 112, where the calories are laid out per serving for some of the more popular drinks often recommended as enhancement beverages before and during exercise. If you feel such drinks do enhance your performance, then select one. But limit your consumption to 6 to 8 ounces, diluting the drink with water to make up the 20-ounce volume, unless you are choosing a low-calorie option. Remember, most of these drinks list 8 ounces as being one serving on the label and provide the drink in a "single-serving" 20-ounce bottle—which is really 2½ servings. Choose your sports drinks carefully and you will enjoy a considerable caloric savings without compromising your ability to run or walk. Although they're a popular choice with many people, I don't recommend 100 percent juices, because of their higher sugar and calorie content, which also can cause cramping or other stomach disturbances unless they are diluted at least by half with water.

Drink	Calories per 8-oz Serving	Calories per 20-oz Bottle
Propel	10	21 (*17-oz bottle)
Vitamin Water	50	150
Powerade	60	150
Gatorade	60	150
Allsport	80	200
SoBe	110	275
100% fruit juice	110	275

Although the extra vitamins and minerals added to these drinks aren't harmful, they haven't been shown to enhance your health, and for most of you, most of the time, the calories aren't worth ingesting. When you are trying to lose weight, every calorie is important—and reducing calories by avoiding most sports drinks is a major savings not only in calories but in cost. Think of the extra fruits and vegetables you can have when you choose not to spend those calories on these products. If you like the idea of this, and don't mind spending money without significant calories, Propel, containing small amounts of sucrose, or other waters containing no calorie sweeteners, like Fruit$_2$0, are better choices. You can also make your own sports drink, using water and a squeeze of fresh lemon or lime. If you simply aren't willing to substitute a lower-calorie choice, then take your beverage of choice and dilute it by half or more with water.

SALT AND WATER GUIDELINES FOR INTENSE EXERCISE: 1 HOUR OR MORE

For intensive exercisers who run for more than an hour, the same fluid guidelines apply, but I do recommend a sports drink. There's abundant evidence that a carbohydrate source can reduce muscle fatigue and enhance your endurance during activities longer than an hour. Consuming a sports drink containing 4 to 8 percent carbohydrate at a rate of about 24 to 30 ounces an hour is a good guideline to sustain muscle energy and avoid cramping and fatigue. Sodium is also recommended at an amount of about 100 milligrams per 8 ounces of replacement fluid—a fact that is less important for a 90-minute run when the rate of fluid depletion is lower, compared with an activity lasting 3 or more hours. It's that sustained activity at the 3-hour mark or more during which your body can lose significant fluid and sodium, and that's where you need steady replacement to avoid muscle exhaustion and mental changes, including confusion and irritability.

As described above, most sports drinks meet these recommendations. (Or you can make your own sports drink by taking 20 ounces of water and adding 3 tablespoons of sugar and ⅛ teaspoon of salt. This mix approximates the standard sports drink, providing 6 percent carbohydrate and 300 milligrams of sodium per 8-ounce serving.) Look for the fewest calories per serving to maximize the calories you'll save. And remember to drink more than you need to take away thirst after your run. Thirst generally is not great enough to encourage you to replace enough fluids. Competitive runners are losing measurable water, reflected in a declining body weight, and the need to make up for this must be met both during and after the run. By the way, you should avoid the impulse to jump on the scale after a run. You'll likely lose 1 to 3 pounds in water weight from a long run. Many people choose not to drink, thinking they will enjoy the weight loss, as temporary as it may be. Make sure you drink fluid at regular intervals.

SPECIAL NEEDS: RESPONDING TO WEATHER CHANGES

Although it's a good idea to maintain regularity and structure in your run or walk to enhance your weight-loss effort, you may need to modify or downscale your efforts based on outside conditions, depending on things like temperature and air quality. Be prepared to walk or run indoors to keep up with your schedule if needed.

Hot and humid weather: The major dangers of extremely hot weather include dehydration, heat exhaustion, and heatstroke. These risks increase when the humidity is above 70 percent and the temperature is higher than 70, because these conditions interfere with your body's natural cooling process. When the humidity is high, you can't lose enough heat by evaporation and can be at risk even if you are drinking more. If the temperature and humidity are extremely high or you feel uncomfortable when you walk outside, don't risk it. Or reduce your exertion to fit the weather: Walk instead of run, allowing extra time for your activity. Or reduce your duration at the same intensity.

Remember that if the outside temperature is greater than your body temperature (around 98°F), body heat cannot be dissipated into the environment. Even worse, if it's humid outside, sweat cannot be absorbed or "wicked" by the environment and simply drips down your body, which is not a means of body cooling.

A few simple guidelines can help.

When dressing, think light: Wear ultra-lightweight, light-colored, and loose-fitting clothing; avoid cotton, which will stay wet during your run; and try nylon, spandex, CoolMax, or polyester blends instead.

Avoid rubberized clothing, which will make you sweat excessively, in order to try to provide a false sense of weight loss. This is particularly risky in hot weather.

Be flexible: Decrease intensity or duration in the heat.

Drink at least 6 to 8 ounces of water every 15 minutes; don't wait until you feel thirsty.

Be aware of the symptoms associated with dehydration or heat exertion (see the table below). If one of these strikes, get out of the heat, drink liquids, and rest until the symptoms are gone.

WARNING SIGNS OF FLUID AND SALT PROBLEMS IN SEVERE WEATHER	
Hot-Weather Symptoms (Hyperthermia: high body temp)	Cold-Weather Symptoms (Hypothermia: low body temp)
Warm, dry skin with no sweating	Lack of coordination
Cold, clammy skin with sweating	Mental confusion
Low blood pressure	Slowed reactions
Confusion	Shivering
High fever	Sleepiness
Slow pulse	Reluctance to keep moving
Ashen, gray skin	

Cold weather: The change of seasons is a great time to vary your run/walk routine, particularly as you feel the urge to get into hibernation mode as the weather turns colder. However, most of us are unaccustomed to the physical stress that cold weather (say, 10°F to 40°F) places on the body. The same caution for high temperature applies when the temperature drops. Although the risk of dehydration is much higher in hot environments, dehydration is not uncommon in cold weather, and cold, dry environments can increase your need for water. Sometimes, extra layers of clothes can cause you to sweat more than you expect, which increases your need for hydration. Even in cold weather, pay attention to your fluid needs, and don't assume your hydration needs are less important because it's colder. If anything, hydration is more important. Besides risking dehydration when the weather drops, you can be at risk for hypothermia— that's low body temperature that occurs when you are unable to produce enough energy to keep your core temperature warm enough. When in doubt, stay inside to run on the treadmill or take a walk in the mall.

Altitude changes: Those running or walking at altitudes of greater than 8,000 feet have a greater need for fluid because of increased urination and extra water loss through breathing (which is an adaptive response of the body to the lower oxygen content of the atmosphere). If you're running or walking in such an environment, say on vacation, increase your fluid intake—at least 24 ounces more than your typical intake—to ensure adequate hydration and normal kidney function.

CAFFEINE

Several studies have correlated caffeine with increases in performance in competitive, conditioned runners. This isn't to suggest you should guzzle caffeine-containing beverages before a run or walk, but rather to suggest that if you do, there is a long, safe history of caffeine use in athletic performance. What does this mean for the average runner trying to lose weight? It simply means that among all the beverages available with few or no calories, the presence or absence of caffeine doesn't need to be a factor in your choice. The amount of caffeine found in typical beverages—50 to 150 milligrams—will not be a deterrent to your run or walk, and might give you a modest boost in energy, depending on your previous caffeine use.

But if you do use caffeine, *do not* use caffeine supplements (including products advertised to help you "stay alert") either as a metabolic booster for running or as a thermogenic (heat-producing) agent for weight loss. More caffeine does not mean better. Caffeine has a number of side effects, including insomnia, headaches, and stomach irritation. It's also a diuretic at higher doses, so you shouldn't use it as a supplement. However, a cup of coffee or tea before a run will not cause increased urination.

Recommendations for a healthy lifestyle suggest a daily caffeine intake of around 300 milligrams per day (or that found in 3 cups of coffee, 6 cups of tea, or 5 cups of diet soda). Caffeine can be a part of your daily diet, as it is a natural flavor enhancer. If you are ingesting more than 300 milligrams per day, you may need to reevaluate your needs. The less caffeine you ingest, the greater your physiological response when you do consume it.

Beverage	Caffeine Content (mg per 8 oz)
Brewed coffee	80–150
Espresso	80–90
Instant coffee	50–70
Soda	25–50
Tea	20–50

Tina, who thought she would have to give up her morning coffee when she wanted to lose weight, had the mistaken idea that caffeine was a bad compound. And she was surprised when I recommended that she have her large mug of regular coffee with skim milk and a glass of water before her 2-mile run 4 days a week. Tina needed a "jump start" before her run, but wasn't ready for breakfast at 6:30 a.m. Her coffee and water gave her the hydration and mild stimulation she was seeking. Upon her return 35 minutes later and after another glass of water and a shower, Tina was ready to face the day with a modest breakfast. She also replaced her second cup with decaffeinated coffee to maximize the energizing boost from caffeine in the early morning, when she needed it most—and would physiologically have the greatest response.

CARBONATION

Discussing fluids without discussing carbonation would be like discussing New York without discussing the Yankees. Carbonation is an issue I leave totally up to the preference of the individual. As Tommy told me, "I gag on anything flat. I don't even like water." Tommy was perfectly free to drink carbonated water, and so are you. Feel free to let your low-calorie soda go flat if you don't like the fizz. A carbonated drink will provide no detriment to your run/walk. The only downside is that drinking a larger (12 ounces or more) volume of carbonated fluids might produce bloating, which could prevent you from consuming enough fluid for your run. If you notice this, switch to noncarbonated (or flat) calorie-free or ultra-low-calorie beverages before your walk or run.

ALCOHOL

Can alcohol be part of your lifestyle program to lose weight? My answer is simple: It can be, if it is a part of your lifestyle that you can manage without overconsumption. Remember, the calories in fluid aren't sensed by the body very well, meaning that your body and brain often ignore the calories in alcohol, resulting in an awful lot of caloric waste. If you can accept the 100 to 150 calories per ounce in alcohol and limit your intake to one serving a day maximum, then the answer is yes, you can have alcohol. If you plan to use alcohol as a tool to rehydrate after a run, then the answer is no. I recall a chat with Oscar, who had a great rationale for his two beers after his three-times-weekly run with his best friend. The two would meet after work, walk/run 3 miles in 35 minutes, and then return to catch up on their week at Oscar's house before going on to their respective family activities. Oscar thought he was doing a healthy thing with his beer consumption: rehydrating after a run, and replenishing carbohydrates. When Oscar realized that beer was a poor source of carbohydrates for restoration, and also acted as a diuretic, he rethought his choice. Oscar compromised with one beer and one large glass of water. He saved 150 calories on his activity days and agreed he felt much better with the change. Oscar saved 450 calories a week, which spurred him on to make some other easy changes in his weight-loss quest.

Alcohol contains 7 calories per gram—almost as many as fat (9 calories per gram), and almost twice as much as protein and carbohydrates (4 calories per gram). If you want alcohol to be a part of your caloric intake, you must plan and count these calories. And remember, the lack of inhibition that can sometimes accompany alcohol consumption can weaken your resolve when tempted by an order of cheese fries. For many runners, it's easier to restrict alcohol calories, because, in the words of Helene, "it's not worth wasting the calories. I'd rather eat." As with so many other concepts in weight loss, it's important not to fool yourself. Alcohol is neither a source of rehydration nor a source of carbohydrates for refueling, but it doesn't have to be eliminated if you use it wisely.

CALORIES IN ALCOHOLIC BEVERAGES

Beverage	Calories per Drink
Beer	150
Light beer	80–120
Wine	100–120
Hard liquor (1 oz) (gin, scotch, bourbon)	90–110
Wine cooler	200
Rum and cola	200
Rum and diet cola	100
Strawberry margarita	300
Mai tai	350

CHAPTER 7

DIETARY SUPPLEMENTS

> When it comes to nutritional supplements, less is always more

Depending on whom you ask, dietary supplements can mean lots of different things to different people. This is partly because we have no standard definition for them and partly because the term "supplements" envelops a whole class of ingredients, nutrients, vitamins, minerals, and other substances that are meant to serve many functions in our bodies. But to me, the really scary part is not only how vague the definition of supplement is but also how little we really know individually about them. When I ask my patients if they take any dietary supplements, they look at me like they're looking at piece of art—curious and not quite sure how to interpret it. Daisy, a 36-year-old self-described former runner who hasn't run in 10 years, told me she didn't take supplements because she doesn't believe in them. But in discussing her need for calcium and vitamins, she chimed in, "Oh, vitamins and minerals. I take those. I didn't realize they counted as supplements."

On the other hand, there are people like Roberto, who filled a large shopping bag with all of his supplements. They ranged from individual vitamins to "fat burners" and "antiaging" compounds. "I'm trying to lose weight," he explained, "so I need to make up all the missing nutrients now." But the most frequent response from the walkers/runners trying to lose weight is the same one I received from Tara: "Oh, yes, I have a great multiple vitamin and mineral supplement at home, but I haven't taken it for a while."

We all have different views about supplements (if we view them at all), but the goal in this chapter is to help you choose supplements that will help you meet your nutritional needs, but by *simplifying your supplement intake.* When it comes to supplements, more is not necessarily better.

I define a dietary supplement as any compound not consumed as part of food ingestion, but having its origins from a dietary source.

Before 1994, federal guidelines reasonably assured us that most over-the-counter supplements were contaminant free and that the health claims were supported by valid scientific data. But with the introduction of the Dietary Supplement Health and Education Act of 1994, all of this changed. Congress allowed any compound—as long as it originated from a dietary source—to be sold to the public without any federal regulation of compound purity, safety, strength, or efficacy. How did this happen? In part, this may be because trying to assemble a definition for a dietary supplement was confusing. When information was circulating to the public that the government was planning on regulating the "dietary supplement industry," many people interpreted this as regulating vitamins and minerals, which were the only dietary supplements generally known to a large sec-

DIETARY SUPPLEMENTS

To check for the latest information, go to www.consumerlab.com for a complete comparison and review of all the dietary supplements described in this chapter.

tion of the population. In fact, reports at the time showed that Congress was flooded with more mail from distressed consumers opposing regulation than regarding any other issue since the Vietnam War. So Congress decided to back off, and the effect was that a cottage industry of supplements popped up everywhere. These supplements were marketed to target every conceivable problem: hair loss, loss of energy, weight gain, and impotence. At best, many of these supplements are a waste of money. At worst, they can cause significant illness or even death.

You need to be a well-informed consumer to weed through the hype and undocumented oversell that can be damaging to runners (current or new) and calorie counters. In fact, for those of us looking for help in both weight control and running, the field of supplements can be a double danger. Claims that sound too good to be true—like burn fat, increase endurance, lose weight while you sleep—usually are. To help you sort through the enormous variety of products available, this chapter divides them into three sections:

1. Micronutrients (vitamins and minerals)
2. Macronutrients (carbohydrates, protein, fat)
3. All others

These three represent either products that are from the food supply (groups one and two) or products found somewhere in nature but not necessarily in foods (group three). Some vitamins and minerals and other supplements *can* support your weight loss and walk/run efforts when used in reasonable quantities to support a healthy lifestyle and food plan. But there's a big world of supplements out there—from your drugstore to the health-food store—and it's important for you to know how to evaluate a product's claims. Use the following four-step approach—which I'll explain in detail throughout the chapter—in evaluating your supplement needs while you are losing or maintaining weight and exercising.

1. Make sure you have no deficiencies in your vitamin and mineral intake. This is the most important way to ensure optimal muscle function and performance in relation to what you eat, particularly when you are reducing caloric intake. *Take a daily multiple vitamin/mineral supplement containing 100 percent of the Reference Daily Intake (RDI).*

2. Understand that most dietary supplements are untested regarding their health claims. *Investigate health claims and compound purity and dosage before considering use.*

3. Know that for supplements that have been tested scientifically, studies have been done in trained athletes. Some effects are substantial, but many are debatable and not supported by medical data. *Give these supplements a try if you feel they contribute to your effort, but they are not required for weight loss or improved performance.*

4. Be wary of product hype and be an informed consumer: Always question and validate product purity and testing. *Always look for the*

USP symbol or at least a toll-free number for more information. Don't put your health at risk. All supplements are not the same when it comes to purity and safety.

VITAMINS AND MINERALS: THE BASICS

Vitamins and minerals are both essential to normal chemical actions in every body cell. They are called "cofactors" to chemical reactions, which are driven by proteins called enzymes. Enzymes convert, build up, and break down nutrients to support all physiologic pathways of every body system. Each enzyme, depending on its function, has different requirements for cofactors. So each vitamin or mineral serves a specific and unique purpose for a specific metabolic pathway. This is why any deficiencies in specific vitamins and minerals produce quite different signs and symptoms, depending on which metabolic pathway is impaired without a sufficient supply.

When it comes to choosing a vitamin, you need to do a reality check of your eating, activity, and other health needs. The best recommendation for anyone is to take a daily multiple vitamin-mineral supplement containing 100 percent of the RDI set by the federal government. These recommendations are based on the summaries of separate scientific review committees that have evaluated all of the available literature on the risks and benefits of individual vitamins and minerals, and it is an unbiased and accurate representation of adequate intake for most adults. Especially as you regulate caloric intake, it becomes exceedingly difficult to ensure that you have 100 percent of all of the nutrients you need each day. Even those following the most nutritious diets will want to ensure dietary adequacy with a daily supplement.

Contrary to what many people may think, there's no particular advantage to taking a costly vitamin and mineral supplement. Make a choice based on content—focusing on completeness of the product. And remember, more of a particular vitamin in a multivitamin doesn't mean it's better. Here's why: There are two types of vitamins, from the chemical point of view: water soluble and fat soluble (see the table on page 128). Water-soluble vitamins carry a low risk for excess, because any extra vitamins not used by the body are dissolved in water and eliminated in the urine. On the other hand, your body retains fat-soluble vitamins and stores them in the liver, a body organ that sequesters fat. As of now, it's unclear what long-term effects high doses of these vitamins have on body functions, so less is always more when it comes to fat-soluble vitamins.

While we are all at a nutritional risk of not getting enough vitamins and minerals when we're cutting calories, some people have a greater need for particular vitamins and minerals. If you are taking prescription medications, are following a vegetarian diet, or have food restrictions due to allergies, you may have increased vitamin and mineral needs. Check with your primary care doctor or other health professional (not the health-food store) for specific advice. Use the following checklist to evaluate your needs.

1. Look for 100 percent RDI of vitamins and minerals in one capsule (less is okay; more is trouble). Everyone losing or maintaining weight should take a daily supplement.

2. Determine your iron need after a visit to your doctor. Avoid iron-containing products except if you are a premenopausal woman (see the special needs section on page 129) or if your doctor determines

you have a special need. Healthy men and postmenopausal women do not need iron supplementation, and including extra iron can put you in danger of iron overload.

3. Take a separate calcium supplement (see the special needs section on page 129). Natural does not mean better (except for vitamin E, where even that change is negligible), because your body doesn't recognize the difference between vitamins made in a factory and vitamins extracted from a food or plant source. "Natural" products are more expensive, but there's no need to spend the extra money.

5. Ignore the terms "chelation" (bound to other compounds) or "no sugar added" (the amount of sugar added to vitamins is negligible). They don't contribute to any health benefit.

6. Don't buy "mega" amounts of vitamins or minerals. Some interactions can block absorption of one or the other ingredients. Even 5 to 10 times the recommended dosage can make a difference. High vitamin C intake can interfere with the absorption of vitamin B_{12}, while copper absorption can be blocked by too much zinc intake.

7. National brands and most supermarket brands are usually equivalent in content and are best choices. Look for the "USP" label on the bottle, indicating standardized manufacturing standards by the US Pharmacopeia.

8. To avoid stomach upset, take your daily supplement with food.

9. Most important: Take your multivitamin every day. Inconsistency is the single biggest mistake you can make with vitamin and mineral supplementation. Choose a time you can reliably remember and stick to it.

GUIDELINES TO 100 PERCENT RDA (RECOMMENDED DIETARY ALLOWANCES) AND UL (UPPER LIMIT) OF VITAMINS AND TRACE MINERALS

	100%	UL**
FAT-SOLUBLE VITAMINS (EXCESS IS ABSORBED AND STORED IN BODY FAT AND BRAIN)		
Vitamin A	3,000 IU	10,000 IU
Vitamin D	400 IU	2,000 IU
Vitamin E	30 IU	1,000 IU
Vitamin K	120 micrograms (mcg)	Not determined
WATER-SOLUBLE VITAMINS (EXCESS IS ELIMINATED IN THE URINE)		
Vitamin B_1 (thiamin)	1.2 mg	Not determined
Vitamin B_2 (riboflavin)	1.3 mg	Not determined
Vitamin B_6	1.3 mg	100 mg
Vitamin B_{12}	2.4 mcg	Not determined
Niacin	16 mg	35 mg
Vitamin C	90 mg	2,000 mg
Folic acid	400 mcg	1,000 mg
MINERALS		
Calcium*	1,000 mg	2,500 mg
Iron*	18 mcg	45 mcg
Phosphorus	700 mg	4,000 mg
Magnesium	400 mg	Not determined
Iodine	150 mcg	1,100 mcg
Zinc	11 mg	40 mg
Selenium	55 mcg	400 mcg
Copper	0.9 mg	10 mg
Molybdenum	45 mcg	2,000 mcg

*Special needs discussed below (source: Institute of Medicine).

** The upper limit is an estimate only, and the true level of excess is not presently known for any of the vitamins or minerals. The estimate may be lower or higher than the number presented.

VITAMINS AND MINERALS: SPECIAL NEEDS

Calcium. When many people start to lose weight, the first category they cut (after the appetizer sampler) is dairy products. In fact, the drop in milk consumption is particularly robust among high school girls trying to lose weight and not "waste" calories from milk or other dairy products. Unfortunately, many adults also take this view. Anne, a walker who was stalled with 20 pounds to lose, said she can live without it. "I'd rather eat other things, and save calories here." I agree that for many, dietary calcium is a struggle to consume, but it cannot be ignored, because of its role in maintaining and strengthening bone density. While calcium needs vary with age (see chart below), at least half of your intake should come from a dietary source. That's because it's not just the calcium that promotes bone health but also the milk solids (the stuff that makes the milk white). Choose a calcium supplement with the RDI for vitamin D if you aren't taking your calcium with your daily vitamin, to optimize calcium absorption. If you can't tolerate dairy products, try nondairy calcium-fortified foods. Choose a 500-milligram dose—whether as a chewable tablet or capsule—and aim for one with the RDI of vitamin D to promote absorption. If your supplement does not contain vitamin D, take it with your daily multivitamin. The effect is the same. If you're convinced that you cannot meet your calcium requirements with one supplement, take a second, but at a different time of day, to optimize absorption.

AGE GROUP	DAILY CALCIUM RECOMMENDATION
18 or under	1,300 mg
19–51	1,000–1,200 mg
51+	1,200–1,500 mg
Women who are nursing, pregnant, or thinking about getting pregnant	1,200–1,500 mg

CALCIUM-CONTAINING FOODS AND SUPPLEMENTS
FOR CALORIE WATCHERS

Food	Calcium (mg) per Serving	Calories per Serving
Fat-free yogurt (8 oz)	450	100
Fat-free milk (8 oz)	300	90
Low-fat cheese (1 oz)	270	70
Light tofu (½ cup)	260	100
Supplements	**Calcium (mg) per Tablet**	**Calories per Tablet**
Calcium carbonate		
Tums (no vitamin D)	500	—
Oscal (with vitamin D)	500	—
Viactiv (with vitamin D)	500	20
Calcium citrate		
Citrical (with vitamin D)	630	—

Iron: While many people believe that fatigue or lack of energy is related solely to iron intake, others think iron can help them boost their energy. The only way to determine your iron adequacy, at first, is to have a blood test measuring circulating iron in blood components (hemoglobin and hematocrit) and blood iron stores (ferritin). Check with your doctor before making any changes in your iron intake. For the majority of people, no supplementation is needed, and sufficient iron is consumed via dietary sources. Premenopausal women are often at increased risk of anemia, due to monthly blood loss, and *do* need an iron-containing multivitamin. For men over 21 and postmenopausal women who have normal blood patterns, iron supplementation is generally discouraged. Regardless of your age and gender, you may be at risk for iron deficiency if you are a vegan (eat no meat, fish, or fowl), have food allergies, or take medication that can interfere with iron absorption. Check with your doctor to evaluate your situation. If you suffer from unusual fatigue that does not disappear with adequate sleep, or if you become fatigued after reducing your caloric intake, see your doctor. Anemia is unusual in the exercising calorie watcher, but must be monitored, particularly at the start of a plan. Overloading on iron has been linked to an increased risk of cardiovascular illness.

VITAMINS AND MINERALS: DO WE NEED SUPERDOSES?

Some runners use vitamins and minerals not in doses to round out nutritional deficiencies but in pharmacological doses (many times as high as in found in foods) as performance enhancers. In using these *nutraceuticals,* many conditioned and professional athletes look at vitamins and minerals for two specific reasons. Reason (1): Vitamins and minerals can act as antioxidants to counteract the negative effects of cellular respiration. When muscle cells use energy, they release fragments called "free radicals," which are produced when muscle is in a metabolically active (called oxidative) phase. The production of these free radicals is sometimes linked to postexercise soreness. Antioxidants theoretically should be able to block the production of such fragments and prevent this soreness. Reason (2): Vitamins and minerals may optimize immune function and reduce susceptibility to upper-respiratory illness. This body of evidence is directed to the highly conditioned athlete and has very little relevance to everyday runners. I am including this short summary because I am frequently asked about the benefits of high vitamin and mineral intake for both running and weight loss.

Antioxidants: The vitamins with antioxidant properties are A, C, E, and beta-carotene (a relative of vitamin A). Their biological actions counteract the negative effects of "free radicals," the compounds produced when muscles are oxidizing. Some studies have attributed this oxidation to the onset of muscle soreness. However, there's no convincing data showing that increasing the amount of antioxidant intake in humans will enhance performance. There have been some limited studies in animals, but they haven't translated when tested in people. In fact, there may be a negative health effect of mega-dosing on antioxidant vitamins. High levels of antioxidants can shift the balance within the muscle cell itself, creating a different change in biochemical balance, called a "reduced state" (the opposite of oxidation). That shift can impair muscle contraction function and exercise performance. Simply put, shifting the balance too far in either direction can influence the way muscle cells perform.

Immune response: Competition and training can lead to impaired immune response in the conditioned athlete and increased susceptibility to upper-respiratory tract infections. It is well known that several vitamins and minerals are essential to normal immune function, including A, C, and E (the antioxidants) and B_6, B_{12}, and zinc. Correcting deficiencies can have a beneficial effect on immune function, but there is no convincing or consistent evidence that ingesting extra supplements will improve immune response or help running performance, even for the conditioned runner. The best course is to include 100 percent of vitamins' and minerals' RDI on a daily basis, which is challenge enough.

Fiber: You don't have to have a raisin bran endorsement contract to know the benefits of fiber: It helps lower cholesterol, manage blood sugar, and improve colon health. There are two types of fiber: *soluble* and *insoluble*. Both are undigested (not absorbed), leaving the body

WEIGHT-LOSS SUPPLEMENTS—STAY AWAY!

You must avoid all supplements promising weight loss. It's tempting to be lured by the product information promising weight loss without effort, especially because some of the explanations sound very scientific and medical. But the medical concepts are often taken from the scientific literature and attributed to the product, which, although not ethical, is not illegal. As with all other non-FDA-approved dietary supplements, there is no guarantee of purity, safety, or efficiency with weight-loss supplements.

relatively intact (almost no calories absorbed!). Soluble fiber (dissolvable in water) forms a gel when mixed with body fluids, while insoluble (nondissolvable in water) doesn't gel and is eliminated by the digestive track untouched.

However, many people still persist in taking a dietary supplement when trying to save calories, instead of consuming it in the diet. "It's too bloating for me and interferes with my running," said Virginia. "I can take a fiber supplement and forget about it, and can time my intake for my run." Many people like Virginia have tried to bulk up on dietary fiber very quickly. True, a high-fiber meal might produce bloating that will interfere with a walk or run, but there's no reason for this to happen. Try to think of fiber as part of your dietary intake, and not use a supplement. It can help your weight-loss effort and enhance your sense of well-being.

Soluble fiber binds fatty acids and slows the rate at which your stomach empties food, which helps in weight loss. When there's food in the stomach, you minimize the physical signs of hunger, prolonging your contentment. Best sources of soluble fiber to limit calories are oats and oat bran, fruits, and vegetables.

Insoluble fiber is a bulking agent and moves food through the intestine, absorbing water and promoting regular bowel movements and preventing constipation. Best sources of insoluble fiber to limit calories are whole wheat products, corn bran, fruits, and vegetables.

Aim for 20 to 25 grams of fiber a day from a dietary source. If you struggle with this amount, consider a fiber supplement, but don't replace the dietary sources. Increase your intake slowly—no more than 5 grams every few days—and make sure you drink plenty of water, whether you are consuming your fiber in foods or getting it from a supplement. You need a lot of fluid to make sure the fiber keeps moving through your digestive tract. Too little fluid can cause gas, bloating, and stomach distension—all unpleasant side effects.

SUPPLEMENT USE FOR PERFORMANCE: PREVENTING MUSCLE FATIGUE

Metabolically, exercise depletes muscle glycogen (another term for stored carbohydrate) and depletes muscle ATP, the energy source that drives muscles. It is also associated with a drop in what's called "phosphocreatine"—the compound that puts the P in ATP. This section provides a short summary of why conditioned athletes try so many supplements, and how those supplements relate to muscle metabolism. While the goal for elite athletes is to go farther and faster and recover quicker, the recreational athletes try to do the same thing on a smaller scale while trying to lose weight. As you'll see, there's really little scientific support for a lot of supplement claims. The main goal is to prevent yourself from dropping below the requirement intake level. If at some point in the future, you become or return to being an elite runner, you may want to consider a supplement. For now, simplest is best.

Carbohydrates: Because muscle glycogen can be depleted during exercise, muscle function can be impaired when the depletion is severe.

Ingested carbohydrates are rapidly digested and appear to spare the internal body from pools of carbohydrate stores, somehow preventing falloff in muscle performance. Having spikes of energy has been the downfall of so many runners when it comes to losing weight. Of course, you must "carb-load" to prevent fatigue and enhance performance under conditions of extended activity (less than 1 hour), but you typically overeat in your attempt to protect your muscle function. This concept of glycogen depletion is true for the conditioned athlete who is exercising for more than an hour at a time. Scientifically, carbohydrates are burned very slowly during the first hour of exercise (20 grams per hour), but the rate of use later triples (60 grams per hour). So, it's okay to replace carbohydrate sources (not just fluid) beyond 1 hour of exercise. Some sources are metabolized at high rates (including glucose, sucrose, maltose, maltodextrins) of up to 1 gram per minute, while others (fructose, galactose, amylase starch) are oxidized at a 25 to 50 percent slower rate. If you are exercising for longer than 1 hour at moderate intensity (unable to carry on a conversation), add a product like Gatorade, Powerade, or a similar product (a 20-ounce bottle) for every hour you exercise. This will provide the necessary mix of carbohydrates needed to sustain muscle glycogen and avoid fatigue. At this point, it is not consuming too many calories and is not a mental crutch but a physiological reality to sustain your best effort.

However, there's no evidence that a supplement to replace carbohydrates will improve performance or add anything other than extra calories for the walker/runner engaging in activity for less than an hour. Realistically, we can suffice just fine with a noncalorie fluid. Calorie-wise, this is the best way to cut out calories for which we have more of a mental dependence than a physical one.

Monica, who enjoyed her walk/run of 2 miles 5 days a week, wanted to lose 12 pounds. Her plan was to cut out some calories that "didn't hurt." She began keeping food logs and was surprised to see that she consumed an energy gel (100 calories) as part of her prerun ritual. "It helps me stay charged," she said. Monica was amazed to learn that just 1 ounce of the sports gel contained 100 calories. Easily digestible or not, these were calories Monica was willing to eliminate as long as her performance was not affected. When I explained the biological realities of glycogen depletion, Monica was willing to try her run without this supplement, substituting a large glass of water with a squirt of lime juice. "I only started this because my old roommate told me this was important to avoid muscle fatigue. I didn't even know what an energy gel was before that," she said. Her performance was the same, and Monica agreed that her dependence on the supplement was only psychological, because it made her feel more like a runner.

AMINO ACIDS (PROTEIN)

Protein powders: Many walkers and runners agree that the aerobic and fitness component of a walk/run is of great benefit but is not the optimal way to build muscle tone. Many people mistakenly try to bulk up using protein powders, thinking that to make more muscle, you need to eat more protein. For recreational athletes, nothing could be further from the truth. First, with the 50-25-25 plan, 25 percent of your total calories will be coming from dietary protein. That will more than cover your protein needs (0.8 grams per kilogram of body weight). Avoid the dense calories of total protein powders. There is no evidence that these supplements do anything for you other than add unneeded calories. In fact, even competitive athletes generally get adequate levels of protein through diet alone.

Amino acids: Although little evidence supports that supplemental total protein provides a benefit, a newer body of literature suggests that certain amino acids might benefit the conditioned athlete. Amino acids, most often referred to as the "building blocks of protein," are the foundation of muscle protein, body enzymes, and some brain neurotransmitters. But the role of amino acids for the runner is quite a bit different. For the elite runner, certain amino acids are the actual energy source for muscles and can help prevent glycogen depletion and save these stores while amino acids are utilized. Whether this applies to the recreational runner/walker is unclear, but this is an active and exciting area of study.

A group of amino acids—*leucine, isoleucine,* and *valine* (called branched-chain amino acids)—are different from other amino acids, because they're metabolized in muscle tissue and not in the liver like the 17 other amino acids. For this reason, muscle utilizes the branched-chain amino acids for energy and muscle repair. When these amino acids are broken down, they're funneled directly into the muscle energy pathway to increase production of ATP (remember, that's the energy component of muscle). As with all other energy substrates, these amino acids can be depleted during intense exercise. Replenishing these specific amino acids before and during exercise may help prevent muscle fatigue and improve performance. This is the case for elite athletes. Two other amino acids—*glutamine* and *arginine*—are also important in supporting the continuous supply of these amino acids for muscle energy.

Amino acids on the market contain all kinds of combinations for muscle metabolism, but it's still unclear whether these dietary supplements will help the moderate walker/runner. The scientific explanation makes sense, but there are no studies yet to support the supplementation of amino acids specifically in the moderate athlete. As with all dietary supplements, there's also no guarantee of amino acid purity in *most* available products. If you want to consider this option, only one product contains pharmaceutical-grade amino acids—a guarantee of purity and lack of contaminants. Named Amino Vital, it's a combination of the five amino acids listed above.

A 20-ounce bottle (75 calories) will provide the hydration needed for longer than 1 hour of activity and a complete supplementation of pure amino acids to replenish amino acid muscle stores and to reduce muscle fatigue. It also contains a modest amount of carbohydrate for energy (3 percent). This product isn't designed to replenish glycogen stores (as is Gatorade) for muscle use, and to prevent fatigue; it acts to replenish amino acid stores for a different and essential source of muscle energy. By replacing amino acid energy stores, remaining glycogen stores will remain intact, preventing muscle fatigue. Amino Vital is also available in a "fast charge" packet. At 15 calories, it is a single-serving packet of these amino acids in a dry form. You toss the crystals back in your mouth and take a swig or two of water to wash them down. (Note to the runner looking for a homemade beverage: You can make a carbohydrate drink similar to Gatorade, as described in Chapter 6, but this will not work for an amino acid supplement. The purity of the amino acids in the Amino Vital mixture is unique to this product, and a similar amino acid mixture cannot be purchased in a retail store.)

FATTY ACIDS (FAT)

Omega-3 fatty acids: Although some have suggested that supplementing with omega-3 fatty acids (a substance found in fish) can enhance running performance and decrease fatigue, there's no evidence that this is so, even in highly trained athletes. Fish oils can be heart healthy and a good choice of dietary fat, but there is no benefit to additional supplementation.

Carnitine: A little-known nutrient, carnitine is essential to normal muscle metabolism, but it's really misunderstood when it comes to supplementation. Because it's a nonessential nutrient, it can be made from other bodily compounds. It's also naturally present in foods, with red meat being the best source (50 to 100 milligrams per 3-ounce serving), with smaller amounts in fish, chicken, and milk (2 to 6 milligrams per 3-ounce serving). Carnitine serves the important function of modulating transport of fatty acids into muscle. For fatty acids to be used by muscle for energy, they must pass from the bloodstream into the muscle's mitochondria, the small cellular elements that turn the fatty acid into energy. The transporter of fatty acids into the muscle is mainly composed of carnitine. This carnitine pathway serves a valuable role, because the use of fatty acids for muscle energy will prevent complete depletion of glycogen, something we want to avoid to maintain muscle performance. Carnitine deficiency is rare, because there are trace amounts in food and the body can synthesize it, but a question remains as to whether carnitine supplementation helps enhance muscle performance. Although not clear-cut, most data does not support carnitine supplementation to enhance performance in conditioned athletes. Even with reduced caloric intake, you can sustain your dietary needs for carnitine.

OTHER COMPOUNDS

Creatine: Muscle contractions depend on the production of ATP, the energy units for muscle function. Like many other things in life, the supply in muscle doesn't last forever; actively exercising muscles may have a depletion of ATP. This ATP can be replenished by the stores of P-creatine (phosphocreatine) already in the muscle, providing the important P to the mix. However, the P-creatine stores are not large, and the question remains as to whether creatine supplementation would raise the pool of P-creatine, leading to greater ATP production in muscle and greater ability to sustain exercise intensity. Most evidence supports a beneficial effect of creatine—but only under certain conditions. Creatine supplementation is helpful for those activities of short-term, high-intensity duration, like sprinting. So, for the regular walker/runner, creatine will not be of particular benefit. Even among athletes, long-term use is not recommended. It's typically used for 4 to 5 days as a "loading" dose of 20 grams per day, then continued with 1 or 2 grams daily for up to 14 days. The safety of long-term use in unknown. By the way, creatine supplementation is often associated with weight gain related to water retention—about 2 to 5 pounds over a 4-day period.

CHAPTER 8

PUTTING IT ALL TOGETHER

> The final push you need to follow the Runner's Diet for life

Sometimes I think a weight-loss plan is a little like soup—throw in a couple of cups of motivation, 2 tablespoons of preparation, and a dash of execution. And when it all comes together, it's incredibly satisfying. Well, my intention is to give you all the ingredients you need to lose weight, maintain energy levels, and have a plan that you can follow for life. Of course, there are many ways you can customize your plan so that you can work on different areas of the package— and I've given you the tools to make the changes. But you don't need to do everything to make it work. In an ideal world, we'd all have unlimited time and money to attend to our weight-management and fitness needs (yeah, and in an ideal world, tiramisu would be calorie free, too!). But in the real world, we need to set realistic goals in areas we know we can manage. To do that, all you need is one thing from yourself—honesty. That's all about the idea of differentiating between what you're willing to do and what you're able to do—and they're not always the same thing.

But the driving force behind your plan should be that being honest with yourself and setting a weight-loss goal for slow, steady progress will bring success. The one we'd rather have with wham-bam instant results—if it worked!—is on the path to failure.

Elizabeth was a former runner who logged 10 miles a week until she graduated from college 20 years earlier. She had a busy life working as a full-time respiratory therapist, running her household, and being a single mother to her high school daughter. Although she hadn't been running for many years, Elizabeth was physically active during the day—primarily by practicing with her daughter, a competitive soccer player.

In her early forties and after a painful divorce, Elizabeth was feeling the weight creep of about 18 pounds since the birth of her daughter and another 20 pounds over the past 8 months from the stress of her divorce. Wanting to lose nearly 40 unwanted pounds, Elizabeth wanted to get back to running—for both weight loss and stress reduction. On her own, Elizabeth tried to set up a plan. She tried getting up at 5:30 instead of 6:30 to walk/run 3 miles on the treadmill (in 35 minutes), shower, and leave the house. She didn't allow any time for eating, and usually left the house with a mug of coffee for the car. Trying to save calories, she ate nothing until lunch—which left her starving and vulnerable to overeating whatever was around throughout the rest of the day.

When Elizabeth came to see me because she was disappointed her plan wasn't working, we had an honest discussion about what she truly was willing and able to do. From there, it was easy to make some practical changes for her to follow. First, we gave her back her much-needed sleep, and she woke up at 6:30. She took a protein bar (170 calories) in the car along with her coffee, which was sufficient until lunch. Elizabeth had either a frozen calorie-controlled lunch with raw fruit if she was at her desk or a salad with grilled chicken if she was out. She liked the minimal choices and felt they kept her on track.

For her exercise, Elizabeth first incorporated her walk/run 3 days a week when she took her daughter to soccer practice. On her way home from work, to prepare for her run/walk she had the sandwich she'd prepared the night before with peanut butter spread on low-calorie bread (200 calories total). Instead of socializing with the other parents, Elizabeth used that time to walk/run her 3 miles. It also left her a little time to socialize and, more importantly, energized her for the evening ahead. She agreed to keep a food record for at least 2 weeks, although she didn't want to at first. She also agreed to a modest goal of losing 5 pounds in the first month ("I'd like it to be 10 pounds," she said).

Keeping her food records helped Elizabeth monitor her food intake, which helped her control herself and feel accountable for her actions. After the first month, Elizabeth exceeded her 5-pound goal and actually lost almost 7 pounds. She was definitely more comfortable with her 3-mile walk/run, and wanted to do more. Not wanting to run outdoors ("I get too cold") and uninterested in a gym membership, Elizabeth purchased a treadmill. She loved the convenience and increased her mileage to 4 miles 4 days a week, with a goal of running as much as she could, with walking in between. This boost in activity energized Elizabeth, and after another month, she had lost another 6 pounds. Although Elizabeth thought she could give her running another boost, she agreed that this was a comfortable activity level, so she revisited her eating. Night eating was her main problem—she ate more than 500 calories at night. Elizabeth agreed to a 200-calorie limit, and she also joined a support group in her community. It has been almost 7 months since she began, and Elizabeth has lost 30 pounds (17 pounds in the past 4 months). The confidence that comes from the control she feels is the secret to her continued success. "I'm down to my last 10 extra pounds. I feel great. I don't even care if I creep down at 2 pounds a month; I know I can reach my goal at some point."

ELIZABETH DID EVERYTHING RIGHT

She matched her lifestyle changes to her internal clock, logged her eating and activity, found some support, and created a plan she could manage for the long term. She rethought both her short-term and long-term goals and set herself up for success—not disappointment. Patient, and confident that she can maintain the present loss, Elizabeth keeps working against the remaining pounds. More importantly, Elizabeth is content with her 30-pound loss. "I am in control. I know I will never be heavier than I am now. I am back to running, because this is what will keep me on track."

The former runner has once again become a runner. And her story is the perfect example of how it's never too late to get back. All it takes is some interest and a pair of running shoes.

Now that you have all the ingredients in place, you can follow these easy tips for setting up a starting plan. So, get a notebook, and start writing.

Match your eating and running style by understanding your biological clock. You need to think about the ups and downs of your own daily energy levels. It's important to think about how and when you prefer to eat, relative to when you choose to set up your walking or running. Whether it's a physical or mental factor, you must meet the needs of your own temperament. Are you a grazer or a three-meal-a-day eater? Do you run in the morning or at night? By answering these questions, you can match your energy needs to your physical activity and select the best combination of times for eating and exercising. Think about the best times to incorporate some walking or running into your program, and don't try to fit someone else's patterns into your lifestyle—it's a setup for disaster. If you're a morning person, then rising earlier is a plus. If you're a night owl, look for late-afternoon or early-evening activity times.

Outline your weekly strategy. Lots of people try to lose weight by outlining what they're going to do every day. Every day is too tough to manage and puts way too much pressure on you. You set yourself up for disappointment. You'll be more successful if you set up a weekly schedule. Set up a walk/run for a number of days per week. Cook and shop for food with a weekly schedule in mind. This attitude makes you proactive and confident and avoids always running to catch up from behind.

Keep your daily food and activity log. As boring and routine as this sounds, it's the best path to success. You won't be doing this forever, but it helps you be accountable for your actions. You want to keep this information in your mental database, but you need to start on paper. Use the food logs in this book, or simply carry around a mini-notepad. Your ultimate goal: Develop mental discipline by recording everything you eat for 2 weeks. I believe that anyone can do anything for 2 weeks. You'll see that food records are either a big help or a major annoyance. The main reason to write it all down is to have a basis on which to change your pattern—so you can see patterns of what's working and what's not and make changes based on that, even if you don't maintain the food log for the long term.

Maximize your commitment by modifying your eating and running patterns. Take a look at your 2-week records for eating and activity. Ask yourself, "Can I stick with this routine for another 2 weeks?" If the answer is yes, go for it. If it is no, ask yourself what *one thing* you need to change to make your plan work. Remember to change only one thing at a time to avoid overwhelming yourself to the point that you abandon your plans. If you review every 2 weeks, you'll be able to stay on track with your goals and not abandon them when you hit rough patches.

Accept slow, steady weight loss as a long-term goal. This is the hardest thing we all have to face, but it's really a plan for life, because it's not a plan you go on and off. It's one you stick to throughout your life. If you are losing at least 2 pounds a month (½ pound per week), that is biological success. You need to determine within yourself whether you are both willing and able to produce a more sustained effort to lose weight at a faster rate. Most of us would like to lose weight faster, and it is possible. But what personal effort do you need to make in order to lose at a faster rate? Can you sustain further changes in your lifestyle? Remember, there's no rush—because it's better to lose weight the slow and steady way than hurry up and fail.

Choose a stable weight. The real barometer to success is choosing a weight-loss and activity level that you can sustain. Sure, we all have our fantasy weights, but you need to find a way to mix your fantasy weight with your reality lifestyle. Here's where you can dream with your feet firmly planted on the ground. When you can select a weight-loss or weight-maintenance and running pattern that suits your present lifestyle, you're well on your way to achieving success. When you can look forward at what you can do—and are willing to extend a modest effort to achieve it—the right combination of eating and exercise will take you to a realistic weight. Even if you maintain a stable weight—and don't gain—that, too, is success, because maintaining your current weight requires significant effort as well.

Get more help. Even with sustained effort, it may be harder than you expected for you to lose weight and improve your walk/run activity. We all have barriers. They may be psychological or biological—and they may apply to eating and/or running. Asking for help is not a weakness (in a way, just buying this book is a way of asking for help); it's a strength. Whether it's visiting your family doctor, a therapist, a nutritionist, a trainer, or a support group or enlisting the help of friends, colleagues, or family, you should seek out the help you need to meet your goals. When you reach out to others, you'll see that we're all working at this. And we're all struggling at times, even those who appear to follow a plan effortlessly. When you take the view that we are all in this together, the pressure is off. And the rest is up to you.

APPENDIX 1

7-DAY FOOD AND EXERCISE LOG

Please record in detail everything that you eat and drink for 7 days and 7 nights. Record food and drinks shortly after having them. Be as exact as possible. Use as many lines as needed to describe items. Please use a separate line for each food item.

HINTS TO HELP YOU WHEN COMPLETING YOUR FOOD RECORD

1. List each item on a separate line.
2. For mixed dishes, such as casseroles and stews:

   Eaten away from home:

   - List ingredients and their amounts.
   - Estimate proportions if exact amounts are unknown.

   Homemade recipe:

   - Write a copy of the recipe in the notes section for each day.
   - Record all the ingredients in the recipe.

- Record the number of servings the recipe makes.
- Record the portion of the recipe that you ate.

Commercial variety:

- List brand name.
- Record whether canned or frozen.
- Record amount eaten.

3. Amount

- Be as exact as possible.
- For foods such as vegetables, juices, soups, or sauces, use measuring cups or spoons.
- For foods such as baked goods, use a ruler to measure length, width, and thickness.
- For foods such as fresh fruit, fresh vegetables, and eggs, give number, dimensions, or size.
- For meat, fish, and poultry, use weighed amount.

When recording amounts, use these abbreviations and equivalents:

Cup = C

Tablespoon = T

Teaspoon = tsp

Ounce = oz

Shake = shk

Slice = sl

Food equivalents:

1 tablespoon = 3 teaspoons

1 cup = 16 tablespoons

1 cup or ½ pint fluid = 8 ounces

1 ounce fluid = 2 tablespoons

1 shot or jigger = 1½ ounces (unless otherwise specified)

4. Description

• Include brand names.
• Include method of preparation (fried, broiled, breaded, baked, etc.).
• Specify if ingredients are unknown.

5. Restaurant meals

• State restaurant name.
• Give price range if other than fast food.

6. Miscellaneous

• When recording pats of butter or margarine, state dimensions.
• When recording ice served with a beverage, give proportion of ice in the glass.
• For meat, fish, and poultry, give weighed amount (state whether raw or cooked weight).
• When measuring in teaspoons or tablespoons, state whether level or heaping.

WHEN COMPLETING YOUR EXERCISE RECORD

• List all of the activity that you do each day.
• Record only activities that last as long as or more than 10 minutes.
• Describe the type of exercise/activity.
• List where you did the exercise/activity.
• Record the total amount of time that you spent performing the exercise/activity.
• Indicate whether you exercised at a slow, medium, or fast pace.
• Estimate the distance that you covered while you were exercising.

DAY 1 FOOD RECORD

Date/day of week:	Check one: Workday: ____ Nonworkday: ____			
Start date of last menstrual period:	Wake-up time: ____ Bedtime: ____ Nap time (if any): ____ to ____			
Time:	Place:		Food, beverages, vitamins, medications, and seasonings:	Amount:
	HOME	OUT		

Today's food intake:	○ **More than usual** ○ **Less than usual** ○ **About usual**
Food intake:	○ **Splurged quite a bit** ○ **Under control** Comments: _____

Description (include brand, fresh, frozen, canned, homemade, recipe, sweetened, etc.):	**Comments:**

DAY 1 EXERCISE RECORD

Date/day of week:	Check one: Workday ____ Nonworkday ____	
Time:	Kind of exercise:	Location of exercise:

	Today's exercise:	○ More than usual ○ Less than usual ○ About usual
Time spent exercising (in minutes):	**Distance (depends on what type of exercise):**	**Speed:**
		○ Minimal ○ Challenging ○ Strenuous
		○ Minimal ○ Challenging ○ Strenuous
		○ Minimal ○ Challenging ○ Strenuous
		○ Minimal ○ Challenging ○ Strenuous
		○ Minimal ○ Challenging ○ Strenuous
		○ Minimal ○ Challenging ○ Strenuous
		○ Minimal ○ Challenging ○ Strenuous
		○ Minimal ○ Challenging ○ Strenuous

DAY 2 FOOD RECORD

Date/day of week:	Check one: Workday: _____ Nonworkday: _____			
Start date of last menstrual period:	Wake-up time: _____ Bedtime: _____ Nap time (if any): _____ to _____			
Time:	Place:		Food, beverages, vitamins, medications, and seasonings:	Amount:
	HOME	OUT		

Today's food intake:	○ **More than usual** ○ **Less than usual** ○ **About usual**
Food intake:	○ **Splurged quite a bit** ○ **Under control** **Comments:** _____

Description (include brand, fresh, frozen, canned, homemade, recipe, sweetened, etc.):	**Comments:**

DAY 2 EXERCISE RECORD

Date/day of week:	Check one: Workday ____ Nonworkday ____	
Time:	Kind of exercise:	Location of exercise:

	Today's exercise:	○ More than usual ○ Less than usual ○ About usual
Time spent exercising (in minutes):	Distance (depends on what type of exercise):	Speed:
		○ Minimal ○ Challenging ○ Strenuous
		○ Minimal ○ Challenging ○ Strenuous
		○ Minimal ○ Challenging ○ Strenuous
		○ Minimal ○ Challenging ○ Strenuous
		○ Minimal ○ Challenging ○ Strenuous
		○ Minimal ○ Challenging ○ Strenuous
		○ Minimal ○ Challenging ○ Strenuous
		○ Minimal ○ Challenging ○ Strenuous

DAY 3 FOOD RECORD

Date/day of week:	Check one: Workday: ____ Nonworkday: ____			
Start date of last menstrual period:	Wake-up time: ____ Bedtime: ____ Nap time (if any): ____ to ____			
Time:	**Place:**		**Food, beverages, vitamins, medications, and seasonings:**	**Amount:**
	HOME	OUT		

Today's food intake:	○ **More than usual** ○ **Less than usual** ○ **About usual**
Food intake:	○ **Splurged quite a bit** ○ **Under control** **Comments:** _____

Description (include brand, fresh, frozen, canned, homemade, recipe, sweetened, etc.):	**Comments:**

DAY 3 EXERCISE RECORD

Date/day of week:	Check one: Workday ___ Nonworkday ___	
Time:	Kind of exercise:	Location of exercise:

	Today's exercise:	○ More than usual ○ Less than usual ○ About usual
Time spent exercising (in minutes):	**Distance (depends on what type of exercise):**	**Speed:**
		○ Minimal ○ Challenging ○ Strenuous
		○ Minimal ○ Challenging ○ Strenuous
		○ Minimal ○ Challenging ○ Strenuous
		○ Minimal ○ Challenging ○ Strenuous
		○ Minimal ○ Challenging ○ Strenuous
		○ Minimal ○ Challenging ○ Strenuous
		○ Minimal ○ Challenging ○ Strenuous
		○ Minimal ○ Challenging ○ Strenuous

DAY 4 FOOD RECORD

Date/day of week:	Check one: Workday: ____ Nonworkday: ____			
Start date of last menstrual period:	Wake-up time: ____ Bedtime: ____ Nap time (if any): ____ to ____			
Time:	Place:		Food, beverages, vitamins, medications, and seasonings:	Amount:
	HOME	OUT		

Today's food intake:	○ More than usual ○ Less than usual ○ About usual
Food intake:	○ Splurged quite a bit ○ Under control Comments: _____
Description (include brand, fresh, frozen, canned, homemade, recipe, sweetened, etc.):	Comments:

DAY 4 EXERCISE RECORD

Date/day of week:	Check one: Workday ____ Nonworkday ____	
Time:	Kind of exercise:	Location of exercise:

	Today's exercise:	○ More than usual ○ Less than usual ○ About usual
Time spent exercising (in minutes):	Distance (depends on what type of exercise):	Speed:
		○ Minimal ○ Challenging ○ Strenuous
		○ Minimal ○ Challenging ○ Strenuous
		○ Minimal ○ Challenging ○ Strenuous
		○ Minimal ○ Challenging ○ Strenuous
		○ Minimal ○ Challenging ○ Strenuous
		○ Minimal ○ Challenging ○ Strenuous
		○ Minimal ○ Challenging ○ Strenuous
		○ Minimal ○ Challenging ○ Strenuous

DAY 5 FOOD RECORD

Date/day of week:	Check one: Workday: ____ Nonworkday: ____			
Start date of last menstrual period:	Wake-up time: ____ Bedtime: ____ Nap time (if any): ____ to ____			
Time:	Place:		Food, beverages, vitamins, medications, and seasonings:	Amount:
	HOME	OUT		

Today's food intake:	○ More than usual ○ Less than usual ○ About usual
Food intake:	○ Splurged quite a bit ○ Under control Comments: _____

Description (include brand, fresh, frozen, canned, homemade, recipe, sweetened, etc.):	Comments:

DAY 5 EXERCISE RECORD

Date/day of week:	Check one: Workday ____ Nonworkday ____	
Time:	Kind of exercise:	Location of exercise:

	Today's exercise:	○ More than usual ○ Less than usual ○ About usual
Time spent exercising (in minutes):	Distance (depends on what type of exercise):	Speed:
		○ Minimal ○ Challenging ○ Strenuous
		○ Minimal ○ Challenging ○ Strenuous
		○ Minimal ○ Challenging ○ Strenuous
		○ Minimal ○ Challenging ○ Strenuous
		○ Minimal ○ Challenging ○ Strenuous
		○ Minimal ○ Challenging ○ Strenuous
		○ Minimal ○ Challenging ○ Strenuous
		○ Minimal ○ Challenging ○ Strenuous

DAY 6 FOOD RECORD

Date/day of week:	Check one: Workday: ____		Nonworkday: ____	
Start date of last menstrual period:	Wake-up time: ____ Bedtime: ____ Nap time (if any): ____ to ____			
Time:	Place:		Food, beverages, vitamins, medications, and seasonings:	Amount:
	HOME	OUT		

Today's food intake:	○ More than usual
	○ Less than usual
	○ About usual

Food intake:	○ Splurged quite a bit
	○ Under control
	Comments: _____

Description (include brand, fresh, frozen, canned, homemade, recipe, sweetened, etc.):	Comments:

DAY 6 EXERCISE RECORD

Date/day of week:	Check one: Workday ____ Nonworkday ____	
Time:	Kind of exercise:	Location of exercise:

	Today's exercise:	○ More than usual
		○ Less than usual
		○ About usual
Time spent exercising (in minutes):	**Distance** (depends on what type of exercise):	**Speed:**
		○ Minimal ○ Challenging ○ Strenuous
		○ Minimal ○ Challenging ○ Strenuous
		○ Minimal ○ Challenging ○ Strenuous
		○ Minimal ○ Challenging ○ Strenuous
		○ Minimal ○ Challenging ○ Strenuous
		○ Minimal ○ Challenging ○ Strenuous
		○ Minimal ○ Challenging ○ Strenuous
		○ Minimal ○ Challenging ○ Strenuous

DAY 7 FOOD RECORD

Date/day of week:	Check one: Workday: ____ Nonworkday: ____			
Start date of last menstrual period:	Wake-up time: ____ Bedtime: ____ Nap time (if any): ____ to ____			
Time:	Place: HOME / OUT		Food, beverages, vitamins, medications, and seasonings:	Amount:

Today's food intake:	○ **More than usual** ○ **Less than usual** ○ **About usual**
Food intake:	○ **Splurged quite a bit** ○ **Under control** **Comments:** _____
Description (include brand, fresh, frozen, canned, homemade, recipe, sweetened, etc.):	**Comments:**

DAY 7 EXERCISE RECORD

Date/day of week:	Check one: Workday ____ Nonworkday ____	
Time:	Kind of exercise:	Location of exercise:

	Today's exercise:	○ **More than usual** ○ **Less than usual** ○ **About usual**
Time spent exercising (in minutes):	**Distance (depends on what type of exercise):**	**Speed:**
		○ Minimal ○ Challenging ○ Strenuous
		○ Minimal ○ Challenging ○ Strenuous
		○ Minimal ○ Challenging ○ Strenuous
		○ Minimal ○ Challenging ○ Strenuous
		○ Minimal ○ Challenging ○ Strenuous
		○ Minimal ○ Challenging ○ Strenuous
		○ Minimal ○ Challenging ○ Strenuous
		○ Minimal ○ Challenging ○ Strenuous

NOTES

FOR DIMENSIONS USE:

Diameter for round foods (example: 2½"-diameter orange)

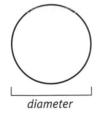

diameter

Diameter and length for cylindrical foods (example: 2"-diameter × 4½"-long sweet potato)

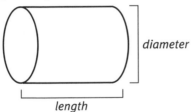

diameter

length

Diameter and thickness for disk foods (example: 3"-diameter × 1"-thick hamburger patty, or 4" diameter × ⅛"-thick bologna slice)

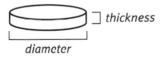

thickness

diameter

Diameter and thickness for rectangles or cubes (example: 1"-high × 3"-wide × 2"-long piece cake, or ½"-high × 2"-wide × 3"-long piece cheese)

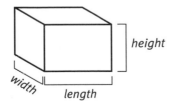

height

width

length

Arc by height by length for wedges (pizza, cheese, etc.) OR fraction of the whole plus diameter and thickness of a total disk for wedges (pizza, cheese, etc.) (example: 3"-arc by 1½"-high by 4"-long wedge of pumpkin pie, or ¹⁄₁₆ of an 8"-diameter pumpkin pie that's 1½" thick)

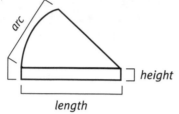

APPENDIX 2

TRACKING YOUR PROGRESS

KEEP RECORDS

Although it may sound time-consuming, monitoring your daily physical activity actually does not take long. An exercise log is a wonderful motivational tool, because it can create a sense of obligation that helps push us to exercise on days when our motivation is low. Moreover, as we progress and reach our fitness goals, our old exercise logs can enhance our sense of accomplishment by helping us see just how far we've come.

Your exercise log should include not just your workouts but also your activities throughout the day. This will provide an accurate picture of how many calories you are burning. You also may begin to think more broadly about exercise as you realize how much of it you are secretly doing.

PEDOMETERS

One of the easiest tools that you can use to monitor the amount of your daily physical activity is the pedometer. A pedometer is a simple gadget that measures steps. If used correctly, the pedometer can give you a good indication of how much your body is "moving" throughout the day. Since you burn calories with each and every movement, the pedometer can also give you a reliable, objective indication of your activity level.

The Japanese were the first to use pedometers as a tool to counteract sedentary lifestyles in the 1950s. One study recommended subjects increase pedometer steps to 12,000 to 15,000 a day to lose weight. More recently, a US study indicated that by wearing a pedometer, research subjects automatically increased daily physical activity. Researchers theorized this happened because the pedometer gave the subjects immediate feedback on their level of physical activity and they were more motivated to improve.

HOW MANY STEPS SHOULD YOU TAKE IN A DAY?

• In terms of weight loss, there is no "right" number of steps to perform.
• The number of steps that you "should" be doing is relative to your baseline level of physical activity.
• Initially, the most important thing is to establish your individual baseline level of steps per day.
• Most sedentary people will do about 3,000 to 4,000 steps per day.
• If you have been sedentary for a long time, it is probably not realistic for you to increase your steps to 12,000 right away.
• You should increase your physical activity only as your body is able to tolerate it.
• In terms of weight loss, the higher the number of steps, the more calories you'll burn on a daily basis.

• You may keep in mind a long-term goal of over 10,000 steps in order to effect weight loss.

• Success is measured in anything above and beyond your baseline level of activity.

HOW DO YOU USE A PEDOMETER?

• Placement of the pedometer is important in terms of accuracy.

• Clip the pedometer onto your waistband directly above the kneecap, in line with the seam on your pants.

• If you're wearing a dress without a waistband, hook it onto your underwear or panty hose.

• If your stomach protrudes, you may want to wear the pedometer at waist level closer to the side of your body, but this will decrease accuracy.

• Put on your pedometer first thing in the morning, and take it off before bedtime.

• Don't immerse your pedometer in water.

• Some pedometers calculate distance based on number of steps (number of steps times stride length in feet divided by 5,280 feet per mile).

• Twenty-five hundred steps equal roughly 1 mile, depending on your stride length (using a stride length of two feet per stride).

• If your pedometer measures 10,000 steps, then you have walked the equivalent of about 4 miles.

• Pedometers may not be as accurate with non-weight-bearing activities like cycling and rowing.

• If you're using an exercise log, you'll want to record these activities in addition to your pedometer steps so that you have an accurate reflection of your total physical activity.

DAILY EXERCISE LOG

Date:	Day/ Time:	Pedometer Reading (Steps):	Warmup and Recovery Activities:	Type of Exercise/ Physical Activity:	Duration (Amount of Time):

APPENDIX 3

STRENGTH TRAINING RECORD

(For each set, include weight in pounds/number of repetitions)

> **EXERCISE** _____

	Week 1	Week 2	Week 3	Week 4	Week 5	Week 6	Week 7	Week 8
Set 1	15/10	etc.						
Set 2								
Set 3								

EXERCISE _____

	Week 1	Week 2	Week 3	Week 4	Week 5	Week 6	Week 7	Week 8
Set 1								
Set 2								
Set 3								

EXERCISE _____

	Week 1	Week 2	Week 3	Week 4	Week 5	Week 6	Week 7	Week 8
Set 1								
Set 2								
Set 3								

EXERCISE _____

	Week 1	Week 2	Week 3	Week 4	Week 5	Week 6	Week 7	Week 8
Set 1								
Set 2								
Set 3								

EXERCISE _____

	Week 1	Week 2	Week 3	Week 4	Week 5	Week 6	Week 7	Week 8
Set 1								
Set 2								
Set 3								

EXERCISE _____

	Week 1	Week 2	Week 3	Week 4	Week 5	Week 6	Week 7	Week 8
Set 1								
Set 2								
Set 3								

EXERCISE _____

	Week 1	Week 2	Week 3	Week 4	Week 5	Week 6	Week 7	Week 8
Set 1								
Set 2								
Set 3								

EXERCISE _____

	Week 1	Week 2	Week 3	Week 4	Week 5	Week 6	Week 7	Week 8
Set 1								
Set 2								
Set 3								

APPENDIX 4

GETTING STARTED: SAMPLE WALKING AND RUNNING PLANS

• Be realistic. The goal is to complete the time segment, not the distance.

• Be patient. Within a month, you'll notice a lot of progress.

• Challenge yourself. When you are comfortable with your walk/run pattern, reevaluate every month to see if it meets your needs, or if it must be increased or reduced to keep up your interest and maintain weight loss goals.

• The 6-week plan is only a guideline. Adjust your goal to earlier weeks if it meets your time and comfort level.

• Make sure you have medical clearance before starting a plan or increasing your intensity of exercise.

• If you want to burn calories faster as well as save time, focus on increasing your intensity—do more running than walking for a given time period. Distance determines total calories. Intensity determines the time it takes to burn them.

6-WEEK WALKING PLAN

Walking Tips:

• Keep your head up.
• Stand up straight but not stiff. Relax.
• Take long, comfortable strides.
• Swing your arms, bent at the elbow.
• Read about the RPE (rate of perceived exertion) to judge effort (Chapter 5).
• Walk at least 3 to 4 times a week.

WEEK 1: Walking time = 20 minutes

Walk 5 minutes; walk 10 minutes *briskly*; walk 5 minutes.

WEEK 2: Walking time = 25 minutes

Walk 5 minutes; walk 12 minutes *briskly*; walk 8minutes.

WEEK 3: Walking time = 30 minutes

Walk 5 minutes; walk 15 minutes *briskly*; walk 10 minutes.

WEEK 4: Walking time = 30 minutes

Walk 5 minutes; walk 20 minutes *briskly*; walk 5 minutes.

WEEK 5: Walking time = 35 minutes

Walk 5 minutes; walk 25 minutes *briskly*; walk 5 minutes.

WEEK 6: Walking time = 40 minutes

Walk 5 minutes; walk 30 minutes *briskly*; walk 5 minutes.

WHAT'S NEXT?

When you can comfortably walk for at least 30 minutes, you may decide to add a little running to your routine. If so, continue with the sample running plan below. If not, maintain your walking pattern regularly—at least 3 to 4 times per week.

6-WEEK RUNNING PLAN

Running Tips:

• Make sure you can first walk at least 30 minutes without stopping.
• Keep your head up.
• Stand up straight but not stiff. Relax.
• Take long comfortable strides.
• Swing your arms, bent at the elbow.
• Read about the RPE (rate of perceived exertion) to judge effort (Chapter 5).
• Walk/run at least 3 to 4 times a week.

WEEK 1: Total Time = 30 minutes (walking = 25 minutes; running = 5 minutes)

Walk 5 minutes; walk 5 minutes *briskly*; alternate walking, brisk walking, and slow jogging for 10 minutes (try for 1- to 2-minute running segments, using the RPE scale as a guide); walk 10 minutes.

WEEK 2: Total time = 30 minutes (walking = 20 minutes; running = 10 minutes)

Walk 5 minutes; walk 5 minutes *briskly*; alternate walking, brisk walking, and slow running for 15 minutes (try for 2- to 3-minute running segments); walk 5 minutes.

WEEK 3: Total time = 30 minutes (walking = 18 minutes; running = 12 minutes)

Walk 5 minutes; alternate walking, brisk walking, and slow running for 20 minutes (try for 3- to 4-minute running segments); walk 5 minutes.

WEEK 4: Total Time = 35 minutes (walking = 20; running = 15 minutes)

Walk 5 minutes *briskly*; walk/run 25 minutes (try for 5- to 6-minute running segments), walk 5 minutes.

WEEK 5: Total time = 35 minutes (walking = 10 minutes; running = 25 minutes)

Walk 5 minutes *briskly*; walk/run 25 minutes (try for 7- to 8-minute running segments), walk 5 minutes.

WEEK 6: Total time = 40 minutes (walking = 10 minutes; running = 30 minutes)

Walk 5 minutes *briskly*; walk/run 30 minutes (try for 10-minute running segments), end with 5 minutes of walking.

WHAT'S NEXT?

When you have mastered the 6-week running program, and can comfortably run for 30 minutes, you may decide to pursue more rigorous workouts, train for races, and become a more serious runner. If you do, great. If you remain a walker/runner, that's great too. You are still a runner regardless of duration and intensity of your effort. Consistent effort—at least 3 to 4 times a week—in whatever plan you choose is what matters most.

APPENDIX 5

7-DAY MEAL PLAN

Using this meal plan:

• Mix and match the meals and snacks to satisfy your own food preferences.

• Purchase a calorie guide and substitute other foods with equivalent calories and food composition.

• Include at least two snacks a day to avoid becoming "overhungry" with too much time between meals.

• You can choose to "save" part of your meal for a later snack if you are satisfied *before* you've eaten everything.

The basic plan provides about 1,200 calories per day. Check out the table on the following page to choose your target calories based on your own calculations. (See below, and also Chapter 4 for more details.)

To calculate your daily calories: Take your present weight and multiply by 13. This is your total daily calories to roughly *maintain* your present weight. As a guideline, to lose about 1 pound a week, subtract 500 calories from this number; to lose about 2 pounds a week, subtract 1,000 calories from that number. One pound equals about 3,500 calories.

ADDING TO THE BASIC 1,200-CALORIE PLAN:

If Your Total Calories Are:	Add:	As:		
		CARBOHYDRATE	PROTEIN	FAT
1,400 calories	200 calories	100 cal	50 cal	50 cal
1,600 calories	400 calories	200 cal	100 cal	100 cal
1,800 calories	600 calories	300 cal	150 cal	150 cal
2,000 calories	800 calories	400 cal	200 cal	200 cal
2,200 calories	1,000 calories	500 cal	250 cal	250 cal
2,400 calories	1,200 calories	600 cal	300 cal	300 cal
2,600 calories	1,400 calories	700 cal	350 cal	350 cal

DAY 1

Breakfast: 1 english muffin + 2 teaspoons peanut butter; coffee or tea (skim milk and/or no calorie sweetener if preferred); ½ grapefruit

Lunch: 1 can High Protein Boost + 1 tangerine

Dinner: 1 cup tomato soup; 1 roasted chicken breast; ½ cup snap peas; ½ cup green beans; ⅓ cup cooked couscous

Snacks:

1 bag Pop Secret light kettle corn (single-serving package)

½ cup sugar-free apple sauce

Free foods (see pages 72 to 73)

DAY 2

Breakfast: ¼ cup egg substitute + 2 cups spinach, tomatoes, and onions; ½ cup cut-up melon; coffee or tea (with skim milk and/or no-calorie sweetener)

Lunch: 2 to 4 ounces white meat turkey sandwich (lettuce, tomato, and mustard on 2 slices light whole wheat bread); 1 cup raw carrots and celery; 1 cup vegetable soup

Dinner: 1½ cup mixed-greens salad tossed with 1 tablespoon light Italian salad dressing and 1 teaspoon grated Parmesan cheese; 3 to 6 ounces grilled flank steak; 1 cup steamed broccoli; ½ cup brown rice

Snacks:

¾ cup dry cereal

1 tortilla + 1 tablespoon salsa + 1 tablespoon low-fat Cheddar cheese

Free foods (see pages 72 to 73)

DAY 3

Breakfast: 2 Kellogg's Eggo waffles Special K + ¼ cup sugar-free syrup; ½ cup skim milk; coffee or tea

Lunch: Ultra Lean Pocket—all varieties; 1 medium apple

Dinner: 4 to 6 ounces grilled salmon with a marinade of your choice; steamed asparagus; ½ cup cracked wheat (bulgur)

Snacks:

1 small banana spread with 1 teaspoon peanut butter

10 sourdough pretzel nuggets

Free foods (see pages 72 to 73)

DAY 4

Breakfast: Egg sandwich (2 slices light whole wheat bread, 4 scrambled egg whites); 1 slice low-fat sharp Cheddar cheese; 1 kiwifruit; coffee or tea

Lunch: Chicken Caesar salad (3 cups mixed greens, 1 sliced grilled chicken breast, 1 tablespoon Parmesan cheese, 2 tablespoons reduced-fat dressing); 1 cup tomato soup

Dinner: Frozen dinner of your choice (limit of 350 calories, 12 grams of fats); 1 cup fresh fruit salad

Snacks:

1 mini-pita bread spread with 2 teaspoons hummus

1 sugar-free Fudgsicle

Free foods (see pages 72 to 73)

DAY 5

Breakfast: Protein bar (up to 200 calories, your choice); 1 medium pear

Lunch: Tuna tortilla (3-ounce can mixed with 1 tablespoon light mayonnaise spread on small tortilla with shredded lettuce and rolled up); 1 cup V8 juice

Dinner: Taco salad (3 cups salad greens topped with ⅔ cup low-fat chili, homemade or purchased, 2 tablespoons shredded low-fat Cheddar cheese, 10 baked tortilla chips)

Snacks:

1 cup skim milk mixed with sugar-free chocolate syrup

2 sugar-free Creamsicles

Free foods (see pages 72 to 73)

DAY 6

Breakfast: ⅔ cup cooked oatmeal; ½ cup skim milk; 1 small orange

Lunch: 1 low-fat hot dog in light bun; ½ cup sauerkraut; 10 baked potato chips; 1 cup mixed raw peppers and cucumbers

Dinner: 1 barbecued chicken breast; ½ cup corn; 1 cup coleslaw in nonfat dressing; 1 cup canteloupe

Snacks:

1 Pria bar (regular, not low carb)

1 Orville Redenbacher Smart Pop or Pop Secret popcorn mini-bag

Free foods (see pages 72 to 73)

DAY 7

Breakfast: Omelet (1 whole egg plus two egg whites) and 1 slice low-fat cheese); 1 slice light whole wheat toast; 5 strawberries

Lunch: Fresh fruit plate (cut up fruits with 1 cup low-fat, calcium-fortified cottage cheese OR 1 cup low-fat, sugar-free yogurt); 8 Triscuit Thin Crisps

Dinner: 4 to 6 ounces grilled shrimp and scallops; 1 cup zucchini; ½ cup brown rice; ½ cup sugar-free applesauce

Snacks:

12 mixed nuts (your choice)

½ cup frozen low-fat, sugar-free ice cream or frozen yogurt

Free foods (see pages 72 to 73)

INDEX

<u>Underscored</u> references indicate boxed text.